LaTeX
Beginner's Guide

Create high-quality and professional-looking texts, articles, and books for business and science using LaTeX

Stefan Kottwitz

[PACKT] open source*
PUBLISHING   community experience distilled

BIRMINGHAM - MUMBAI

LaTeX
Beginner's Guide

First published: March 2011

Production Reference: 1150311

Published by Packt Publishing Ltd.
32 Lincoln Road
Olton
Birmingham, B27 6PA, UK.

ISBN 978-1-847199-86-7

www.packtpub.com

Cover Image by Asher Wishkerman (a.wishkerman@mpic.de)

Credits

Author

Stefan Kottwitz

Reviewers

Kevin C. Klement

Joseph Wright

Acquisition Editor

Eleanor Duffy

Development Editor

Hyacintha D'Souza

Technical Editor

Sakina Kaydawala

Copy Editor

Leonard D'Silva

Indexer

Hemangini Bari

Editorial Team Leader

Mithun Sehgal

Project Team Leader

Lata Basantani

Project Coordinator

Vishal Bodwani

Proofreader

Aaron Nash

Graphics

Nilesh Mohite

Production Coordinator

Adline Swetha Jesuthas

Cover Work

Adline Swetha Jesuthas

About the Author

Stefan Kottwitz studied mathematics in Jena and Hamburg. Afterwards, he worked as an IT Administrator and Communication Officer onboard cruise ships for AIDA Cruises and for Hapag-Lloyd Cruises. Following 10 years of sailing around the world, he is now employed as a Network & IT Security Engineer for AIDA Cruises, focusing on network infrastructure and security such as managing firewall systems for headquarters and fleet.

In between contracts, he worked as a freelance programmer and typography designer. For many years he has been providing LaTeX support in online forums. He became a moderator of the web forum `http://latex-community.org/` and of the site `http://golatex.de/`. Recently, he began supporting the newly established Q&A site `http://tex.stackexchange.com/` as a moderator.

He publishes ideas and news from the TeX world on his blog at `http://texblog.net`.

I would like to thank Joseph Wright and Kevin C. Klement for reviewing this book. Special thanks go to Markus Kohm for his great valuable input. I would also like to thank the people of Packt Publishing, who worked with me on this book, in particular my development editor Hyacintha D'Souza.

About the Reviewers

Kevin C. Klement is an Associate Professor of Philosophy at the University of Massachusetts, Amherst. Besides using LaTeX in his academic work in the history of logic and analytic philosophy, he is a maintainer of the PhilTeX blog, and an active participant in many online LaTeX communities, including PhilTeX, LaTeX Community, and TeX.SE.

Joseph Wright is a research assistant at the University of East Anglia. As well as using LaTeX for his academic work as a chemist, he is a member of the LaTeX3 Project, runs the blog Some TeX Developments and is one of the moderators on the TeX.SE site.

www.PacktPub.com

Support files, eBooks, discount offers, and more

You might want to visit www.PacktPub.com for support files and downloads related to your book.

Did you know that Packt offers eBook versions of every book published, with PDF and ePub files available? You can upgrade to the eBook version at www.PacktPub.com and as a print book customer, you are entitled to a discount on the eBook copy. Get in touch with us at service@packtpub.com for more details.

At www.PacktPub.com, you can also read a collection of free technical articles, sign up for a range of free newsletters, and receive exclusive discounts and offers on Packt books and eBooks.

 PACKTLiB®

http://PacktLib.PacktPub.com

Do you need instant solutions to your IT questions? PacktLib is Packt's online digital book library. Here, you can access, read, and search across Packt's entire library of books.

Why Subscribe?

- Fully searchable across every book published by Packt
- Copy and paste, print, and bookmark content
- On demand and accessible via web browser

Free Access for Packt account holders

If you have an account with Packt at www.PacktPub.com, you can use this to access PacktLib today and view nine entirely free books. Simply use your login credentials for immediate access.

Table of Contents

Preface

LaTeX is a high-quality open source typesetting software that produces professional prints and PDF files. However, as LaTeX is a powerful and complex tool, getting started can be intimidating. There is no official support and certain aspects such as layout modifications can seem rather complicated. It may seem more straightforward to use Word or other WYSIWG programs, but once you've become acquainted, LaTeX's capabilities far outweigh any initial difficulties. This book guides you through these challenges and makes beginning with LaTeX easy. If you are writing mathematical, scientific, or business papers, then this is the perfect book for you.

LaTeX Beginner's Guide offers you a practical introduction to LaTeX. Beginning with the installation and basic usage, you will learn to typeset documents containing tables, figures, formulas, and common book elements like bibliographies, glossaries, and indexes. Lots of step-by-step examples start with fine-tuning text, formulas and page layout and go on to managing complex documents and using modern PDF features. It's easy to use LaTeX, when you have LaTeX Beginner's Guide at hand.

This practical book will guide you through the essential steps of Latex, from installing LaTeX, formatting, and justification, to page design. Finally, you will learn how to manage complex documents and how to benefit from modern PDF features. Right from the beginning, you will learn to use macros and styles to maintain a consistent document structure while saving typing work. This book will help you learn to create professional looking tables as well as include figures and write complex mathematic formulas. You will see how to generate bibliographies and indexes with ease. Detailed information about online resources like software archives, web forums, and online compilers complement this introductory guide.

What this book covers

Chapter 1, Getting Started with LaTeX, introduces LaTeX and explains its benefits. It guides you through the download and installation of a comprehensive LaTeX distribution and shows you how to create your first LaTeX document.

Chapter 2, Formatting Words, Lines, and Paragraphs, explains how to vary font, shape, and style of text. It deals with centering and justification of paragraphs and how you can improve line breaks and hyphenation. It introduces the concept of logical formatting and teaches you how to define macros and how to use environments and packages.

Chapter 3, Designing Pages, shows how you can adjust the margins and change the line spacing. It demonstrates portrait, landscape, and two-column layout. In this chapter, we will create dynamic headers and footers and learn how to control page breaking and how to use footnotes. Along the way, you will also learn about redefining existing commands and using class options. Furthermore, you will get familiar with accessing package documentation.

Chapter 4, Creating Lists, deals with arranging text in bulleted, numbered, and definition lists. We will learn how to choose bullets and numbering style and how to design the overall layout of lists.

Chapter 5, Creating Tables and Inserting Pictures, shows you how to create professional-looking tables and how to include external pictures in your documents. It deals with typesetting captions to tables and figures. We will learn how to benefit from LaTeX's automated tables and figures placement and how to fine-tune it.

Chapter 6, Cross-Referencing, introduces means of intelligent referencing to sections, footnotes, tables, figures, and numbered environments in general.

Chapter 7, Listing Content and References, deals with creating and customizing of a table of contents and lists of figures and tables. Furthermore, it teaches how to cite books, how to create bibliographies, and how to generate an index.

Chapter 8, Typing Math Formulas, explains mathematical typesetting in depth. It starts with basic formulas and continues with centered and numbered equations. It shows how to align multi-line equations. In detail, it shows how to typeset math symbols such as roots, arrows, Greek letters, and operators. Moreover, you will learn how to build complex math structures such as fractions, stacked expressions, and matrices.

Chapter 9, Using Fonts, takes us into the world of fonts and demonstrates various fonts for Roman, sans-serif, and typewriter fonts in different shapes. By the way, you will learn about character encoding and font encoding.

Chapter 10, *Developing Large Documents*, helps in managing large documents by splitting them into several files. It shows how to swap out settings, how to reuse code, and how to compile just parts of a bigger documents. After reading this chapter, you will be able to create complex projects building upon sub-files. Furthermore, we deal with front matter and back matter with different page numbering and separate title pages. We will work it out by creating an example book. By doing this, you will get familiar with using document templates, finally being able to write our own thesis, book, or report.

Chapter 11, *Enhancing Your Documents Further*, brings color into your documents. It shows you how to modify headings of chapters and all kinds of sections. We will learn how to create feature-rich PDF documents with bookmarks, hyperlinks, and meta-data. While doing this, we visit the TeX Catalogue Online to look out for further useful LaTeX packages and we will go through a package installation.

Chapter 12, *Troubleshooting*, provides us with tools for problem-solving. We will learn about different kinds of LaTeX's errors and warnings and how to deal with them. After reading this chapter, you will understand LaTeX's messages and you will know how to use them for fixing errors.

Chapter 13, *Using Online Resources*, guides you through the vast amount of LaTeX information on the Internet. We will visit a LaTeX online forum and a LaTeX Question & Answer site. This chapter points the way to huge LaTeX software archives, to homepages of TeX user groups, to mailing lists, Usenet groups, and LaTeX blogs. It tells you where you can download LaTeX capable editors and where you can find enhanced versions of TeX, such as XeTeX, LuaTeX, and ConTeXt. Finally, you will know how to access the knowledge of the world-wide LaTeX community and how to become a part of it.

What you need for this book

You need access to a computer with LaTeX on it. An online connection would be helpful regarding installation and updates. LaTeX can be installed on most operating systems, so you can use Windows, Linux, Mac OS X, or Unix.

This book uses the freely available TeX Live distribution, which runs on all mentioned platforms. You just need an online connection or the TeX Live DVD to install it. In the book, we work with the cross-platform editor TeXworks, but you could use any editor you like.

Who this book is for

If you are about to write mathematical or scientific papers, seminar handouts, or even plan to write a thesis, then this book offers you a fast-paced and practical introduction. Particularly when studying in school and university you will benefit a lot, as a mathematician and a physicist as well as an engineer or a humanist. Everybody with high expectations who plans to write a paper or a book may be delighted by this stable software.

Conventions

In this book, you will find several headings appearing frequently. To give clear instructions of how to complete a procedure or task, we use:

Time for action - heading

1. Action 1

2. Action 2

3. Action 3

Instructions often need some extra explanation so that they make sense, so they are followed with:

What just happened?

This heading explains the working of tasks or instructions that you have just completed.

You will also find some other learning aids in the book, including:

Pop quiz

These are short multiple choice questions intended to help you test your own understanding.

Have a go hero - heading

These set practical challenges and give you ideas for experimenting with what you have learned.

You will also find a number of styles of text that distinguish between different kinds of information. Here are some examples of these styles, and an explanation of their meaning.

Code words in text are shown as follows: "The command `\chapter` produced a large heading. This command will always begin on a new page."

A block of code is set as follows:

```
\documentclass[a4paper,12pt]{book}
\usepackage[english]{babel}
\usepackage{blindtext}
\begin{document}
\chapter{Exploring the page layout}
In this chapter we will study the layout of pages.
\section{Some filler text}
\blindtext
\section{A lot more filler text}
More dummy text will follow.
\subsection{Plenty of filler text}
\blindtext[10]
\end{document}
```

When we wish to draw your attention to a particular part of a code block, the relevant lines or items are set in bold:

```
\documentclass[a4paper,11pt]{book}
\usepackage[english]{babel}
\usepackage{blindtext}
\usepackage[a4paper, inner=1.5cm, outer=3cm, top=2cm,
bottom=3cm, bindingoffset=1cm]{geometry}
\begin{document}
\chapter{Exploring the page layout}
In this chapter we will study the layout of pages.
\section{Some filler text}
\blindtext
\section{A lot more filler text}
More dummy text will follow.
\subsection{Plenty of filler text}
\blindtext[3]
\end{document}
```

Any command-line input or output is written as follows:

```
texdoc geometry
```

New terms and **important words** are shown in bold. Words that you see on the screen, in menus or dialog boxes for example, appear in the text like this: "Save the document and **Typeset** it."

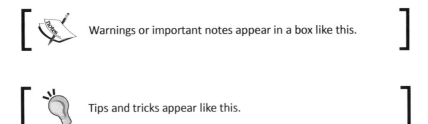

Warnings or important notes appear in a box like this.

Tips and tricks appear like this.

Reader feedback

Feedback from our readers is always welcome. Let us know what you think about this book—what you liked or may have disliked. Reader feedback is important for us to develop titles that you really get the most out of.

To send us general feedback, simply send an e-mail to feedback@packtpub.com, and mention the book title via the subject of your message.

If there is a book that you need and would like to see us publish, please send us a note in the **SUGGEST A TITLE** form on www.packtpub.com or e-mail suggest@packtpub.com.

If there is a topic that you have expertise in and you are interested in either writing or contributing to a book on, see our author guide on www.packtpub.com/authors.

Customer support

Now that you are the proud owner of a Packt book, we have a number of things to help you to get the most from your purchase.

Downloading the example code

You can download the example code files for all Packt books you have purchased from your account at http://www.PacktPub.com. If you purchased this book elsewhere, you can visit http://www.PacktPub.com/support and register to have the files e-mailed directly to you.

Errata

Although we have taken every care to ensure the accuracy of our content, mistakes do happen. If you find a mistake in one of our books—maybe a mistake in the text or the code—we would be grateful if you would report this to us. By doing so, you can save other readers from frustration and help us improve subsequent versions of this book. If you find any errata, please report them by visiting http://www.packtpub.com/support, selecting your book, clicking on the **errata submission form** link, and entering the details of your errata. Once your errata are verified, your submission will be accepted and the errata will be uploaded on our website, or added to any list of existing errata, under the Errata section of that title. Any existing errata can be viewed by selecting your title from http://www. packtpub.com/support.

Piracy

Piracy of copyright material on the Internet is an ongoing problem across all media. At Packt, we take the protection of our copyright and licenses very seriously. If you come across any illegal copies of our works, in any form, on the Internet, please provide us with the location address or website name immediately so that we can pursue a remedy.

Please contact us at copyright@packtpub.com with a link to the suspected pirated material.

We appreciate your help in protecting our authors, and our ability to bring you valuable content.

Questions

You can contact us at questions@packtpub.com if you are having a problem with any aspect of the book, and we will do our best to address it.

1

Getting Started with LaTeX

Are you ready to leave those "what you see is what you get" word processors behind and to enter the world of real, reliable, and high-quality typesetting? Then let's go together!

It's great that you decided to learn LaTeX. This book will guide you along the way to help you get the most out of it. Let's speak briefly about LaTeX's benefits and the challenges, and then we shall prepare our tools.

In this chapter, we will:

- ◆ Get to know LaTeX and talk about the pros and cons compared to word processors
- ◆ Install a complete LaTeX software bundle, including an editor
- ◆ Write our first LaTeX document

So, let's get started.

What is LaTeX?

LaTeX is a software for typesetting documents. In other words, it's a document preparation system. LaTeX is not a word processor, but is used as a document markup language.

LaTeX is a free, open source software. It was originally written by Leslie Lamport and is based on the TeX typesetting engine by Donald Knuth. People often refer to it as just TeX, meaning LaTeX. It has a long history; you can read about it at `http://www.tug.org/whatis.html`. For now, let's continue by looking at how we can make the best use of it.

How we can benefit

LaTeX is especially well-suited for scientific and technical documents. Its superior typesetting of mathematical formulas is legendary. If you are a student or a scientist, then LaTeX is by far the best choice, and even if you don't need its scientific capabilities, there are other uses — it produces very high quality output, it is extremely stable, and handles complex documents easily no matter how large they are.

Further remarkable strengths of LaTeX are its cross-referencing capabilities, its automatic numbering and generation of lists of contents, figures and tables, indexes, glossaries, and bibliographies. It is multilingual with language-specific features, and it is able to use PostScript and PDF features.

Apart from being perfect for scientists, LaTeX is incredibly flexible—there are templates for letters, presentations, bills, philosophy books, law texts, music scores, and even for chess game notations. Hundreds of LaTeX users have written thousands of templates, styles, and tools useful for every possible purpose. It is collected and categorized online on archiving servers.

You could benefit from its impressive high quality by starting with its default styles relying on its intelligent formatting, but you are free to customize and to modify everything. People of the TeX community have already written a lot of extensions addressing nearly every formatting need.

The virtues of open source

The sources of LaTeX are completely free and readable for everyone. This enables you to study and to change everything, from the core of LaTeX to the latest extension packages. But what does this mean for you as a beginner? There's a huge LaTeX community with a lot of friendly, helpful people. Even if you cannot benefit from the open source code directly, they can read the sources and assist you. Just join a LaTeX web forum and ask your questions there. Helpers will, if necessary, dig into LaTeX sources and in all probability find a solution for you, sometimes by recommending a suitable package, often providing a redefinition of a default command.

Today, we're already profiting from about 30 years of development by the TeX community. The open source philosophy made it possible, as every user is invited to study and improve the software and develop it further. *Chapter 13, Using Online Resources*, will point the way to the community.

Separation of form and content

A basic principle of LaTeX is that the author should not be distracted too much by the formatting issues. Usually, the author focuses on the content and formats logically, for example, instead of writing a chapter title in big bold letters, you just tell LaTeX that it's a chapter heading—you could let LaTeX design the heading or you decide in the document's settings what the headings will look like—just once for the whole document.

LaTeX uses style files extensively called **classes** and **packages**, making it easy to design and to modify the appearance of the whole document and all of its details.

Portability

LaTeX is available for nearly every operating system, like Windows, Linux, Mac OS X, and many more. Its file format is plain text—readable and editable, on all operating systems. LaTeX will produce the same output on all systems. Though there are different LaTeX software packages, so called **TeX distributions**, we will focus on **TeX Live**, because this distribution is available for Windows, Linux, and Mac OS X.

LaTeX itself doesn't have a graphical user interface; that's one of the reasons why it's so portable. You can choose any text editor. There are many editors, even specialized in LaTeX, for every operating system. Some editors are available for several systems. For instance, **TeXworks** runs on Windows, Linux, and Mac OS X; that's one of the reasons why we will use it in our book. Another very important reason is that it's probably best-suited for beginners.

LaTeX generates PDF output—printable and readable, on most computers and looks identical regardless of the operating system. Besides PDF, it supports DVI, PostScript, and HTML output, preparing the ground for distribution both in print and online, on screen, electronic book readers, or smart phones.

To sum up, LaTeX is portable in three ways—source, its implementation, and output.

Protection for your work

LaTeX documents are stored in human readable text format, not in some obscure word processing format, that may be altered in a different version of the same software. Try to open a 20 year old document written with a commercial word processor. What might your modern software show? Even if you can read the file, its visual appearance would certainly be different than before. LaTeX promises that the document will always be readable and will result in the same output. Though it's being further developed, it will remain backwards compatible.

Word processor documents could be infected with viruses, malicious macros could destroy the data. Did you ever hear of a virus "hiding" in a text file? LaTeX is not threatened by viruses.

Comparing it to word processor software

We've already described some advantages of the typesetting system LaTeX compared to word processing software. While LaTeX encourages structured writing, other word processors may compel you to work inconsistently. They might hide the real formatting structure and encrypt your document in some proprietary file format. Compatibility is a big problem, even between versions of the same software.

There are some interesting articles available online comparing LaTeX to other software. Of course, they are expressions of opinion. Some are years old and therefore do not cover the most recent software, but they discuss important points that are still valid today. You will find them listed in *Chapter 13, Using Online Resources*.

What are the challenges?

The learning curve could be steep, but this book will to help you master it.

Though writing LaTeX looks like programming, don't be afraid. Soon you will know the frequently used commands. Text editors with auto completion and keyword highlighting will support you. They might even provide menus and dialogs with commands for you.

Do you now think it will take a long time until you would learn to achieve creditable results? Don't worry; this book will give you a quick start. You will learn by practicing with a lot of examples. Many more examples can be read and downloaded from the Internet. In *Chapter 13*, we will explore the Internet resources.

We shall continue with the setup of LaTeX on our computer.

Installing LaTeX

Let's start off with the installation of the LaTeX distribution—TeX Live. This distribution is available for Windows, Linux, Mac OS X, and other Unix-like operating systems. TeX Live is well maintained and it is being actively developed.

 Another very good and user-friendly LaTeX distribution for Windows is MiKTeX. It's easy to install like any other Windows application, but it's not available for other systems like Linux or Mac OS X. You can download it from http://miktex.org.

At first, we will visit the TeX Live homepage and take a survey of the installation possibilities. Feel free to explore the homepage in depth to study the information offered there.

Open the TeX Live homepage at http://tug.org/texlive.

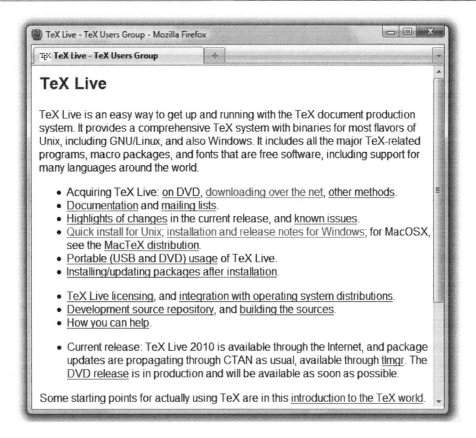

We will cover two ways of installation. The first will be online and requires an Internet connection. The other method starts with a huge download, but may be finished offline.

Let's check out the two installation methods.

Time for action – installing TeX Live using the net installer wizard

We will download the TeX Live net installer and install the complete TeX Live distribution on our computer.

1. Click on **downloading over the net** or navigate to `http://tug.org/texlive/acquire-netinstall`.

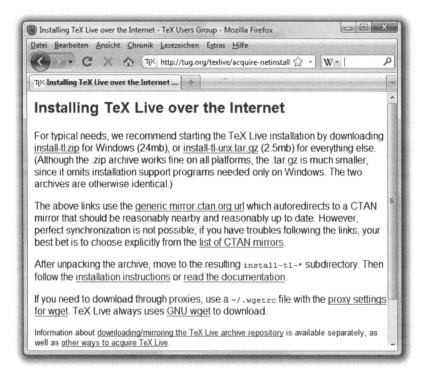

2. Download the net installer for Windows by clicking on **install-tl.zip**.

3. Extract the file `install-tl.zip` using your favorite archiving program. For example, WinZip, WinRar, or 7-Zip can do it for you.

4. Open the folder `install-tl-*`and double-click the Windows batch file `install-tl`:

5. The net installer will automatically detect your language. If it's showing the wrong language, you can force the choice of the language using the `lang` option at the command prompt such as `install-tl -lang=en`:

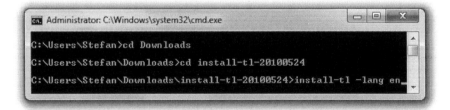

6. The installation wizard will pop up, as shown in the following screenshot:

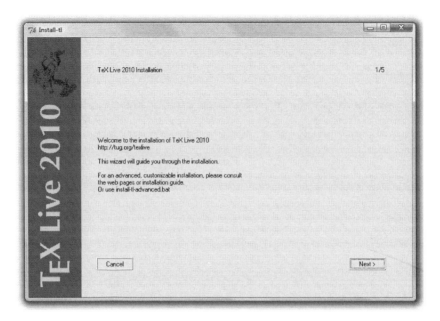

7. Click on the **Next** button, now it offers to change the installation folder, but it's fine to retain it. In our book, we will refer to this default location:

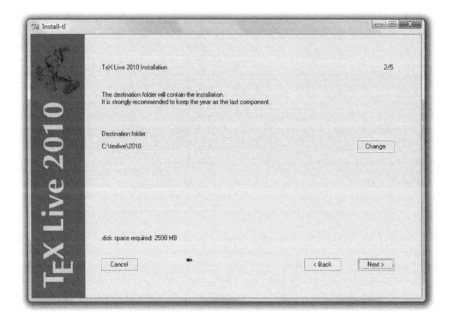

8. Click on the **Next** button. As shown in the following screenshot, choose one of the options, for example, for the creation of shortcuts:

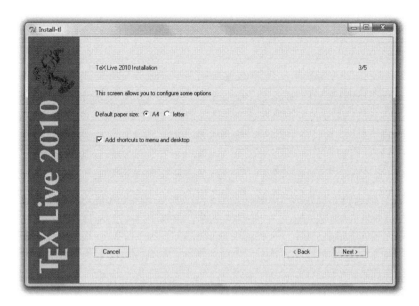

9. Click on the **Next** button. You can then confirm the settings and actually start the installation by clicking on the **Install** button:

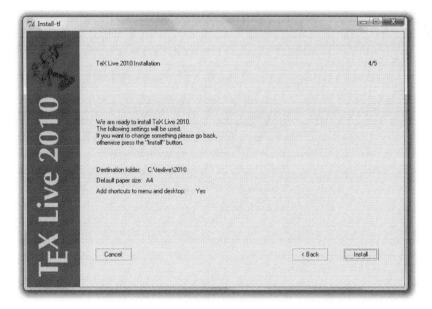

10. The next screenshot shows how you can monitor the installation progress:

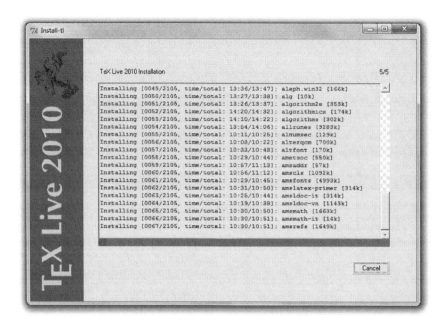

11. Finally, click on the **Finish** button and you're done.

What just happened?

You have completed the installation of TeX Live 2010. Now your **Start** menu contains a folder called **TeX Live 2010** containing six programs:

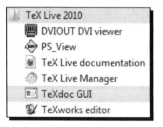

◆ **DVIOUT DVI viewer**—a viewer program for the classic LaTeX output format DVI. Today, most people choose PDF output, so you probably won't need it.

- ◆ **PS_VIEW**—a viewer program for the PostScript format; again you probably won't need it, except if you would like to use the PostScript language or read such documents.

- ◆ **TeX Live documentation**—well, that's useful regarding setup and use of your software!

- ◆ **TeX Live Manager**—that's your tool for package management, for example, installation and update of LaTeX packages.

- ◆ **TeXdoc GUI**—it's a graphical user interface offering access to a huge amount of LaTeX-related information. There's a lot of it stored in your computer by now. Use it to gather information whenever needed; it could be quicker than searching online.

- ◆ **TeXworks editor**—this is an editor developed to create LaTeX documents comfortably. We will make extensive use of it.

 TeXworks is also shipped with MiKTeX 2.8 and higher.

If you would like to stay in control over what should be installed on your computer, start the **install-tl-advanced** batch file instead of **install-tl**:

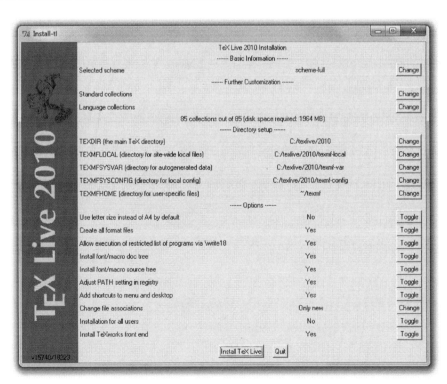

The TeX documentation available online contains more information for advanced users.

Now, we will go through the offline installation of TeX Live 2010.

Time for action – installing TeX Live offline

We will download a compressed ISO image of TeX Live 2010 with a size of about 1.2 gigabytes. After extraction, we can choose to burn it on DVD or to extract it to our hard disk drive and run the installation from there:

1. Visit the download area at `http://www.tug.org/texlive/acquire-iso.html`.

2. Download `texlive2010.xz`. If possible, use a download manager, especially if your Internet connection is not stable.

3. Extract `texlive2010.xz` and you will get the file `texlive2010.iso`. If your archiving program doesn't support the `.xz` file format, obtain, for instance, the program 7-Zip version 9 or later from `http://7zip.org` and use it for extraction.

4. Either burn the ISO file on a DVD using a burning software supporting the ISO format or extract it to your hard disk drive. 7-Zip is also capable of doing that for you.

5. Among the extracted files or on your DVD, you will find the installer batch files `install-tl` and `install-tl-advanced` that we've already seen. Choose one, start it, and go through the installation like in the previous installation.

What just happened?

It was similar to the first installation, but this time you've got all the data and you won't need an Internet connection. This complete download is especially recommended if it's foreseeable that you will do another installation of TeX Live later or if you would like to give it to friends or colleagues.

 After an offline installation, it's recommended to run an update of TeX Live soon, because packages on a DVD or within an image could already be outdated. Use the **TeX Live Manager** to keep your system up-to-date if you are connected to the Internet.

Installation on other operating systems

If you work on Mac OS X, you may download a customized version of TeX Live at `http://www.tug.org/mactex/`. Download the huge `.zip` file and double-click on it to install.

On most Linux systems, installation is easy. Use your system's package manager. With Ubuntu, you may use Synaptic, on SUSE systems use YaST, with Red Hat a RPM frontend, and on Debian systems use Aptitude. In the respective package manager, look out for `texlive`.

If you want to stay on the edge, you could download and install the most current version of TeX Live from its homepage, instead of the version from the operating system's repositories. But be aware that installing third party sources may harm the integrity of your system.

Now that we've prepared the ground, let's start to write LaTeX!

Creating our first document

We have installed TeX and launched the editor; now let's jump in at the deep end by writing our first LaTeX document.

Time for action – writing our first document with TeXworks

Our first goal is to create a document that's printing out just one sentence. We want to use it to understand the basic structure of a LaTeX document.

1. Launch the TeXworks editor by clicking on the desktop icon or open it in the **Start** menu.

2. Click on the **New** button.

3. Enter the following lines:
```
\documentclass{article}
\begin{document}
This is our first document.
\end{document}
```

4. Click on the **Save** button and save the document. Choose a location where you want to store your LaTeX documents, ideally in its own folder.

5. In the drop-down field in the TeXworks toolbar, choose **pdfLaTeX**:

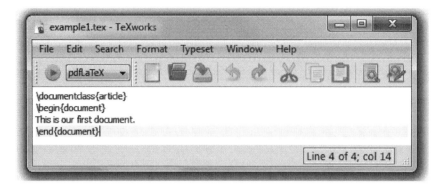

6. Click the **Typeset** button 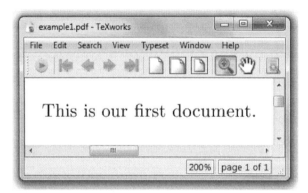.

7. The output window will automatically open. Have a look at it:

What just happened?

You have just seen the first few minutes of the life of a LaTeX document. Its following hours and days will be determined by editing, typesetting, and so on. Don't forget to save your document frequently.

As announced in contrary to the classic word processor software, you cannot see the effect of changes immediately—but the result is just one click away.

Have a go hero – checking out advanced LaTeX editors

Do you have experience in working with complex programs? Do you like using a feature-rich and powerful editor? Then have a look at these LaTeX editors. Visit their websites to find screenshots and to read about their features:

- **TeXnicCenter**— a very powerful editor for Windows, `http://texniccenter.org/`
- **Kile**— a user-friendly editor for operating systems with KDE, such as Linux, `http://kile.sourceforge.net/`
- **TeXShop**—an easy-to-use and very popular editor for Mac OS X, `http://pages.uoregon.edu/koch/texshop/`
- **Texmaker**—a cross-platform editor running on Linux, Mac OS X, Unix, and Windows systems, `http://www.xm1math.net/texmaker/`

The mentioned editors are free open source software.

Summary

We learned in this chapter about the benefits of LaTeX. It will be our turn to use the virtues of LaTeX to achieve the best possible results.

Furthermore, we covered:

- Installation of TeX Live
- Using the editor TeXworks
- Creation of a LaTeX document and generation of output

Now that we've got a functional and tested LaTeX system, we're ready to write our own LaTeX documents. In the next chapter, we will work out the formatting of text in detail.

2
Formatting Words, Lines, and Paragraphs

In the last chapter, we installed LaTeX and used the TeXworks editor to write our first document. Now we will speak about the structure of a document and we will focus on the text details and its formatting.

In this chapter, we shall:

- ◆ Speak about logical formatting
- ◆ Learn how to modify font, shape, and style of text
- ◆ Use boxes to limit the text width
- ◆ See how to break lines and how to improve hyphenation
- ◆ Explore justification and formatting of paragraphs

By working with examples and trying out new features, we shall learn some basic concepts of LaTeX. By the end of this chapter, we will be familiar with commands and environments. You will even be able to define your own commands.

Understanding logical formatting

In the previous chapter, we wrote a small example document. Let's extend it a bit to get an illustrative example for understanding the typical document structure.

Time for action – titling your document

We will take the first example and insert some commands that will produce a nice-looking title.

1. Type the following code in the editor; modify the previous example if you like:

```
\documentclass[a4paper,11pt]{article}
\begin{document}
\title{Example 2}
\author{My name}
\date{January 5, 2011}
\maketitle
\section{What's this?}
This is our second document. It contains a title and a section
with text.
\end{document}
```

2. Click the **Typeset** button.

3. View the output:

Example 2

My name

January 5, 2011

1 What's this?

This is our second document. It contains a title and a section with text.

What just happened?

In the first chapter, we talked about logical formatting. First, let's look at this example from that point of view. We told LaTeX that:

- Our document is of the type `article`. It will be printed on A4 paper using a size of 11 points for the base font.
- The title is "Example 2".
- You are the author.
- The document was written on January 5, 2011.

- Concerning the content of the document:

    - It begins with a title.

    - The first section shall have the heading "What's this?"

    - The following text is "This is our second document."

Note, we did not choose the font size of the title or heading; neither did we make something bold or centered. Such formatting is done by LaTeX but nevertheless you're free to tell LaTeX how it actually should look.

[We did not need to press the **Save** button. TeXworks automatically saves the document if we click the **Typeset** button.]

Exploring the document structure

Let's look at the details. A LaTeX document doesn't stand alone—commonly the document is based on a versatile template. Such a fundamental template is called a **class**. It provides customizable features, usually built for a certain purpose. There are classes for books, for journal articles, for letters, for presentations, for posters, and many more; hundreds of reliable classes can be found in Internet archives but also on your computer now, after you've installed TeX Live. Here we have chosen the article class, a standard LaTeX class suitable for smaller documents.

The first line starts with \documentclass. This word begins with a backslash; such a word is called a **command**. We used commands to specify the class and to state document properties: title, author, and date.

This first part of the document is called the **preamble** of the document. This is where we choose the class, specify properties, and in general, make document-wide definitions.

\begin{document} marks the end of the preamble and the beginning of the actual document. \end{document} marks the end of it. Everything that follows would be ignored by LaTeX. Such a piece of code, framed by a \begin ... \end command pair, is called an **environment**.

In the actual document, we've used the command \maketitle that prints the title, author, and date in a nicely formatted manner. By the \section command, we produced a heading, bigger and bolder than normal text. Then we let some text follow. What we wrote here, in the document environment, will be printed out. On the contrary, the preamble will never produce any output.

Let's look at commands in detail.

Understanding LaTeX commands

LaTeX commands begin with a backslash, followed by big or small letters. LaTeX commands are usually named with small letters and in a descriptive way. There are exceptions: you will see some commands consisting of a backslash and just one special character.

Commands may have **arguments**, given in curly braces or in square brackets.

Calling a command looks like the following:

```
\command
```

Or:

```
\command{argument}
```

Or:

```
\command[optional argument]{argument}
```

There could be several arguments, each of them in braces or brackets. Arguments in curly braces are mandatory. If a command is defined to require an argument, one has to be given. For example, calling `\documentclass` would be futile if we hadn't stated a class name.

Arguments in square brackets are optional; they may be given but it's not a must. If no optional argument is provided, the command will use a default one. For instance, in the first example in *Chapter 1, Getting Started with LaTeX*, we wrote `\documentclass{article}`. This document has been typeset with a base font size of 10pt, because this is the class default base font size. In the second document, we wrote `\documentclass[a4paper,11pt]{article}`; this way, we replaced default values with the given values, so now the document will be adjusted for A4 paper using a base font size of 11pt.

There are commands generating output—try `\LaTeX`—and commands setting properties, changing fonts or layout. Generally, the names of commands are chosen according to their purpose. We will have a more detailed look in this chapter, but first let's see how LaTeX treats what we type.

How LaTeX reads your input

Before we continue writing, let's look at how LaTeX understands what you've written in the editor.

Time for action – trying out the effect of spaces, line breaks, and empty lines

We will take the first example and insert spaces and line breaks.

1. Modify the previous example as follows:

```
\documentclass[a4paper,11pt]{article}
\begin{document}
\title{Example 3}
\author{My name}
\date{January 5, 2011}
\maketitle
\section{What's this?}
This          is     our
second document.

It contains two paragraphs. The first line of a paragraph will be
indented, but not when it follows a heading.
% Here's a comment.
\end{document}
```

2. **Typeset**.

3. View the output:

Example 3

My name

January 5, 2011

1   What's this?

This is our second document.

    It contains two paragraphs. The first line of a paragraph will be indented, but not when it follows a heading.

What just happened?

Though we've inserted some spaces, the distances between the words in the output remained the same. The reason is that LaTeX treats multiple spaces just like a single space. Also, a single line break has the same effect like a single space. It doesn't matter how you arrange your text in the editor using spaces or breaks, the output will stay the same.

A blank line denotes a paragraph break. Like spaces, multiple empty lines are treated as one.

Briefly said, spaces separate words, empty lines separate paragraphs.

Commenting your source text

You've seen that the last line seems to be missing in the output. That's because the percent sign introduces a **comment**. Everything following a percent sign until the end of the line will be ignored by LaTeX and won't be printed out. This enables you to insert notes into your document. It's often used in templates to inform the user what the template does at that certain place. Note also that the end of the line, normally behaving like a space, will be ignored after a percent sign.

Easing experimenting by trial and error

If you want to disable a command temporarily, it may be favorable to insert a percent sign instead of deleting the command. That way, you're able to undo this change easily by removing the %.

If the percent sign behaves that way, what should we do if we want to write **100%** in our text? Let's figure out how to do it.

Printing out special symbols

Common text mostly contains upper and lowercase letters, digits, and punctuation characters. Simply type them with your editor. However, some characters are reserved for LaTeX commands; they cannot be used directly. We already encountered such characters, and besides the percent sign, there are the curly braces and so on. There are LaTeX commands to print such symbols.

Time for action – writing special characters in our text

We will write a very short example printing out an amount of dollars and a percent number, then we shall try more symbols:

1. Create a new document and enter the following lines:

```
\documentclass{article}
\begin{document}
Statement \#1:
50\% of \$100 makes \$50.
More special symbols are \&, \_, \{ and \}.
\end{document}
```

2. **Typeset** and view the output:

> Statement #1: 50% of $100 makes $50.
> More special symbols are &, _, { and }.

What just happened?

By putting a backslash before such a special symbol, we turned it into a LaTeX command. This command has the only purpose of printing out that symbol.

 The command for printing a backslash is \textbackslash. If you would like to know what \\ might be used for, it is used as a shortcut for a line break command. That's a bit odd, but line breaks occur frequently whereas backslashes are rarely needed in the output, therefore this shortcut has been chosen.

There's a wealth of symbols that we can use for math formulas, chess notation, zodiac signs, music scores, and more. We don't need to deal with those symbols for now, but we shall return to that subject in *Chapter 8, Typing Math Formulas*, when we will need symbols to typeset math formulas.

Now that we know how to enter pure text, let's find out how we can format it.

Formatting text – fonts, shapes, and styles

LaTeX already does some formatting. For example, we've seen that section headings are bigger than normal text and bold faced. Now we will learn how to modify the appearance of the text ourselves.

Time for action – tuning the font shape

We will emphasize an important word in a text and we will see how to make words appear bold, italic, or slanted. We shall figure out how to highlight words in a part of some text that's already emphasized:

1. Create a new document containing the following code:

```
\documentclass{article}
\begin{document}
Text can be \emph{emphasized}.

Besides being \textit{italic} words could be \textbf{bold},
\textsl{slanted} or typeset in \textsc{Small Caps}.

Such commands can be \textit{\textbf{nested}}.

\emph{See how \emph{emphasizing} looks when nested.}
\end{document}
```

2. **Typeset** and have a look at the output:

> Text can be *emphasized*.
> Besides being *italic* words could be **bold**, *slanted* or typeset in SMALL CAPS.
> Such commands can be ***nested***.
> *See how* emphasizing *looks when nested.*

What just happened?

At first, we used the command \emph, giving one word as an argument to this command. This argument will be typeset in italic shape, because this is the default way how LaTeX emphasizes text.

Text-formatting commands usually look like \text**{argument}, where ** stands for a two letter abbreviation like bf for bold face, it for italic, and sl for slanted. The argument will then be formatted accordingly like we've seen. After the command, the subsequent text will be typeset as it was before the command—precisely after the closing curly brace marking the end of the argument. We checked it out.

We've nested the commands \textit and \textbf, which allowed us to achieve a combination of those styles, and the text appears both italic and bold.

Most font commands will show the same effect if they are applied twice like `\textbf{\textbf{words}}`: the words won't become bolder. Only `\emph` behaves differently. We've seen that emphasized text will be italic, but if we use `\emph` onto a piece of this text again, it will change from italic to normal font. Imagine an important theorem completely typeset in italics—you should still have the opportunity to highlight words inside this theorem.

`\emph` is so called **semantic markup**, because it refers to the meaning, not just to the appearance of text.

 Emphasizing twice, such as marking bold and italic at the same time, might be considered to be a questionable style. Change the font shape wisely—and consistently.

Choosing the font family

Compare the font of our examples and the standard font you see in this book. While the LaTeX font has a decorative appearance, the text font of this book looks simple and clean. Our code examples are different in another way: every letter has the same width. Let's see how we can implement this in our writings.

Time for action – switching to sans-serif and to typewriter fonts

Imagine that we start to write an article about LaTeX's Internet resources. To get a clearly readable heading, we shall use a font without frills. The body text will contain a web address; we choose a typewriter font to stress it:

1. Create a LaTeX document with the following code:

```
\documentclass{article}
\begin{document}
\section{\textsf{\LaTeX\ resources on the internet}}
The best place for downloading LaTeX related software is CTAN.
Its address is \texttt{http://www.ctan.org}.
\end{document}
```

2. **Typeset** and look at the result:

> # 1   LaTeX resources on the internet
>
> The best place for downloading LaTeX related software is CTAN. Its address is `http://www.ctan.org`.

What just happened?

We encountered more font commands. By using `\textsf`, we've chosen the sans-serif font in the section heading. We used the command `\texttt` to get the typewriter font for the web address. Those commands can be used just like the font commands we've learned before.

The letters in the LaTeX standard font have so-called **serifs**, those small decorative details at the end of a letter's strokes. Serifs shall improve readability by leading the reader's eyes along the line. Therefore, they are widely used in body text. Such fonts are also called **Roman** fonts. This name led to the command `\textrm` for the Roman text—the default font with serifs.

Headings are often done without serifs; the used font is called a **sans-serif** font. Such fonts are also a good choice for screen text because of the better readability on lower resolutions. So you might want to choose a sans-serif font when you produce an e-book.

If every letter of a font has the same width, the font is called **monospaced** or a **typewriter** font. Besides, on typewriters, such fonts were used with early computers; today they are still preferred for writing source code of computer programs, both in print and in text editors. So if you want to typeset a program listing or LaTeX source code, consider using a typewriter font. Like we did in the previous example, this book is using a typewriter font to distinguish code and web addresses from the normal text.

Switching fonts

Putting too much text into a command's argument could be unhandy. Sometimes we would like to set font properties of longer passages of text. LaTeX provides other commands, which work like switches.

Time for action – switching the font family

We will modify the previous example using font family switching commands:

1. Modify the example to get the following code:

```
\documentclass{article}
\begin{document}
\section{\sffamily\LaTeX\ resources in the internet}
The best place for downloading LaTeX related software is CTAN.
Its address is \ttfamily http://www.ctan.org\rmfamily.
\end{document}
```

2. **Typeset** and compare the output to the previous one; it's the same.

What just happened?

By using the command \sffamily, we switched over to sans serif font. This change has been made inside an argument, so it's valid only there.

We used the command \ttfamily to switch to a typewriter font. The typewriter font will be used from this point onwards. By using\rmfamily, we returned to Roman font.

These commands don't produce any output, but they will affect the following text. We will call such a command a **declaration**.

Now have a closer look at the section number: it's a digit with serifs, which doesn't match the remaining sans-serif heading. Moreover, changing the font within a\section command feels wrong—and rightly so! The better way is to declare the section heading font once for the complete document. We will learn how to globally modify heading fonts in *Chapter 11*, *Enhancing Your Documents Further*, after we prepared some more tools.

Summarizing font commands and declarations

Let's list the font commands and their corresponding declarations together with their meanings:

Command	Declaration	Meaning
\textrm{...}	\rmfamily	roman family
\textsf{...}	\sffamily	sans-serif family
\texttt{...}	\ttfamily	typewriter family
\textbf{...}	\bfseries	**bold-face**
\textmd{...}	\mdseries	medium
\textit{...}	\itshape	*italic shape*
\textsl{...}	\slshape	*slanted shape*
\textsc{...}	\scshape	SMALL CAPS SHAPE
\textup{...}	\upshape	upright shape
\textnormal{...}	\normalfont	default font

 The corresponding declaration to \emph is \em.

Delimiting the effect of commands

In the previous example, we've reversed the effect of \ttfamily by writing \rmfamily. To be safe, we could write \normalfont to switch back to the base font. However, there's an easier way.

Time for action – exploring grouping by braces

We shall use curly braces to tell LaTeX where to apply a command and where to stop that:

1. Modify our first font shape example to get this code:

    ```
    \documentclass{article}
    \begin{document}
    {\sffamily
    Text can be {\em emphasized}.

    Besides being {\itshape italic} words could be {\bfseries bold},
    {\slshape slanted} or typeset in {\scshape Small Caps}.

    Such commands can be {\itshape\bfseries nested}.}

    {\em See how {\em emphasizing} looks when nested.}
    \end{document}
    ```

2. **Typeset** and check out the output:

> Text can be *emphasized*.
> Besides being *italic* words could be **bold**, *slanted* or typeset in SMALL CAPS.
> Such commands can be **nested**.
> *See how* emphasizing *looks when nested.*

What just happened?

We started with an opening curly brace. The effect of the following command `\sffamily` lasted until we stopped it with the corresponding closing brace. That closing brace came at the end of the highlighted code. This highlighting shows the area of the code where `\sffamily` is valid.

We replaced every font command by the corresponding declaration. Remember, `\em` is the declaration version of `\emph`. Further, we surrounded every declaration and the affected text by curly braces.

An opening curly brace tells LaTeX to begin a so called **group**. The following commands are valid for the subsequent text until a closing curly brace appears causing LaTeX to stop using the commands or declarations written in this group. Till a command is valid, that's called its **scope**.

Groups can be nested as follows:

```
Normal text, {\sffamily sans serif text {\bfseries and bold}}.
```

We have to be careful to close each group; opening and closing braces should match.

> Braces which enclose an argument of a command don't form a group. Together with the argument, these braces are gobbled by the command. If necessary, use additional braces.

Time for action – exploring font sizes

We will try out every font size available by LaTeX's default font size commands. For testing, we exceptionally use them in the body text—their main use is in the macro definitions:

1. Create a document with the following code:

```
\documentclass{article}
\begin{document}
\noindent\tiny We \scriptsize start \footnotesize \small small,
\normalsize get \large big \Large and \LARGE bigger,
```

```
\huge huge and \Huge gigantic!
\end{document}
```

2. **Typeset** and observe the output:

> We start small, get big and bigger, huge and gigantic!

What just happened?

At first, we used \noindent. This command suppresses the paragraph indentation. Then we used all 10 available size declarations, starting small with \tiny and ending really big with \Huge. There are no corresponding commands taking arguments, so we would have to use curly braces to delimit their scope, as we learned to before.

The actual resulting font size depends on the base font. If your document has a base font of 12 pt, then \tiny would result in text bigger than with a base font of 10 pt. We have to see it in relation. Use \footnotesize, if you wish to get the same size like LaTeX uses for footnotes; use \scriptsize, if you create a style with a size matching LaTeX subscripts and superscripts. It's still a kind of logical formatting though they are quite low-level commands.

Normally, font size declarations are used only in definitions of macros in the preamble, just as it does apply to the other font commands. You will rarely encounter font size or shape commands in good body texts, except freely designed passages like title pages—and test examples like the ones here.

Using environments

When you use several declarations and you group them by curly braces, will you always know which closing brace matches which of the previously entered declarations? An environment forms a group. Using an environment instead of just curly braces improves the readability of your code.

Time for action – using an environment to adjust the font size

We will produce a title with a larger and bigger font:

1. Create another small document with this code:

```
\documentclass{article}
\begin{document}
\begin{huge}
\bfseries
A small example
```

```
\end{huge}
\bigskip
This is just another small illustrative example.
\end{document}
```

2. **Typeset** to see the result:

> # A small example
>
> This is just another small illustrative example.

What just happened?

By writing `\begin{huge}`, we told LaTeX to switch to a huge font size just like with the `\huge` command. `\end{huge}` informs LaTeX that this size change should end now. From this point onwards, the font size is the same as before `\begin{huge}`.

Inside this environment, we use the declaration `\bfseries`. Note that the effect of this declaration ended together with the end of the environment.

The empty line before `\end{huge}` denotes a paragraph break. Using the command `\bigskip`, we skipped some space vertically.

For every declaration there's a corresponding environment carrying the same name except the backslash. Using environments instead of braces might make complex code easily understandable.

> Commonly it's advisable to end the paragraph before a font size change, not after it. That's because TeX calculates the interline spacing depending on the current font size when it reaches the end of the paragraph. That's the reason we used the blank line before `\end{huge}` instead of afterwards.

Saving time and effort – creating your own commands

If you're frequently using the same term in your document, it would be annoying to type it again and again. What if you later decided to change that term or its formatting? To avoid searching and replacing in the whole document, LaTeX allows you to define your own commands in your preamble. They are also called **macros**. Give it a name. Later in the document you just need to use this name whenever you want to change this term. We need to do it just once in the macro definition. This will affect the whole document. Let's see how it works.

Time for action – creating our first command using it as an abbreviation

We will define a short command printing out the name of the TeX Users Group:

1. Type this code into a new document:

```
\documentclass{article}
\newcommand{\TUG}{TeX Users Group}
\begin{document}
\section{The \TUG}
The \TUG\ is an organization for people who are interested in
\TeX\ or \LaTeX.
\end{document}
```

2. **Typeset** and look at the result:

> # 1   The TeX Users Group
>
> The TeX Users Group is an organization for people who are interested in TEX or LATEX.

What just happened?

\newcommand in the highlighted line defines our command. The first argument is the name we chose for it, and the second argument is the text we want it to put out in the document.

Now, whenever we type \TUG in our document, the complete name will appear. If we later decide to change the name or its formatting, we just need to change this \newcommand line. Then it will be applied for the complete document.

You may use formatting commands inside your command definition. Let's say you would like to change the formatting of all occurrences of this name to be typeset in small caps; just change the definition to the following:

```
\newcommand{\TUG}{\textsc{TeX Users Group}}
```

You have also seen that we've used the command \TeX. This command just prints out the name of the basic typesetting system formatted like in its logo. It's an abbreviation command like we've written now and \LaTeX works similarly. Note that we had to use a backslash after \TeX! The following space would just separate the command from the following text; it won't produce a space in the output. Using the backslash followed by a space forces the output of the space that would otherwise be ignored. You may try omitting that backslash to be convinced.

Gentle spacing after commands

A backslash following a command could easily be forgotten. Can't we modify the command in order to automate that? Tasks like this, which aren't supported by LaTeX directly, could be solved by using **packages**. These are collections of styles and commands.

Time for action – adding intelligent spacing to command output

We will load the package `xspace`. Its only purpose is to fulfill this need.

1. Modify the previous example to get the following code:

```
\documentclass{article}
\usepackage{xspace}
\newcommand{\TUG}{\textsc{TeX Users Group}\xspace}
\begin{document}
\section{The \TUG}
The \TUG is an organization for people who are interested in \TeX\
or \LaTeX.
\end{document}
```

2. **Typeset**, see that the spacing between the words is correct, even without the backslash:

> ## 1   The TeX Users Group
>
> The TeX Users Group is an organization for people who are interested in TeX or LaTeX.

What just happened?

`\usepackage{xspace}` tells LaTeX to load the package called `xspace` and to read in all of its definitions. From now on we may use all commands contained in that package. This package provides the command `\xspace` that inserts a space depending on the following character: If a dot, a comma, an exclamation, or a quotation mark follows, it won't insert a space, but if a normal letter follows, then it will. Usually, that's exactly what we want.

Imagine you've mentioned the TUG several times in your document and now you've got the idea to use the TeX logo style in its name. There's no need for changes in the document. Now only the command in the preamble needs adjustment:

```
\newcommand{\TUG}{\textsc{\TeX\ Users Group}\xspace}
```

> ## 1   The TEX Users Group
>
> The TEX USERS GROUP is an organization for people who are interested in TEX or LATEX.

 The heading in our last example doesn't contain small caps—have you seen it? Not all font properties can be combined, depending on the chosen font. For instance, fonts with small caps together with variations like bold and italic are rare. Therefore, some people even fake small caps if they don't want to change to a more complex font.

By defining and using commands, you can ensure that the formatting remains consistent throughout your whole document.

Creating more universal commands – using arguments

Imagine that your text contains a lot of keywords that you want to be printed in bold. If you use the \textbf{} command on all the keywords, what would happen if you later decide to use an italic shape instead or a typewriter font? You would have to change that formatting for each keyword. There's a better way: defining your own macro and using \textbf{} only inside that.

Time for action – creating a macro for formatting keywords

We will use \newcommand again, but this time we will introduce a parameter that will contain our keyword. Let's just use it on some terms that we've got to know in this chapter:

1. Type this code example:

```
\documentclass{article}
\newcommand{\keyword}[1]{\textbf{#1}}
\begin{document}
\keyword{Grouping} by curly braces limits the
\keyword{scope} of \keyword{declarations}.
\end{document}
```

2. **Typeset** and notice the look of the keywords in the output:

> **Grouping** by curly braces limits the **scope** of **declarations**.

What just happened?

Let's look at the highlighted line in the code. The number 1 in the square brackets marks the number of arguments that we want to use in the command. #1 will be replaced by the value of the first argument. #2 would refer to a second argument, and so on.

Now if you want to modify the appearance of all keywords to be italic, just modify the definition of \keyword and the change will be global.

Using optional arguments

In one preceding example, we've used \newcommand with two arguments. In the previous example, there were three arguments. The additional argument has been put in square brackets. That's the way we mark **optional arguments**: those arguments may be given or may be omitted. If omitted, they would have a default value. We've already noticed that with the \documentclass command. But how can we define a command with optional arguments ourselves?

Time for action – marking keywords with optional formatting

We will use \newcommand another time, this time with an optional parameter concerning the formatting and a mandatory argument for the keyword:

1. Modify the previous example to get this code:

```
\documentclass{article}
\newcommand{\keyword}[2][\bfseries]{{#1#2}}
\begin{document}
\keyword{Grouping} by curly braces limits the
\keyword{scope} of \keyword[\itshape]{declarations}.
\end{document}
```

2. **Typeset** and check out the result:

> **Grouping** by curly braces limits the **scope** of *declarations*.

What just happened?

Let's look again at the bold marked line in the code. By using [\bfseries], we introduced an optional parameter. We refer to it with #1. Its default value is \bfseries. Since we used a declaration this time, we added a pair of braces to ensure that only the keyword is affected by the declaration.

Later in the document, we gave [\itshape] to \keyword, changing the default formatting to italics.

Here's the definition of the \newcommand:

\newcommand{command} [arguments] [optional] {definition}

command	The name of the new command, starting with a backslash followed by lowercase and/or uppercase letters or a backslash followed by a single non-letter symbol. That name must not be already defined and is not allowed to begin with \end.
arguments	An integer from 1 to 9, the number of arguments of the new command. If omitted, the command will have no arguments.
optional	If this is present, then the first of the arguments would be optional with a default value given here. Otherwise all arguments are mandatory.
definition	Every occurrence of the command will be replaced by definition and every occurrence of the form #n will then be replaced by the nth argument.

\newcommand is our key to introduce logical formatting. We should avoid using LaTeX font commands inside the document—you are on the right track if they appear only in the preamble of the document. Use \newcommand to create styles for keywords, code snippets, web addresses, names, notes, information boxes, or differently emphasized text. How did we achieve the consistent structure of this book? Using styles is the key!

Pop quiz – commands

1. Imagine your document contains some addresses of websites. Let's say we want them to be typeset in typewriter font. According to this book, which of the following possibilities would be the best way to print out, for instance, http://ctan.org?

   a. \texttt{http://ctan.org}

   b. {\ttfamilyhttp://ctan.org}

   c. \newcommand{\CTAN}{\texttt{http://ctan.org}} in the preamble and \CTAN in the body text

   d. \newcommand{\site}[1]{\texttt{#1}} and \newcommand{\CTAN} {http://ctan.org} in the preamble and \site{\CTAN} in the body text

2. Which kind of punctuation marks are used to enclose optional arguments?

   a. Parentheses: ()

   b. Square brackets: []

   c. Curly braces: { }

Have a go hero – saving effort using optional arguments

Most website addresses begin with `http://`. But there are sites that differ—some may start with `ftp://`, so called FTP server, some sites begin with `https://`, so called secure web server. Visit, for instance, `ftp://ctan.org`, and you will enter a file server instead of a web server.

Extend the definition of `\site` of our last pop quiz. Introduce an optional argument denoting the protocol of the site, that is, how the address starts. Default should start with `http://`. It shall work like the following:

- `\site{www.tug.org}` prints out `http://www.tug.org` in typewriter font

- `\site[ftp]{ctan.org}` prints out `ftp://ctan.org` in typewriter font

Web addresses in texts

There's a package called **url** designed for typesetting web addresses. Write `\usepackage{url}` in your preamble; this will provide the command `\url`. This command takes an address for the argument and will print it out with typewriter font. Furthermore, it is able to handle special characters in addresses like underscores and percent signs. It even enables hyphenation in addresses, which is useful for websites with a very long name.

Using boxes to limit the width of paragraphs

We won't always write the text just from left to right over the complete text width. Sometimes, we'd like a paragraph to have a smaller width, for instance, when we would like to put text and a picture side-by-side.

Time for action – creating a narrow text column

We would like to explain the acronym TUG in a text column of only 3 cm width:

1. Create a new document containing these four lines:

```
\documentclass{article}
\begin{document}
\parbox{3cm}{TUG is an acronym. It means \TeX\ Users Group.}
\end{document}
```

2. **Typeset** and take a critical look at the output:

TUG　　　is　　　an
acronym.　　　　　　It
means　TeX　Users
Group.

What just happened?

We used the command \parbox to create a column. We stated the width of 3 cm in the first argument and the contained text in the second argument to \parbox.

\parbox takes the argument text and formats the output to fit the specified width. We see that the text is fully justified. Our example shows an obvious problem: insisting on full justification could lead to undesirable big gaps in the text. Possible solutions are:

◆   Introducing hyphenation: the word acronym could easily be divided

◆   Improving justification: LaTeX could do better

◆   Giving up full justification: narrow text could look better when it's only left justified

We will check out all of these options. But first, let's see how \parbox is working.

Common paragraph boxes

Usually we just need a text box with a certain width; occasionally we would like to have some additional alignment to the surrounding text. So the common definition of the \parbox command is:

```
\parbox[alignment]{width}{text}
```

`alignment`	Optional argument for the vertical alignment. State t to align at the top line of the box; write b to align at its bottom line. The default behavior is to place the box such that its center is in line with the center of the current text line.
`width`	The width of the box. It can be given for example in ISO units like 3 cm, 44 mm, or 2 in.
`text`	The text that you want to put in that box. It should be a short piece of common text. For complicated contents, we will get to know other methods.

Here's a demonstration of the effect of the alignment parameters:

```
\documentclass{article}
\begin{document}
Text line
\quad\parbox[b]{1.8cm}{this parbox is aligned at its bottom line}
\quad\parbox{1.5cm}{center-aligned parbox}
\quad\parbox[t]{2cm}{another parbox aligned at its top line}
\end{document}
```

The command \quad produces some space; we used it to separate the boxes a bit. Here's the output:

```
              this parbox
              is aligned at
              its  bottom   center-
Text line     line          aligned        another par-
                            parbox          box   aligned
                                            at its top line
```

From now on we will call such a box a **parbox**.

Have a go hero – exploring further features of \parbox

\parbox is capable of doing even more. Here's the complete definition:

```
\parbox[alignment][height][inner alignment]{width}{text}
```

height	If this optional argument isn't given, the box will have just the natural height of the text inside. Use this argument if you want to change the height of the box to make it bigger or smaller.
inner alignment	Especially, if the height of the box is different to the natural height of the contained text, you might want to adjust the text position. The argument means:

- c—vertically center the text in the box
- t—place text at the top of the box
- b—place text at its bottom
- s—stretch the text vertically if possible

If you omit this argument, the alignment argument will be used here as the default value.

Take our previous demonstration example and try the effect of the optional arguments. Use the command \fbox that helps to visualize the effect; if you write \fbox{\parbox[...] {...}{text}}, the complete parbox will be framed.

Boxes containing more text

Parboxes are suitable for boxes with only a little text inside. In case of a box containing a large amount of text, the closing brace could easily be forgotten or overlooked. The **minipage** environment would then be a better choice.

Time for action – using the minipage environment

We will use the minipage environment instead of \parbox to get a text with a width of just 3 cm.

1. Modify the parbox example to get the following code:
    ```
    \documentclass{article}
    \begin{document}
    \begin{minipage}{3cm}
    TUG is an acronym. It means \TeX\ Users Group.
    \end{minipage}
    \end{document}
    ```

2. **Typeset** and look at the output:

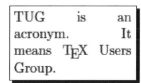

What just happened?

By using\begin{minipage}, we started a "page in a page". We specified the width of 3cm by the mandatory argument. From this point onwards, the text lines will have a width of 3cm. They will be automatically wrapped and fully justified. We ended this restriction with \end{minipage}. Any text typed afterwards would run over the complete body text width.

Note: There won't be a page break in such a "minipage".

Have you been a hero struggling with the \parbox and all of its optional arguments? The minipage environment accepts all those arguments as well with the same meaning.

Have a go hero – creating a footnote inside a minipage

Of course, LaTeX supports footnotes. You guessed it right—the corresponding command is called \footnote{text}. Try it in one of our examples. You will get a footnote mark inside the text and the text of the footnote will be put into the bottom of the page.

A minipage is like a small page inside a normal page. Think of using a footnote inside such a "page"; do you want to see the footnote text inside this small page? The minipage environment supports it, just try it—use \footnote inside the minipage in the previous example.

Understanding environments

LaTeX environments are started with \begin and ended with \end. Both commands require the name of the environment as their argument.

Simple environments look like the following:

```
\begin{name}
   ...
\end{name}
```

Such environments can be used for each declaration called \name.

Like commands, environments may also have arguments. Exactly like in the case of commands, mandatory arguments are written in curly braces and optional arguments in square brackets. So you will encounter:

```
\begin{name}{argument}
   ...
\end{name}
```

And:

```
\begin{name}[optional argument]{argument}
   ...
\end{name}
```

Environments are like declarations with a built-in scope. With `\begin`, the environment introduces a change in layout, font, or other properties. There must be an `\end` command, where this change will be canceled. The effect of the environment `name` is delimited to the piece of code between `\begin{name}` and `\end{name}`.

Furthermore, the effect of all local declarations used inside an environment will end together with the surrounding environment.

Breaking lines and paragraphs

Generally, when you're writing text, you don't need to care about the line wrapping. Just type the text with your editor; LaTeX will make it fit to the line and take care of the justification. If you want to begin a new paragraph, in consequence of getting a line break in the output, just insert an empty line before you continue with your text.

Now we will find out how to control the line wrapping. First we will see how to improve the automatic line breaking. Then we will learn commands to insert breaks directly.

Improving hyphenation

If you look at longer texts, you will notice that it's outstanding how the text is fully justified by LaTeX and how the spacing between words is evenly distributed on the lines. If necessary, LaTeX will divide words and put hyphens at the end of the line in order to break the lines in a better way. LaTeX already uses very good algorithms to hyphenate words, but it may happen that it can't find an acceptable way to divide a word. The previous example pointed out this problem: breaking the word **acronym** would improve the output, but LaTeX does not know where to divide it. We shall find out how to solve that.

Time for action – stating division points for words

No matter how good the justification skill is, text in very narrow columns is extremely hard to justify. The previous example showed it pitiless. We will tell LaTeX how a word could be divided:

1. Insert the following line into the preamble of the previous example:

   ```
   \hyphenation{acro-nym}
   ```

2. **Typeset** and look at the output:

   > TUG is an acro-
   > nym. It means TEX
   > Users Group.

What just happened?

We've told LaTeX that the word **acronym** may have a division point between **acro** and **nym**. That means a hyphen might be put after **acro** at the end of the line and **nym** goes to the following line.

The `\hyphenation` command tells LaTeX where the division points of a word may be. Its argument may contain several words separated by spaces. For each word, we can indicate several points. For instance we could extend the argument by more division points and more word variants like this:

```
\hyphenation{ac-ro-nym ac-ro-nym-ic a-cro-nym-i-cal-ly}
```

You could also indicate division points in the body text by inserting a backslash followed by a hyphen, like `ac\-ro\-nym`. But if you do it in the preamble, you'll collect all rules there and they will be used consistently. Use it especially in the rare cases when LaTeX's automation fails.

Preventing hyphenation

If you want to prevent the hyphenation of a certain word at all, there are two ways: either declare it in the preamble by using it in the `\hyphenation` argument without any division points, like `\hyphenation{indivisible}`, or you protect it inside the text using the `\mbox` command: `The following word is \mbox{indivisible}`.

Have a go hero – exploiting the hyphenat package

The **hyphenat** package extends the possibilities:

- ◆ \usepackage[none]{hyphenat} prevents hyphenation throughout the document.

- ◆ \usepackage[htt]{hyphenat} enables hyphenation for typewriter text. Otherwise such monospaced fonts won't be hyphenated by LaTeX.

Such optional arguments to \usepackage are called package **options**. They configure the behavior of a package. The mentioned options may be combined, separated by commas. Even if you don't use the option none, you can disable hyphenation for short pieces of text using the command \nohyphens{text}. Try out these features if you want to profit from them. The package documentation explains more features that you might need sometimes, such as hyphenation after special characters like numerals and punctuation characters—TeX would not break there.

Improving the justification further

Today's most popular TeX compiler is pdfTeX, which directly produces PDF output. When Hàn Thế Thành developed **pdfTeX**, he extended TeX by micro-typographic capabilities. When we typeset directly to PDF, we're actually using **pdfLaTeX** and we can benefit from the new features by using the microtype package.

Time for action – using microtype

We will improve our previous example by loading the microtype package:

1. Insert the following line into the preamble of the previous example:

   \usepackage{microtype}

2. **Typeset** and look at the output:

   TUG is an acronym.
   It means TEX Users
   Group.

What just happened?

We have loaded the `microtype` package without any options, relying on its default behavior. It introduces font expansion to tweak the justification and uses hanging punctuation to improve the optical appearance of the margins. This may reduce the need of hyphenation and improves the "grayness" of the output. You've seen its effect on a narrow column—imagine the improvement on wide text—keep that in mind and try it out later!

Though `microtype` provides powerful features and options for the advanced typesetter, we usually won't need to do more than just load it to profit from it. There's an extensive package documentation if you want to study it in depth.

`microtype` does nice tweaking, but it's not a cure-all; we should still take care of proper hyphenation.

Breaking lines manually

We might choose to end a line overriding the automatism. There are several commands with different effects.

Time for action – using line breaks

We will type the beginning of a famous poem by Edgar Allan Poe. As the author has specified where a verse has to end, we shall insert line breaks there.

1. Create a document containing these lines:

```
\documentclass{article}
\begin{document}
\emph{Annabel Lee}\\
It was many and many a year ago,\\
In a kingdom by the sea,\\
That a maiden there lived whom you may know\\
By the name of Annabel Lee
\end{document}
```

2. **Typeset** and view the output:

> *Annabel Lee*
> It was many and many a year ago,
> In a kingdom by the sea,
> That a maiden there lived whom you may know
> By the name of Annabel Lee

What just happened?

The very short command \\ ended a line; the following text was put to the next line. That's different to a paragraph break: we're still in the same paragraph. The command called \newline has the same effect.

There's another command called \linebreak, which tells LaTeX to end the line but to keep the full justification. Therefore, the space between the words would be stretched to reach the right margin. This could cause unpleasant gaps—that's why that command is rarely used.

Have a go hero – exploring line breaking options

Both introduced commands understand optional arguments.

- ◆ \\[value] would insert additional vertical space after the break depending on the value, like \\[3mm].

- ◆ *[value] is a variation of the same but prevents a page break before the next line of text.

- ◆ \linebreak[number] can be used to influence the line break slightly or strongly: If number is 0, a line break is allowed, 1 means it's desired, 2 and 3 mark more insistent requests, and 4 will force it. The latter is the default behavior if no number was given.

Change the heading of our poem example to the following:

```
\emph{Annabel Lee}\\[3mm]
```

This will insert some space between our heading and the poem fragment. Try the options further and check out their effects. If you're daring, try \linebreak instead of \\ to end a poem line just to see its effect.

Preventing line breaks

The command \linebreak has a direct counterpart: \nolinebreak. This command prevents a line break at the current position. Like its counterpart, it takes an optional argument. If you write \nolinebreak[0], you recommend to not break the line there. Using 1, 2, or even 3 makes the request stronger and \nolinebreak[4] forbids it completely. The latter will be presumed if you don't provide an argument.

The already mentioned command, \mbox[text], does not only disable hyphenation of a word, it will also prevent a line break for the complete text.

LaTeX will break lines at spaces between words if meaningful. The symbol ~ stands for an interword space where no break is allowed: if you would write `Dr.~Watson`, the title **Dr.** would never stand lonely at the end of a line.

Managing line breaks wisely

Bad hyphenation could still disappear as the document grows, so stating some sensible hyphenation rules would not do any harm but could prove to be useful.

But only use `\\`, `\newline`, and `\linebreak` for line adjustment when you're working on the final version of your document! While you're still editing your text, you don't need to worry about line breaks. They still may change during the writing process. Bad looking justification could still change and become better without intervention. On the other hand, if you break a line manually but later insert text before, the result could be an unwanted short line.

So don't waste your energy on formatting while you're writing.

Exploring the fine details

Typographic conventions may require paying attention to small details; there are different dashes, and the space around a dot may vary depending on the context. The space after some letters may depend on the following one, so much so that some letters may even be joined to a single one. Such constructions are called **ligatures**. Let's have a closer look at them.

Time for action – exploring ligatures

We will check out **Example 3** to discover a ligature. Afterwards, we will have a close look at the default ligatures:

1. Open **Example 3** in TeXworks, click the **Typeset** button. Move the mouse pointer into the output window, right over the word **first**, and then click the left button.

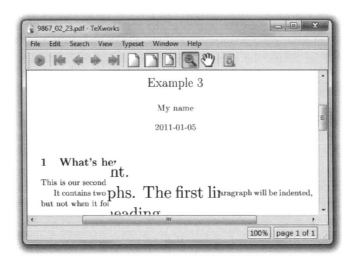

2. Go to the editor window, and then add a paragraph break by with empty line and the following letter combinations: `ff fi flffiffl -- ---`

3. Add a paragraph break, repeat the preceding line, but this time insert `\/` between the letters: `f\/f f\/i f\/l f\/f\/i f\/f\/l -\/- -\/-\/-`

4. **Typeset** and compare the letters in the output:

What just happened?

By left-clicking the mouse in the output window, you activated TeXworks' magnifying glass. It allows inspecting the output in detail as the area around the mouse pointer will be enlarged. You can see that two or even three letters have been joined, but not in the last line: the command `\/` prevented this.

Understanding ligatures

If the letter i follows the letter f, the dot of the letter i could collide with the head of the f. It could be avoided in two ways: either by increasing the space between those two letters or by combining them. The latter will result in a ligature. This will automatically be done by LaTeX when the used font provides such ligatures.

Sometimes this behavior might be undesirable, for instance, in compound words like "halflife". In this case, you can suppress this behavior by inserting \/ getting `half\/life`.

Curly braces can be used to achieve the same effect. For instance, in `-{}-` and `{-}{-}`, the dashes cannot be joined because this would cross group boundaries.

 If you don't like ligatures, for instance, because your PDF reader doesn't support search or copy and paste of ligatures, completely suppressing ligatures could be done easily by passing the option `noligatures` to the `microtype` package: `\usepackage[noligatures]{microtype}`.

Choosing the right dash

We've seen several kinds of dashes up until now. Let's sort them out:

- A short dash is used to mark hyphenation or compound words. In LaTeX: -

- A longer dash is used to indicate a range of some values, such as 2-3 hours. Generally this dash has the same width like a digit. In LaTeX: --

- Even wider is the dash commonly used to mark a parenthetical thought. In LaTeX: ---

Hyphenation is always done using the short dash. Regarding the wider dashes, it's a matter of style which kind of dash should be used, and further whether there should be a space around the dash or not. You decide—but now you know how to typeset those dashes.

Setting dots

How wide is the space following a dot? Some styles require additional space after the period that ends a sentence, but not after the period marking an abbreviation. Furthermore, three consecutive dots, forming an **ellipsis**, aren't usually written by just typing three dots. Let's figure this out.

Time for action – using differently spaced dots

We shall typeset a short text containing periods to see the default behavior. Afterwards, we will create an example where LaTeX's automation fails; we shall see how to correct it. We will learn how to simplify all this spacing using a different style.

1. Create a new document in TeXworks:

```
\documentclass{article}
\begin{document}
\TeX\ was designed by Donald E. Knuth.
It has become a de facto standard in mathematics.
\end{document}
```

2. **Typeset** to see the output:

> TeX was designed by Donald E. Knuth. It has become a de facto standard

3. Now add a paragraph break followed by this line:

```
Look at the spacing etc. in LaTeX. See it?
```

4. Check out the spacing after the two periods in the output:

> Look at the spacing etc. in LaTeX. See it?

5. Correct the spacing by inserting a backslash and \@:

```
Look at the spacing etc.\ in LaTeX\@. See it?
```

> Look at the spacing etc. in LaTeX. See it?

6. Now remove the extra \ and \@ we've added, insert the declaration \frenchspacing into the preamble, and typeset to see the difference:

> TeX was designed by Donald E. Knuth. It has become a de facto standard in mathematics.
> Look at the spacing etc. in LaTeX. See it?

What just happened?

The first step shows typical text and its output. As you can see, LaTeX adds a little space after the period ending a sentence. But not following the letter E: in case of periods after capital letters, LaTeX assumes that it's an abbreviation, therefore it doesn't add the extra space.

Generally, this automatism is helpful. However, you might encounter exceptions: in step 3, we constructed such a situation where LaTeX's assumptions are wrong. We've got unwanted extra space after **etc.** and missed a space after the last period.

In step 5, we corrected it: the backslash followed by a space (a "quoted space") produces the normal interword space, the `\@` before the dot states that the following dot stands at the end of a sentence. Now the spacing is correct.

If you prefer to avoid this extra space or if the style you're following requires it, you could switch off this default sentence spacing. We've done it in step 6 with the declaration `\frenchspacing`. Now the spacing after sentences will be as it is between words.

The counterpart to `\frenchspacing` is `\nonfrenchspacing`, which is default.

Time for action – comparing dots to ellipsis

We will write an ellipsis in two ways: firstly by simply writing dots, secondly by using a dedicated command. Let's compare!

1. Create a new document in TeXworks:

   ```
   \documentclass{article}
   \begin{document}
   Here are three dots... compare them to the ellipsis\ldots
   \end{document}
   ```

2. Check out the difference:

   > Here are three dots... compare them to the ellipsis...

What just happened?

We used the command `\ldots` to print out an ellipsis—three consecutive dots with a wider spacing. Such dots may indicate a pause, an unfinished thought, or an omitted word. When we just accumulated dots, they were typeset tightly together. However, it's common to print those dots wider.

Setting accents

Some languages have letters with accents that you can't simply type with your editor. In case you need to write such letters: let's see how to do it.

Time for action – experimenting with accents

We will write some words having letters with accents in Portuguese and in French.

1. Create a new document:

```
\documentclass{article}
\begin{document}
N\~{a}o compreendo. H\'{a} aqui algu\'{e}mque fale ingl\^{e}s?

Comment \c{c}a va? O\`{u} se trouve l'a\'{e}roport?
\end{document}
```

2. **Typeset** to see the generated accents:

> Não compreendo. Há aqui alguém que fale inglês?
> Comment ça va? Où se trouve l'aéroport?

What just happened?

LaTeX provides some special commands to produce a variety of accents. They may be combined with any letter. Such a command consists of a backslash followed by one character. The accent will be put above or below the letter that has to follow in curly braces. The following table will list these commands and their effect:

Command	Output	Command	Output
\'{a}	á	\u{a}	ă
\`{o}	ò	\v{e}	ě
\^{e}	ê	\H{a}	a̋
\"{u}	ü	\t{oo}	o͡o
\~{n}	ñ	\c{c}	ç
\={o}	ō	\d{n}	ṇ
\.{a}	ȧ	\b{i}	i̲

Using special characters directly in the editor

It might be a bit cumbersome to use those accent commands. There's a package that extends LaTeX basic capabilities. It allows you to enter at least some commonly used accented and other special characters directly.

Time for action – using accents directly

We will modify the previous example daring to enter accented letters directly in the editor.

1. Create a new document:

```
\documentclass{article}
\usepackage[utf8]{inputenc}
\begin{document}
Não compreendo. Há aqui alguém que fale inglês?

Comment çava? Où se trouve l'aéroport?
\end{document}
```

2. **Typeset** and compare to the previous output:

> Não compreendo. Há aqui alguém que fale inglês?
> Comment ça va? Où se trouve l'aéroport?

What just happened?

We loaded the **inputenc** package. The option `utf8` tells the package to use Unicode input encoding, which provides many more symbols than just the ASCII code. Now we just need to find the symbol on the keyboard and to type it.

TeXworks supports Unicode/UTF-8. Depending on operating system and editor, you might need to use another option when loading `inputenc`. A rule of thumb: `utf8` works on most Linux and Unix systems, like Mac OS X, and `latin1` works with most Windows editors.

 Today, many Windows editors move to UTF-8. This is seemingly becoming the cross-platform standard.

Turning off full justification

Though commonly your text will look fine if full justification is used, there may be occasions when it's not the optimum. For instance, full justification could be displeasing if the text lines are short. In such a case, it could be sufficient to justify only to the left side. We shall see how to put this into practice, further how to right-justify, and how to get centered lines.

Time for action – justifying a paragraph to the left

Remember the first parbox example which was fully justified but had those big gaps between the words. We shall give up justification to the right side to avoid such gaps.

1. Create a new document containing these lines:

    ```
    \documentclass{article}
    \begin{document}
    \parbox{3cm}{\raggedright
        TUG is an acronym. It means \TeX\ Users Group.}
    \end{document}
    ```

2. **Typeset** and look at the output:

    ```
    TUG is an
    acronym. It means
    TeX Users Group.
    ```

What just happened?

We inserted the declaration `\raggedright`. From this point onwards, the text will be ragged-right. In other words, the text will be moved to the left margin - "flushed-left". There won't be hyphenation.

Because we used this declaration inside a box, it's only valid there, like inside environments. After the box, the text will be fully justified again.

If we want the whole document to be ragged-right, we just need to use `\raggedright` in our preamble.

Creating ragged-left text

There might be occasions when we would like to achieve the opposite effect: flushing the text to the right margin. We can do it similarly by inserting the declaration `\raggedleft`. Remember, you're able to control where lines are broken by inserting `\\`.

Time for action – centering a title

We shall create a nice looking title for our document. It should contain the title, the author, and the date. All those lines have to be centered.

1. Write a document containing this code:

```
\documentclass{article}
\pagestyle{empty}
\begin{document}
{\centering
    \huge\bfseries Centered text \\
    \Large\normalfont written by me \\
    \normalsize\today

}
\end{document}
```

2. **Typeset** to see the output:

What just happened?

Because only the title should be centered, we opened a group to limit the centering. Through the declaration \centering, we made the remaining text of this group horizontally aligned to the center. We inserted a paragraph break: it's always a good idea to do it before ending the group when paragraph-affecting commands were used. By the brace after \today, we ended the group. If you complement some following text, it will be typeset normally, not centered.

\centering is commonly used when pictures or tables are inserted, further on title pages and sometimes for headings.

Using environments for justification

As there's a corresponding environment for every declaration, as we learned, we could have written \begin{centering} ... \end{centering} in our previous example. It could be done similarly for ragged-right and ragged-left text. There's a couple of predefined environments acting similarly but starting a new paragraph at the same time.

Time for action – centering verses

Let's reuse the fragment of the poem "Annabel Lee". This time we shall center all verses:

1. Create a document containing these lines:

```
\documentclass{article}
\usepackage{url}
\begin{document}
\noindent This is the beginning of a poem
by Edgar Allan Poe:
\begin{center}
    \emph{Annabel Lee}
\end{center}
\begin{center}
    It was many and many a year ago,\\
    In a kingdom by the sea,\\
    That a maiden there lived whom you may know\\
    By the name of Annabel Lee
\end{center}
The complete poem can be read on
\url{http://www.online-literature.com/poe/576/}.
\end{document}
```

2. **Typeset** and see the output:

This is the beginning of a poem by Edgar Allan Poe:

Annabel Lee

It was many and many a year ago,
In a kingdom by the sea,
That a maiden there lived whom you may know
By the name of Annabel Lee

The complete poem can be read on http://www.online-literature.com/poe/576/.

What just happened?

We began with \noindent avoiding the paragraph indentation. \begin{center} started the **center** environment. It begins a new paragraph, leaving some space to the preceding text. \end{center} ended this environment. We used the environment twice. In the second one, we inserted \\ to end the verses.

After the `center` environment ended, some space followed and the next paragraph began at the left margin.

The corresponding environment for ragged-right text is called **flushleft**, and for ragged-left text it's **flushright**.

Displaying quotes

Imagine your text contains a quotation of another author. It might be hard to read if it's just embedded in your words. A common way to improve the readability is displaying: setting the text off by indenting on both margins.

Time for action – quoting a scientist

We will quote thoughts of famous physicists.

1. Create a new document containing these lines:

```
\documentclass{article}
\begin{document}
Niels Bohr said: ``An expert is a person who has made
all the mistakes that can be made in a very narrow field.''
Albert Einstein said:
\begin{quote}
Anyone who has never made a mistake has never tried anything new.
\end{quote}
Errors are inevitable. So, let's be brave trying something new.
\end{document}
```

2. **Typeset** to see the result:

> Niels Bohr said: "An expert is a person who has made all the mistakes that can be made in a very narrow field." Albert Einstein said:
>
> Anyone who has never made a mistake has never tried anything new.
>
> Errors are inevitable. So, let's be brave trying something new.

What just happened?

Firstly we quoted inline. ` produced a left quotation mark; the character is also called a **backtick**. ' gave a right quotation mark. We just typed two such symbols to get double quotes.

Then we used the **quote** environment to display a quotation. We did not begin a new paragraph for it, because the quotation is already set a bit off. That's the reason we don't use a blank line before and after the environment.

Quoting longer text

When writing short quotations, the quote environment looks very good. However, when you would like to quote a text containing several paragraphs, you might wish to have the same paragraph indentation like in your surrounding text. The **quotation** environment will do it for you.

Time for action – quoting TeX's benefits

We will quote some of the benefits of TeX and LaTeX found on a web page on CTAN.

1. Start a new document. This time, it will be a bit longer:

```
\documentclass{article}
\usepackage{url}
\begin{document}
The authors of the CTAN team listed ten good reasons
for using \TeX. Among them are:
\begin{quotation}
    \TeX\ has the best output. What you end with,
the symbols on the page, is as useable, and beautiful,
as a non-professional can produce.

    \TeX\ knows typesetting. As those plain text samples
show, \TeX's has more sophisticated typographical algorithms
such as those for making paragraphs and for hyphenating.

    \TeX\ is fast. On today's machines \TeX\ is very fast.
    It is easy on memory and disk space, too.

    \TeX\ is stable. It is in wide use, with a long history.
    It has been tested by millions of users, on demanding input.
    It will never eat your document. Never.
\end{quotation}
The original text can be found on
\url{ http://www.ctan.org/what_is_tex.html}.
\end{document}
```

2. **Typeset** and look at the output:

> The authors of the CTAN team listed ten good reasons for using TeX. Among them are:
>
> > TeX has the best output. What you end with, the symbols on the page, is as useable, and beautiful, as a non-professional can produce.
> >
> > TeX knows typesetting. As those plain text samples show, TeX's has more sophisticated typographical algorithms such as those for making paragraphs and for hyphenating.
> >
> > TeX is fast. On today's machines TeX is very fast. It is easy on memory and disk space, too.
> >
> > TeX is stable. It is in wide use, with a long history. It has been tested by millions of users, on demanding input. It will never eat your document. Never.
>
> The original text can be found on `http://www.ctan.org/what_is_tex.html`.

What just happened?

This time, we used the `quotation` environment to display some paragraphs. As in normal text, blank lines separate the paragraphs. They are left-indented at their beginning just like in all our body text.

But what if we don't like that paragraph indentation? Let's check out an alternative.

Time for action – spacing between paragraphs instead of indentation

We like to avoid the paragraph indentation. Instead, we shall separate the paragraphs by some vertical space.

1. Create copy of the previous example and reuse most of it this way:

```
\documentclass{article}
\usepackage{parskip}
\usepackage{url}
\begin{document}
The authors of the CTAN team listed ten good reasons
for using \TeX. Among them are:

\TeX\ has the best output. What you end with,
the symbols on the page, is as useable, and beautiful,
as a non-professional can produce\ldots

The original text can be found on
\url{ http://www.ctan.org/what_is_tex.html}.
\end{document}
```

2. See the effect:

> The authors of the CTAN team listed ten good reasons for using TEX. Among them are:
>
> TEX has the best output. What you end with, the symbols on the page, is as useable, and beautiful, as a non-professional can produce...
>
> The original text can be found on `http://www.ctan.org/what_is_tex.html`.

What just happened?

The highlighted line shows that we've loaded the **parskip** package. Its only purpose is to remove the paragraph indentation completely. At the same time, this package introduces a skip between paragraphs. But this package doesn't affect the definition of the quotation environment—you still could use the quote environment.

In order to distinguish paragraphs, there are two common ways. One is to indent the beginning of each paragraph; this is the default LaTeX style. The other way is to insert vertical space between paragraphs while omitting the indentation, which is suitable for narrow columns where indenting would cost too much width.

Pop quiz – lines and paragraphs

1. Which of the following designates the end of a paragraph?

   a. `\newline`

   b. `\\`

   c. A blank line

2. How do the words in a `\hyphenation` command be separated?

   a. By commas

   b. By semicolons

   c. By spaces

3. Which command switches to left-aligned text?

   a. `\raggedleft`

   b. `\raggedright`

   c. `\flushright`

Summary

In this chapter, we developed the basics: editing, arranging, and formatting of text.

Specifically, we covered:

◆ Modifying shape and style of text and its font

◆ Breaking lines and improving hyphenation

◆ Controlling justification of text

We got to know the basic LaTeX concepts:

◆ Commands and declarations, mandatory and optional arguments

◆ Definition of new commands

◆ Using environments

◆ Using packages, how they can be loaded and options to packages

Keep in mind that even though we've used formatting commands directly in the text when exploring them, you should use them inside command definitions in the preamble to allow easy changes for the future. During your learning and writing process, you probably will get to know further useful commands and packages that could improve your previously written commands.

We've learned general practices:

◆ As often as possible, create your own macros to achieve a logical structure. You will be rewarded with consistent formatting and changes could easily be applied to the whole document.

◆ Deal with line or page breaking issues at the earliest when you go for your final version.

Now that we've learned about the detailed formatting of text, we're ready to enter the next chapter that deals with formatting and layout of whole pages and documents.

3
Designing Pages

After the previous chapter, formatting text should be easy for us. So, let's turn to whole pages!

In this chapter, we will learn how to:

- ◆ Adjust the margins
- ◆ Change the line spacing
- ◆ Section the document
- ◆ Create a table of contents
- ◆ Design headers and footers
- ◆ Control page breaking
- ◆ Set footnotes and modify their appearance

In learning this, we shall gain a deeper insight into classes and packages.

Defining the overall layout

We shall write an example document spanning over several pages. This will be our test object for modifying margins, line spacing, headers, footers, and more.

Time for action – writing a book with chapters

We will start to write a book. At first, we shall choose a class, further we will use some filler text to work out the page layout.

1. Create a new document with the following code:

```
\documentclass[a4paper,12pt]{book}
\usepackage[english]{babel}
\usepackage{blindtext}
\begin{document}
\chapter{Exploring the page layout}
In this chapter we will study the layout of pages.
\section{Some filler text}
\blindtext
\section{A lot more filler text}
More dummy text will follow.
\subsection{Plenty of filler text}
\blindtext[10]
\end{document}
```

2. Save the document and **Typeset** it. Look at the first page:

Chapter 1

Exploring the page layout

In this chapter we will study the layout of pages.

1.1 Some filler text

Hello, here is some text without a meaning. This text should show, how a printed text will look like at this place. If you read this text, you will get no information. Really? Is there no information? Is there a difference between this text and some nonsense like »Huardest gefburn«. Kjift – Never mind! A blind text like this gives you information about the selected font, how the letters are written and the impression of the look. This text should contain all letters of the alphabet and it should be written in of the original language. There is no need for a special contents, but the length of words should match to the language.

1.2 A lot more filler text

More dummy text will follow.

1.2.1 Plenty of filler text

Hello, here is some text without a meaning. This text should show, how a printed text will look like at this place. If you read this text, you will get no information. Really? Is there no information? Is there a difference between this text and some nonsense like »Huardest gefburn«. Kjift – Never mind! A blind text like this gives you information about the selected font, how the letters are written and the impression of the look. This text should contain all letters of the alphabet and it should be written in of the original

1

What just happened?

We have chosen the document class **book**. As the name implies, this class is suitable for book-like documents. Books are commonly two-sided and consist of chapters which usually start at right-hand pages. They may have a front matter with one or more title pages and a back matter with bibliography, index, and so on. The book class supports all of this.

We loaded the **babel** package. This is useful especially for typesetting in other languages than English regarding hyphenation, language-specific characters, and more.

Even for English language, there are several options: USenglish, american, english, UKenglish, british, canadian, australian, and newzealand. Obviously, some mean the same, such as UKenglish and british. However, there are differences in hyphenation rules between USenglish (american, english) and UKenglish (british).

For now, we just need babel to load **blindtext**: this package has been developed to produce filler text. It requires babel to detect the language of the document. We stated the language English to babel, which means American English.

The command \chapter produced a large heading. This command will always begin on a new page.

We've already seen the \section command. It's our second sectioning level and generates a smaller heading than \chapter. It's automatically numbered per chapter. The command \blindtext followed, printing some dummy text just to fill the space with some text.

At last, we refined the sectioning with a \subsection command followed by more dummy text to fill up the page.

There's another popular package for generating dummy text. It's called **lipsum** and it produces the famous LoremIpsum text which has been the typesetter's dummy text for hundreds of years.

Reviewing LaTeX's default page layout

For the example in the current chapter, we used A4 paper and a font size of 12 pt. We let LaTeX define the margins. Let's look at them:

- The right margin is the outer margin of the book, because the chapter starts on a right-hand page. It might seem to be a bit wide—but good text isn't just intended to fill as much space as possible: it should be well-readable for our eyes. Therefore the lines shouldn't be too long.

- The left margin is the inner margin on such a right-hand page. A user asked why the inner margin is smaller than the outer, even further some space will get lost because of the binding. The explanation is simple, if we imagine the book lies opened right before us: the inner margins would look joined. It's a good idea to aim at equal margins—left, middle, and right. In this sense, we could choose the inner margin to be half of the size of the outer margin—plus some offset for the binding.

- The bottom margin contains the page number.

- The top margin looks very tall. It's caused by the chapter heading, there's always more space left above. By looking at the second page, you will see that normal pages have a smaller top margin.

If you ever doubt LaTeX's design, look at some books in your shelves and compare, whether it's regarding margins, ligatures, numbering, or anything else.

Defining the margins yourself

A publisher or a supervisor may request you to follow his specifications. Besides font size, interline spacing, and other style issues, this might also apply to the margins. In this case, you would need to override LaTeX's recommendations specifying the margins precisely. There's a package fulfilling these demands.

Time for action – specifying margins

We shall load the **geometry** package and state the exact width and height of all margins.

1. Extend the preamble of the previous example with this command:

```
\usepackage[a4paper, inner=1.5cm, outer=3cm, top=2cm,
bottom=3cm, bindingoffset=1cm]{geometry}
```

2. **Typeset** and examine the margins:

Chapter 1

Exploring the page layout

In this chapter we will study the layout of pages.

1.1   Some filler text

Hello, here is some text without a meaning. This text should show, how a printed text
will look like at this place. If you read this text, you will get no information. Really?
Is there no information? Is there a difference between this text and some nonsense like
»Huardest gefburn«. Kjift – Never mind! A blind text like this gives you information
about the selected font, how the letters are written and the impression of the look.
This text should contain all letters of the alphabet and it should be written in of the
original language. There is no need for a special contents, but the length of words
should match to the language.

1.2   A lot more filler text

More dummy text will follow.

1.2.1   Plenty of filler text

Hello, here is some text without a meaning. This text should show, how a printed text
will look like at this place. If you read this text, you will get no information. Really?
Is there no information? Is there a difference between this text and some nonsense like
»Huardest gefburn«. Kjift – Never mind! A blind text like this gives you information
about the selected font, how the letters are written and the impression of the look.
This text should contain all letters of the alphabet and it should be written in of the
original language. There is no need for a special contents, but the length of words
should match to the language. Hello, here is some text without a meaning. This text
should show, how a printed text will look like at this place. If you read this text, you
will get no information. Really? Is there no information? Is there a difference between
this text and some nonsense like »Huardest gefburn«. Kjift – Never mind! A blind
text like this gives you information about the selected font, how the letters are written
and the impression of the look. This text should contain all letters of the alphabet and
it should be written in of the original language. There is no need for a special contents,
but the length of words should match to the language. Hello, here is some text without

1

What just happened?

We loaded another package with the name **geometry**. This package takes care of our layout
regarding the paper size, margins, and more dimensions. We chose A4 paper size, an outer
margin of 3 cm, and an inner margin of just 1.5 cm, remembering that the two inner margins
will be perceived as one space when the two-sided book is opened. We stated the top and
the bottom margin. At last, we specified a value of 1 cm for the binding correction. We need
the inner margins to be wider because we expect to lose this space later because of the
binding like gluing or stapling.

Using the geometry package

In the early days of LaTeX, it was common to manipulate the layout dimensions directly. This
approach had some disadvantages. We could easily make mistakes in calculating the lengths,
for instance left margin + right margin + text width might not fit to the paper width. The
`geometry` package comes to the rescue. It provides a comfortable interface for specifying
layout parameters. Further, it provides auto-completion. It calculates missing values to match
the paper size. It even adds missing lengths using a heuristic approach to achieve a good
layout. Let's look at it in detail.

The `geometry` package understands arguments of the form "key=value", separated by commas. If you load `geometry` without arguments, those arguments could alternatively be used by calling `\geometry{argument list}`. We shall look at some of them.

Choosing the paper size

Geometry provides several options to set the paper size and orientation:

- `paper=name` states the paper name, for example, `paper=a4paper`. It may be abbreviated like we did in our example. The package supports a lot of paper sizes, such as `letterpaper, executivepaper, legalpaper, a0paper, ... ,a6paper, b0paper, ... , b6paper`, and more.

- `paperwidth, paperheight` allow you to choose the paper dimensions freely, like `paperwidth=7in, paperheight=10in`.

- `papersize={width,height}` sets width and height of the paper like `papersize={7in,10in}`. This is an example of a double-valued argument.

- `landscape` changes the paper orientation to landscape mode.

- `portrait` switches to portrait mode. This is the default.

 If you already specified the paper name to the document class, `geometry` will inherit it. That's valid in general: all document class options will be automatically given to the packages that recognize them.

Specifying the text area

The text area may be adjusted by these options:

- `textwidth` sets the width of the text area, like `textwidth=140mm`.

- `textheight` states the height of the text area, like `textheight=180mm`.

- `lines` gives another way to specify the text height by the number of lines, like `lines=25`.

- `includehead` causes the header of the page to be included into the body area; set `false` by default.

- `includefoot` causes the footer of the page to be included into the body area; set `false` by default.

Setting the margins

The size of the visible margins can be specified by these options:

- ◆ `left`, `right` set the width of the left and the right margin, like `left=2cm`. Use it for one-sided documents.

- ◆ `inner`, `outer` set the width of the inner and the outer margin, like `inner=2cm`. Use it for two-sided documents.

- ◆ `top`, `bottom` set the height of the top and the bottom margin, like `top=25mm`.

- ◆ `twoside` switches to two-sided mode. This means that left and right margins would be swapped on left-hand pages, also called verso pages.

- ◆ `bindingoffset` reserves space on the left margin (one-side), respectively the inner margin (two-sided) for the binding.

That's just a selection of commonly used options—there are many more. You could choose and set some options intuitively—for instance, `\usepackage[margin=3cm]{geometry}` will result in a 3 cm margin on each edge of the paper and the paper size comes from the document class option.

The auto-completion works like this:

- ◆ `paperwidth = left + width + right`, where `width=textwidth` by default

- ◆ `paperheight = top + height + bottom`, where `height=textheight` by default

If you decide to include marginal notes within the text body when calculating, `width` could get wider than `textwidth`. If two dimensions of the right side of each formula are given, the missing dimension would be calculated. That's why it may be enough to specify `left` and `right`, `top` and `bottom`, respectively. Even if just one margin is specified, the other dimensions would be determined using default margin ratios:

- ◆ `top:bottom = 2:3`

- ◆ `left:right = 1:1` for one-sided documents

- ◆ `inner:outer = 2:3` for two-sided documents

Sounds complicated? That's just intended to help you to achieve practical dimensions even if some values were missing.

> In 2010, version 5 of `geometry` introduced the commands `\newgeometry{argument list}` and `\restoregeometry`, allowing users to change margin dimensions in the middle of a document. Their auto-completion may also differ a bit from previous versions.

The `geometry` package provides an extensive manual. Don't be worried by the amount of documentation: it's an offer to guide you through the variety of features.

Obtaining package documentation

There are hundreds of LaTeX packages available. No book could ever explain all of their features on its own. But most of those packages offer good documentation that you can read for free. If you work your way through this book and supplement it with the documentation of the mentioned packages, you're on the right track to become a LaTeX power user.

Time for action – finding the geometry package manual

We would like to examine the documentation of the geometry package. At first, we shall look for it locally on our computer. Afterwards, we will see how to find the documentation online:

1. Click the **Start** button and choose **All Programs| Accessories |Command prompt**

2. Type the following:

   ```
   texdoc geometry
   ```

3. A PDF viewer should start and show the package manual. The same command works at the command prompt on Linux/Unix computers.

4. Hit the **Start** button again; this time, choose **All Programs | TeX Live 2010 |TeXdoc GUI**. Click on **Search texdoctk's database**, enter the keyword **geometry**, and press *Enter*:

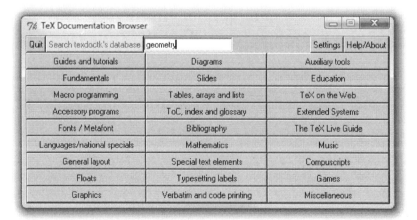

5. Have a look at the search result. Open it by double-clicking or hit the **View** button. A viewer should open the documentation.

6. Open an Internet browser and visit the site `http://ctan.org/pkg/geometry`. Scroll down to **Documentation on CTAN** and hit the link **User's manual**. Again, your PDF viewer or a browser plug-in will show the documentation.

What just happened?

We've tried three ways of obtaining the documentation. At first, we used **texdoc**. This is a tool to find and to view LaTeX documentation. It can be used at the command prompt; just type `texdoc` followed by a keyword. For this, it's required to be in the operating system's search path. The TeX distribution installer takes care of it. The argument to `texdoc` doesn't have to be the package name, as `texdoc` understands aliases. Further, we used a GUI for `texdoc` providing a search feature supplemented by a category classification. Perhaps browse for a little while through the categories.

If `texdoc` doesn't help you, there's another opportunity: visit CTAN. You just need to know the package name. Simply visit `http://ctan.org/pkg/packagename` to get to the package homepage, there you may find documentation.

In case you don't know the package name or you just have a vague idea what you're looking for, visit the TeX Catalogue Online on `http://texcatalogue.sarovar.org/bytopic.html`. It lists hundreds of packages sorted by topic.

Note: The online documentation might match a different package version than the one on your computer.

Have a go hero – constructing the page layout with typearea

Now that you know how to open package documentation, you could figure out if you want to benefit from the **typearea** package. While the `geometry` package allows you to control all margins yourself, `typearea` provides a different approach. It supports you in creating a page layout based on proven typography standards. `typearea` is explained within the KOMA-Script manual, so the keywords for `texdoc` and CTAN would be **koma-script** or **typearea**. Reading Chapter 2 of the manual on Page Layout could give you an insight into typography, even if you decide not to use `typearea`.

Changing the line spacing

Without some vertical space between the lines, the readability of a text could suffer. Adding such space would help lead the eye along the line.

Time for action – increasing line spacing

Though LaTeX already takes care of good readability by choosing a meaningful interline spacing, publishers might require different spacing. We shall modify our example by adding half of a line height to the line spacing.

1. Extend the preamble of our example with this command:

   ```
   \usepackage[onehalfspacing]{setspace}
   ```

2. **Typeset** to see the change:

What just happened?

We loaded the **setspace** package. Its only purpose is to adjust the line spacing. We provided the option `onehalfspacing`. This increases the spacing by half of a line height for the whole document.

`setspace` understands three options:

- ◆ `singlespacing` is the default. No additional space will be inserted. The text will be typeset with LaTeX's default interline spacing, which is about 20 percent of the line height.

- ◆ `onehalfspacing` means one-and-a-half spacing like in our example.

- ◆ `doublespacing` can be used for even more spacing: the distance between the baselines of successive text lines would be twice as high as a single line.

Commonly, we choose the spacing for the complete document. In that case, such an option would be sufficient. For each of the options, there's a corresponding environment. They are called `singlespace`, `onehalfspace`, and `doublespace`. Those environments may be used to adjust the spacing within the document. They shouldn't be nested. For the need of a different stretching factor, the `spacing` environment is provided. It may be used like the following:

```
\begin{spacing}{2.4}
This text is stretched by a factor of 2.4.
\end{spacing}
```

> In typesetter's jargon, the distance between the baselines of consecutive text lines is called **leading**.

Have a go hero – examining a package source file

In some cases the documentation of a package is not easily accessible. This applies to `setspace`: the explanation of the options, commands, and environments is contained in the package source file itself. How can we obtain it? We could visit CTAN, as we described before, or locate the file on our computer. A package filename usually ends with `.sty`, standing for **style file**. TeX Live provides a tool for locating such source files. Try it: open the command prompt, that is, hit the **Start** button and click **All Programs | Accessories | Command prompt**. Then type the following:

`kpsewhich setspace.sty`

And press *Enter*. The program will print the location of the file, as follows:

`c:/texlive/2010/texmf-dist/tex/latex/setspace/setspace.sty`

Open the file using TeXworks or any text editor. There are a lot of comment lines explaining the package features.

The kpsewhich tool belongs to the **kpathsea** library. kpathsea's fundamental purpose is filename lookup.

Using class options to configure the document style

We already know that a document class is the basis of our document. It provides commands and environments extending the LaTeX standard features. Though the class provides a default style, it's still customizable with options.

Time for action – creating a two-column landscape document

We shall change the orientation of our example to landscape. We would also like to typeset our text in two columns:

1. Add the options landscape and twocolumn to the \documentclass statement of our example, as follows:

```
\documentclass[a4paper,12pt,landscape,twocolumn]{book}
```

2. **Typeset** and see how the layout has changed:

Chapter 1

Exploring the page layout

In this chapter we will study the layout of pages.

1.1 Some filler text

Hello, here is some text without a meaning. This text should show, how a printed text will look like at this place. If you read this text, you will get no information. Really? Is there no information? Is there a difference between this text and some nonsense like »Huardest gefburn«. Kjift – Never mind! A blind text like this gives you information about the selected font, how the letters are written and the impression of the look. This text should contain all letters of the alphabet and it should be written in of the original language. There is no need for a special contents, but the length of words should match to the language.

1.2 A lot more filler text

More dummy text will follow.

1.2.1 Plenty of filler text

Hello, here is some text without a meaning. This text should show, how a printed text will look like at this place. If you read this text, you will get no information. Really? Is there no information? Is there a difference between this text and some nonsense like »Huardest gefburn«. Kjift – Never mind! A blind text like this gives you information about the selected font, how the letters are written and the impression of the look. This text should contain all letters of the alphabet and it should be written in of the original language. There is no need for a special contents, but the length of words should match to the language. Hello, here is some text without a meaning. This text should show, how a printed

1

What just happened?

By using the `landscape` option, we switched the orientation. By stating the `twocolumn` option, we caused the body text to be divided into two columns.

 There's a command `\twocolumn[opening text]` starting a two-column page with optional opening text over the whole width. `\onecolumn` begins a one-column page.

If you'd like to balance the columns on the last page or if you wish to have more than two columns, use the **multicols** package.

The LaTeX base classes are **article**, **book**, **report**, **slides**, and **letter**. As the name suggests, the last one can be used to write letters, though there are further suitable classes like **scrlttr2**. `slides` can be used to create presentations, but today there are more powerful and feature rich classes like **beamer** and **powerdot**.

Let's sum up the options of the base classes:

- ♦ `a4paper`, `a5paper`, `b5paper`, `letterpaper`, `legalpaper`, or `executivepaper`: The output will be formatted according to this paper size, that is, A4: 210 mm x 297 mm. `letterpaper` (8.5 in x 11 in) is the default. Loading the `geometry` package allows more sizes.

- ♦ `10pt`, `11pt`, or `12pt`: The size of normal text in the document; the default is ten points (`10pt`). The size of headings, footnotes, indexes, and so on, will be adjusted accordingly.

- ♦ `landscape`: Switches to landscape format; width and height of the output size will be interchanged.

- ♦ `onecolumn` or `twocolumn`: Decides whether the pages will be one-column (default) or two-column. It's not supported by the letter class.

- ♦ `oneside` or `twoside`: Formatting for printing on one side or both sides of a page. `oneside` is the default, except for the book class. `twoside` is not usable with the `slides` class and the `letter` class.

- ♦ `openright` or `openany`: The first decides that chapters have to begin on a right-hand page (the default for the `book` class), `openany` allows chapters to start on any page (default for the `report` class). These options are only supported by the book and the report class because the other classes don't provide chapters.

- ♦ `titlepage` or `notitlepage`: The first causes a separate title page when `\maketitle` is used and is the default, except for the `article` class. The default of `article` is `notitlepage`, which means that normal text may follow the title on the same page.

- ◆ `final` or `draft`: If `draft` is set, then LaTeX will mark overfull lines with a black box, which is helpful in reviewing and improving the output. Some packages support these option as well, behaving differently then, such as omitting embedding of graphics and listings when `draft` has been chosen. `final` is the default.

- ◆ `openbib`: When this option is set, a bibliography would be formatted in open style instead of compressed style.

- ◆ `fleqn`: Causes displayed formulas to be left-aligned.

- ◆ `leqno`: For numbered displayed formulas, the number would be put to the left side. The right side is the default.

Many other classes support these options as well and even more. For the need of an uncommon base font size, the classes `extarticle`, `extbook`, `extreport`, and `extletter` provide base font sizes from 8 pts to 20 pts. The so called **KOMA-Script** classes allow arbitrary base font sizes. They understand such a large amount of options that they're additionally supporting a "key=value" interface like we've seen with the `geometry` package.

Have a go hero – trying KOMA-Script classes

Have you been so brave to check out the `typearea` package documentation? Then you've already seen the KOMA-Script manual accessible by `texdoc koma-script`. Open it again; this time, read it with the idea of choosing KOMA classes for your documents. They may be used like the base classes: for each base class, there's a corresponding KOMA class. They differ in some meaningful presets; for instance, headings use a sans-serif font by default. However, the presets can easily be changed. Those classes extend the base classes very much, providing a huge amount of commands. Web forums frequently show user questions being hard to solve using base classes, but being easily achievable by a single KOMA class command.

Creating a table of contents

A book commonly begins with a table of contents, so let's create one.

Time for action – adding a table of contents

We shall create a table of contents based on our numbered headings.

1. Let's remove the options `landscape` and `twocolumn`. We also don't load the `setspace` package. Add the command `\tableofcontents` right after `\begin{document}`. Our code shall now be:

```
\documentclass[a4paper,12pt]{book}
\usepackage[english]{babel}
\usepackage{blindtext}
\usepackage[a4paper, inner=1.5cm, outer=3cm, top=2cm,
bottom=3cm, bindingoffset=1cm]{geometry}
\begin{document}
\tableofcontents
\chapter{Exploring the page layout}
In this chapter we will study the layout of pages.
\section{Some filler text}
\blindtext
\section{A lot more filler text}
More dummy text will follow.
\subsection{Plenty of filler text}
\blindtext[10]
\end{document}
```

2. **Typeset** twice. Afterwards, the first page of your output will contain this table:

Contents

What just happened?

The command `\tableofcontents` tells LaTeX to produce a file with the extension `.toc`. This file will be used to generate a table of contents. We had to typeset twice: in the first run, the `.toc` file was written and in the second run, LaTeX read it and processed it.

The entries are created by the sectioning commands. We used `\chapter`, `\section`, and `\subsection`, and we've got an entry for each.

Sectioning and the contents

A heading might be very long; it could span over two or more lines. In that case, we might wish to shorten its corresponding table of contents entry. Let's see how.

Time for action – shortening the table of content entries

We will use the optional argument of the sectioning commands to produce shorter entries, different to the actual headings:

1. Take our example and modify the sectioning commands as shown in the highlighted lines:

```
\documentclass[a4paper,12pt]{book}
\usepackage[english]{babel}
\usepackage{blindtext}
\usepackage[a4paper, inner=1.5cm, outer=3cm, top=2cm,
bottom=3cm, bindingoffset=1cm]{geometry}
\begin{document}
\tableofcontents
\chapter[Page layout]{Exploring the page layout}
In this chapter we will study the layout of pages.
\section[Filler text]{Some filler text}
\blindtext
\section[More]{A lot more filler text}
More blindtext will follow.
\subsection[Plenty]{Plenty of filler text}
\blindtext[10]
\end{document}
```

2. **Typeset** twice and look at the modified table of contents:

Contents

What just happened?

Besides the mandatory argument producing the heading, each sectioning command understands an optional argument. If this is given, it will be used instead of the mandatory heading for the table of contents entry.

Again, we had to typeset twice to notice a change. This is not unusual. You will encounter more situations when several LaTeX runs would be necessary, like creating an index or a bibliography.

In *Chapter 7, Listing Content and References*, we shall take a further look and learn how to customize the table of contents. Let's look again at the sectioning commands of book, report, and article. There are seven levels in those base classes:

- ◆ \part: For dividing the document in major units. The numbering of other sectional units is independent of \part. A part heading will use a whole page in book and report documents.

- ◆ \chapter: A large heading that will start at a new page, available in the book and report classes.

- ◆ \section, \subsection, \subsubsection: Bold headings available in all classes, the following text comes below.

- ◆ \paragraph, \subparagraph: Available in all classes, produces a run-in heading.

Except \part, all sectioning commands reset the counter of the section that's one level below in the hierarchy. For instance, \chapter resets the section counter. This way, the sections will be numbered per chapter.

To sum up, though these commands are easy to use, they do a lot, such as:

- ◆ Cause a page break (\part and \chapter with book and report classes)

- ◆ Generate a number and a presentation for it, some depending on the higher-level counters (like **2.1**)

- ◆ Reset the counter of the next-level sectional unit (except \part)

- ◆ Produce a table of contents entry storing it in the .toc file

- ◆ Format the heading, usually bold-faced and the larger the higher in the hierarchy

- ◆ If needed, save the heading for use in a page header

All sectioning commands provide a **starred form**, as follows:

```
\section*{title}
```

If you use this form, the numbering will be suppressed and there won't be an entry in the table of contents or in a header. Look at the heading **Contents** in our example; this has actually been typeset by \chapter* inside the \tableofcontents macro.

As page headers have been mentioned, let's explore them now.

Designing headers and footers

Already during testing of the first version of our example, you might have noticed that except for the page where the chapter started, all pages already showed the page number, chapter title, and section title in their header:

2	*CHAPTER 1. EXPLORING THE PAGE LAYOUT*	*1.2. A LOT MORE FILLER TEXT*	3

language. There is no need for a special contents, but the length of words should match to the language. Hello, here is some text without a meaning. This text should show, how a printed text will look like at this place. If you read this text, you will get no information. Really? Is there no information? Is there a difference between this text and some nonsense like »Huardest

of the alphabet and it should be written in of the original language. There is no need for a special contents, but the length of words should match to the language. Hello, here is some text without a meaning. This text should show, how a printed text will look like at this place. If you read this text, you will get no information. Really? Is there no information? Is there a difference

Though these standard headers are already quite useful, we shall see how to customize them to meet our individual requirements.

Time for action – customizing headers with the fancyhdr package

The default shape of the page headings is slanted. Furthermore, they are written in capital letters. We shall use bold typeface instead and we will use capital letters only for the chapter title. We will load the **fancyhdr** package and use its commands to achieve that:

1. Load the first version of our example. Insert the highlighted lines:

```
\documentclass[a4paper,12pt]{book}
\usepackage[english]{babel}
\usepackage{blindtext}
\usepackage{fancyhdr}
\fancyhf{}
\fancyhead[LE]{\leftmark}
\fancyhead[RO]{\nouppercase{\rightmark}}
\fancyfoot[LE,RO]{\thepage}
\pagestyle{fancy}
\begin{document}
\chapter{Exploring the page layout}
In this chapter we will study the layout of pages.
\section{Some filler text}
```

```
\blindtext
\section{A lot more filler text}
More dummy text will follow.
\subsection{Plenty of filler text}
\blindtext[10]
\end{document}
```

2. **Typeset**—the footers will contain the page number on their outer side and the headers should look like the following:

CHAPTER 1. EXPLORING THE PAGE LAYOUT

language. There is no need for a special contents, but the length of words should match to the language. Hello, here is some text without a meaning. This text should show, how a printed text will look like at this place. If you read this text, you will get no information. Really? Is there no information?

1.2. A lot more filler text

of the alphabet and it should be written in of the original language. There is no need for a special contents, but the length of words should match to the language. Hello, here is some text without a meaning. This text should show, how a printed text will look like at this place. If you read this text, you will

What just happened?

We loaded the `fancyhdr` package. Our first action was calling `\fancyhf{}`; this command clears the headers and footers. Further, we used the following:

- `\leftmark`: Used by the `book` class to store the chapter title together with the chapter number. Capital letters are used as default.

- `\rightmark`: Used by the `book` class to store the section title together with its number. Capital letters are used as well.

We used the command `\fancyhead` with the optional argument LE to put the chapter title into the header. LE stands for left-even and means that this chapter title will be put on the left side of the header on even-numbered pages.

Analogous, we called the command `\fancyhead` with RO to put the section title into the header. RO stands for right-odd and means that this section heading shall be displayed on right side of the header on odd-numbered pages.

Afterwards, we used `\fancyfoot` to display the page number in the footer. This time, we used LE and RO that showed the page number on even as well as on odd pages, always on the outer side. The command `\thepage` prints the page number.

All those commands are used to modify a page style provided by `fancyhdr`; this style is called **fancy**. We had to tell LaTeX to use this style and we did it through `\pagestyle{fancy}`.

Emphasizing by writing all letters capitalized, like `fancyhdr` does by default, is called **all caps**. It is widely regarded as a questionable style. If it's used at all, then it's recommended to slightly increase the spacing between the capital letters. For adjusting this so called **letterspacing**, you can use the `microtype` package or the `soul` package.

Understanding page styles

LaTeX and its base classes provide four page styles:

- `empty`: Neither a header nor a footer is shown.
- `plain`: No header. The page number will be printed and centered in the footer.
- `headings`: The header contains titles of chapters, sections, and/or subsections, depending on the class and also the page number. The footer is empty.
- `myheadings`: The header contains a user-defined text and the page number; the footer is empty.

`fancyhdr` adds one page style:

- `fancy`: Both the header and footer may be customized by the user.

Two commands may be used to choose the page style:

- `\pagestyle{name}`: Switches to the page style `name` from this point onwards.
- `\thispagestyle{name}`: Chooses the page style `name` only or the current page; the following pages will have the style that's been used before.

You have seen that where a chapter starts, the page style is different to the style of other pages. Such pages will have `plain` style. If you thought all pages should use the same style, look into some books: it's very common that chapter beginnings differ in style. They usually have a blank header. `\thispagestyle` could be used to override that.

Customizing header and footer

Let's divide the header and footer into six pieces: left, center, and right (l, c, r) both for the header and footer. The commands to modify those areas are as follows:

- For the header: `\lhead`, `\chead`, `\rhead`
- For the footer: `\lfoot`, `\cfoot`, `\rfoot`

Each of these commands requires a mandatory argument, like `\chead{User's guide}` or `\cfoot{\thepage}`. This argument will be put into the corresponding area of the page.

Alternatively, you could use these versatile commands:

- For the header: `\fancyhead[code]{text}`
- For the footer: `\fancyfoot[code]{text}`

Here, `code` may consist of one or more letters:

Symbol	Meaning
L	left
C	center
R	right
E	even page
O	odd page
H	header
F	footer

It doesn't matter if we choose uppercase or lowercase letters. We already used such combinations in our example.

Using decorative lines in header or footer

We can introduce or delete lines between header and body text and body text and footer, respectively, with these two commands:

- `\renewcommand{\headrulewidth}{width}`
- `\renewcommand{\footrulewidth}{width}`

Where `width` may be a value like `1pt`, `0.5mm`, and so on. Just set it to `0pt` if you don't like such a line. The default is `0.4pt` for the header line and `0pt` for the footer line.

`\renewcommand` works exactly like `\newcommand`, except that the command must already exist. It will get the new meaning. Incidentally, we've got to know a new concept: a lot of LaTeX commands may be redefined in this way. We shall take advantage of it from now on.

 There are starred versions-`\newcommand`, and `\renewcommand`, respectively. They are called short commands. Their arguments must not contain paragraph breaks. This limitation eases troubleshooting, as TeX would be able to pick up an error earlier. That's why many people use them whenever possible.

Changing LaTeX's header marks

As we already know, LaTeX classes and packages store sectioning numbers and headings in the macros \leftmark and \rightmark automatically. It will be done when we call \chapter, \section, or \subsection. So, we could just use \leftmark and \rightmark in the arguments of the fancyhdr commands.

We will sometimes want to change those entries manually, even if we rely on this automatism. For instance, the starred sectioning commands like \chapter* and \section* won't produce a header entry, like indicated earlier. In such a case, two commands will help us:

- \markright{right head} sets the right heading
- \markboth{left head}{right head} sets both left and right heading

The default style headings is easy-to-use and gives good results. myheadings can be used together with \markright and \markboth. However, the most flexible way is given by fancy, especially in combination with \markright and \markboth.

> There's a very good alternative to fancyhdr, which is a package called **scrpage2**. It belongs to KOMA-Script, but works with other classes as well. It provides a similar functionality and offers even more features.

Breaking pages

As you've seen in our example, LaTeX took care of the page breaking. There might be occasions where we'd like to insert a page break ourselves. LaTeX offers several commands to do it; with vertical balance or without.

Time for action – inserting page breaks

We will go back to the first version of our example and we shall manually insert a page break right before the subsection 1.2.1.

1. Insert the highlighted line into our example:
   ```
   \documentclass[a4paper,12pt]{book}
   \usepackage[english]{babel}
   \usepackage{blindtext}
   \begin{document}
   \chapter{Exploring the page layout}
   In this chapter we will study the layout of pages.
   \section{Some filler text}
   ```

```
\blindtext
\section{A lot more filler text}
More dummy text will follow.
\pagebreak
\subsection{Plenty of filler text}
\blindtext[10]
\end{document}
```

2. **Typeset** and have a look:

Chapter 1

Exploring the page layout

In this chapter we will study the layout of pages.

1.1 Some filler text

Hello, here is some text without a meaning. This text should show, how a printed text
will look like at this place. If you read this text, you will get no information. Really?
Is there no information? Is there a difference between this text and some nonsense like
»Hnardest gefburne. Kjift – Never mind! A blind text like this gives you information
about the selected font, how the letters are written and the impression of the look.
This text should contain all letters of the alphabet and it should be written in of the
original language. There is no need for a special contents, but the length of words
should match to the language.

1.2 A lot more filler text

More dummy text will follow.

1

3. **Replace** \pagebreak **by** \newpage.

4. **Typeset** and compare:

> ## Chapter 1
>
> ## Exploring the page layout
>
> In this chapter we will study the layout of pages.
>
> ### 1.1 Some filler text
>
> Hello, here is some text without a meaning. This text should show, how a printed text will look like at this place. If you read this text, you will get no information. Really? Is there no information? Is there a difference between this text and some nonsense like »Huardest gefburn«. Kjift – Never mind! A blind text like this gives you information about the selected font, how the letters are written and the impression of the look. This text should contain all letters of the alphabet and it should be written in of the original language. There is no need for a special contents, but the length of words should match to the language.
>
> ### 1.2 A lot more filler text
>
> More dummy text will follow.
>
> 1

What just happened?

At first, we inserted the command \pagebreak. Like its name suggests, it causes a page break. Furthermore, the text has been stretched to fill the page down to the bottom.

Afterwards, because of the obviously unpleasant whitespace between the paragraphs and the headings, we replaced \pagebreak with \newpage. This command breaks the page as well, but it doesn't stretch the text: the remaining space of the page will stay empty.

So, \pagebreak behaves like \linebreak and \newpage works like \newline, for pages instead of lines. There's even a command \nopagebreak that's analogous to \nolinebreak and forbids page breaking.

\pagebreak won't break a line. Furthermore, \nopagebreak doesn't refer to the middle of a line: both commands apply at the end of the current line. Of course, they immediately have effect when used between paragraphs.

If you use the two-column format, both \pagebreak and \newpage would begin on a new column instead of a new page.

> There are two further variants: \clearpage works like \newpage, except that it will start on a new page, even in two-column mode. \cleardoublepage does the same, but causes the following text to start on a right-hand page, inserting a blank page if necessary. The latter is useful for two-sided documents.
>
> More importantly, both commands cause all figures and tables that LaTeX has in its memory to be printed out immediately.

Sometimes you may notice large gaps between headings and paragraphs. Those could be the result of a bad page break like in our example. In that case, you could assist LaTeX by such a page break command or you switch off vertical justification by the command \raggedbottom. Its counterpart \flushbottom will switch it on, which is the default in the book class.

What we learned about line breaking is valid for page breaking as well: don't worry about it while your work is still in progress. Only when you're done with your document and you're preparing the final version, will it be time to tweak the page breaks.

Have a go hero – exploring page breaking options

Remember the optional arguments for \linebreak and \nolinebreak. \pagebreak and \nopagebreak are able to take an optional argument as well, an integer between 0 and 4. While 0 recommends, 4 demands. Again, try the previous example. This time use an optional argument for \pagebreak. Test with 0, 1, 2, 3, 4. Only \pagebreak[4] will cause the page break because the necessary stretching is so much that LaTeX doesn't like to follow either a weak or a strong request.

Enlarging a page

LaTeX's rules are not set in stone; they also apply to page balancing. There may be occasions where we want to put a little more text onto a page, even if the text would be squeezed a bit or the text height increases. There's a command that will help us out: \enlargethispage.

Time for action – sparing an almost empty page

We shall modify our example a bit. This time, we will try to avoid a nearly empty page by squeezing their text to the preceding page.

1. Remove the command `\newpage` from our example and switch to `11pt` base font. This time, use less filler text in the subsection:

```
\documentclass[a4paper,11pt]{book}
\usepackage[english]{babel}
\usepackage{blindtext}
\usepackage[a4paper, inner=1.5cm, outer=3cm, top=2cm,
bottom=3cm, bindingoffset=1cm]{geometry}
\begin{document}
\chapter{Exploring the page layout}
In this chapter we will study the layout of pages.
\section{Some filler text}
\blindtext
\section{A lot more filler text}
More dummy text will follow.
\subsection{Plenty of filler text}
\blindtext[3]
\end{document}
```

2. **Typeset**, and the result will consist of two pages:

> 2   *CHAPTER 1. EXPLORING THE PAGE LAYOUT*
>
> and it should be written in of the original language. There is no need for a special contents, but the length of words should match to the language.

3. Insert this command right after the `\subsection` line:

`\enlargethispage{\baselineskip}`

4. **Typeset**. Now our document fits in only one page:

> ## Chapter 1
>
> # Exploring the page layout
>
> In this chapter we will study the layout of pages.
>
> ### 1.1 Some filler text
>
> Hello, here is some text without a meaning. This text should show, how a printed text will look like at this place. If you read this text, you will get no information. Really? Is there no information? Is there a difference between this text and some nonsense like ≫Huardest gefburn≪. Kjift – Never mind! A blind text like this gives you information about the selected font, how the letters are written and the impression of the look. This text should contain all letters of the alphabet and it should be written in of the original language. There is no need for a special contents, but the length of words should match to the language.
>
> ### 1.2 A lot more filler text
>
> More dummy text will follow.
>
> #### 1.2.1 Plenty of filler text
>
> Hello, here is some text without a meaning. This text should show, how a printed text will look like at this place. If you read this text, you will get no information. Really? Is there no information? Is there a difference between this text and some nonsense like ≫Huardest gefburn≪. Kjift – Never mind! A blind text like this gives you information about the selected font, how the letters are written and the impression of the look. This text should contain all letters of the alphabet and it should be written in of the original language. There is no need for a special contents, but the length of words should match to the language. Hello, here is some text without a meaning. This text should show, how a printed text will look like at this place. If you read this text, you will get no information. Really? Is there no information? Is there a difference between this text and some nonsense like ≫Huardest gefburn≪. Kjift – Never mind! A blind text like this gives you information about the selected font, how the letters are written and the impression of the look. This text should contain all letters of the alphabet and it should be written in of the original language. There is no need for a special contents, but the length of words should match to the language. Hello, here is some text without a meaning. This text should show, how a printed text will look like at this place. If you read this text, you will get no information. Really? Is there no information? Is there a difference between this text and some nonsense like ≫Huardest gefburn≪. Kjift – Never mind! A blind text like this gives you information about the selected font, how the letters are written and the impression of the look. This text should contain all letters of the alphabet and it should be written in of the original language. There is no need for a special contents, but the length of words should match to the language.
>
> 1

What just happened?

We used the command \enlargethispage to squeeze more text onto a page. This command takes the additionally requested height as its argument. The command \baselineskip returns the height of a text line that we used as the argument. So, LaTeX could put one extra line onto the page, and even the remaining line fitted in as well because LaTeX compressed some whitespace.

We could use factors: write \enlargethispage{2\baselineskip} to get two more lines on a page. It doesn't even need to be an integer value. Like always, when you state a length, you could use other units such as 10pt, 0.5in, 1cm, or 5mm, and even negative values.

Only the current page will be affected by this command.

> There's a starred version: \enlargethispage* would additionally shrink all vertical spaces on the page to their minimum.

Using footnotes

As briefly mentioned in *Chapter 2, Formatting Words, Lines, and Paragraphs*, LaTeX provides a command to typeset footnotes. Let's see it in action.

Time for action – using footnotes in text and in headings

Let's go back to the very first example of this chapter. We shall insert one footnote in the body text and one in a section heading:

1. Modify the example inserting a footnote, as shown in the highlighted line:

```
\documentclass[a4paper,12pt]{book}
\usepackage[english]{babel}
\usepackage{blindtext}
\begin{document}
\chapter{Exploring the page layout}
In this chapter we will study the layout of pages.
\section{Some filler text}
\blindtext
\section{A lot more filler text}
More dummy text\footnote{serving as a placeholder} will follow.
\subsection{Plenty of filler text}
\blindtext[10]
\end{document}
```

2. **Typeset** to see how the footnote looks in print:

> ## 1.2   A lot more filler text
>
> More dummy text[1] will follow.
>
> ### 1.2.1   Plenty of filler text
>
> Hello, here is some text without a meaning. This text should show, how a printed text will look like at this place. If you read this text, you will get no information. Really? Is there no information? Is there a difference between this text and some nonsense like »Huardest gefburn«. Kjift – Never mind! A blind text like this gives you information about the selected font,
>
> ---
> [1]serving as a placeholder
>
> 1

3. Insert a footnote in the second section header. This time, put `\protect` right before:

```
\section{A lot more filler text\protect\footnote{to fill the
page}}
```

4. **Typeset** to check that it works:

> ## 1.2   A lot more filler text[1]
>
> More dummy text[2] will follow.
>
> ### 1.2.1   Plenty of filler text
>
> Hello, here is some text without a meaning. This text should show, how a printed text will look like at this place. If you read this text, you will get no information. Really? Is there no information? Is there a difference between this text and some nonsense like »Huardest gefburn«. Kjift – Never
>
> ---
> [1]to fill the page
> [2]serving as a placeholder

What just happened?

The command \footnote{text} placed a superscripted number at the current position. Further, it prints its argument text into the bottom of the page, marked by the same number. As we've seen, such notes are separated from the main text by a horizontal line.

The other \footnote command has been preceded by the command \protect. If we omitted that, an error would be raised—try it. Such an error may occur when we use \footnote inside an argument, where it's being further processed. \protect simply prevents this processing error. As a rule of thumb, if a command causes an error when it's used inside an argument, like in headings, try to fix it by putting \protect right before that command. Cases where \protect would hurt instead of helping are rare.

Generally, a heading might not be a good place for footnotes. If you simply use \footnote in headings, be aware that they would appear in the table of contents and perhaps also in page headers. If you want to avoid that, use the optional parameter of the sectioning commands without \footnote, that is, \section[title without footnote]{title with footnote}. The same applies to \chapter, and so on, and even further to \caption.

The complete definition of \footnote is:

- \footnote[number]{text} produces a footnote marked by this optional number, an integer. If we don't give the optional number, an internal counter would be stepped and used. This would be done automatically; we don't need to worry.

Nevertheless, if we encounter difficulties in placing footnotes, there are two commands that help us:

- \footnotemark[number] produces a superscripted number in the text as a footnote mark. If the optional argument wasn't given, it's also stepping and using the internal footnote counter. No footnote will be generated.

- \footnotetext[number]{text} generates a footnote without putting a footnote mark into the text without stepping the internal footnote counter.

Both the commands may be used together in circumstances when \footnote would fail.

Set a footnote command right after the related text. Don't leave a space in-between. Otherwise, you would get a gap between the text and the following footnote mark.

Modifying the dividing line

The line that separates footnotes from the text is produced by the command \footnoterule. If we wish to omit that line or if we want to modify it, we must redefine it. We learned about \renewcommand—so, let's use it.

Time for action – redefining the footnote line

We will use `\renewcommand` to override the default `\footnoterule` command:

1. Take the previous example and add the following lines to the preamble:

    ```
    \renewcommand{\footnoterule}
        {\noindent\smash{\rule[3pt]{\textwidth}{0.4pt}}}
    ```

2. Typeset and see how the line has changed:

    ## 1.2   A lot more filler text[1]

    More dummy text[2] will follow.

    ### 1.2.1   Plenty of filler text

    Hello, here is some text without a meaning. This text should show, how
    a printed text will look like at this place. If you read this text, you will
    get no information. Really? Is there no information? Is there a difference
    between this text and some nonsense like ›Huardest gefburn‹. Kjift – Never

    ---
    [1] to fill the page
    [2] serving as a placeholder

What just happened?

Remember the definition of `\newcommand`—here it's analogous. The existing command
`\footnoterule` will be replaced by a new definition that we wrote in the second line. The
command `\rule[raising]{width}{height}` draws a line, here 0.4 pt thick, and as
wide as the text, raised a bit by 3 pt. Through the command `\smash`, we let our line pretend
to have a height and a depth of zero, so it's occupying no vertical space at all. This way,
the page balancing will not be affected. You already know `\noindent`, which avoids the
paragraph indentation.

If you want to omit that line completely, you just need to write:

```
\renewcommand{\footnoterule}{}
```

Now the command is defined to do nothing.

Using packages to expand footnote styles

There are different habits for setting footnotes. Some styles require footnotes numbered per page, they might have to be placed in the document as so called endnotes, and symbols instead of numbers may be used. More demands exist and therefore several packages have been developed to comply with them. Here's a selection:

- **endnotes**: Places footnotes at the end of the document
- **manyfoot**: Allows nested footnotes
- **bigfoot**: Replaces and extends `manyfoot`, improves page break handling with footnotes
- **savefnmark**: Useful when you need to use footnotes several times
- **footmisc**: All-round package; introduces numbering per page, is able to save space when many short footnotes are used, offers symbols instead of numbers as footnote marks, provides hanging indentation and other styles

Have a look at the respective package documentation to learn more—now you know how to obtain it.

Pop quiz

1. According to the text, which of the following points should be the goal when designing the page layout?
   a. Fill the page as much as possible
   b. Achieve an artistic design
   c. Improve readability
   d. Distinguish the work from other publications

2. Which options are preset by the book class?
   a. `openright` and `twoside`
   b. `openany` and `twoside`
   c. `openright` and `oneside`
   d. `openany` and `oneside`

3. Which page style is used as default on the first page of a chapter?
   a. `empty`
   b. `plain`
   c. `headings`
   d. `myheadings`
   e. `fancy`

4. One of these page breaking commands is able to stretch the text to the bottom to fill the page. Which one?

    a. `\newpage`

    b. `\clearpage`

    c. `\cleardoublepage`

    d. `\pagebreak`

5. We would like to put a footnote into a chapter heading. Choose the best way!

    a. `\chapter{title\footnote{text}}`

    b. `\chapter*{title\footnote{text}}`

    c. `\chapter{title\protect\footnote{text}}`

    d. `\chapter[title]{title\footnote{text}}`

Summary

In this chapter, we have worked out how to design the overall layout of a document.

Specifically, we learned about:

- Adjusting the page dimensions and margins
- Using landscape orientation and two-column layout
- Modifying the spacing between lines
- Breaking pages and paying attention to the vertical justification
- Designing headers and footers with titles and page numbers
- Using footnotes

Further, we covered some general topics:

- Obtaining documentation of packages in several ways
- Changing document properties by choosing class options
- Redefining existing commands

Now it's time to deal with further text structures. In the next chapter, we shall learn how to create lists for presenting text in an easy-to-read way.

4
Creating Lists

Arranging text in the form of a list can be very reader-friendly. You can present several ideas by a clear structure which is easy to survey. Commonly, three types of lists are used:

1. *Bulleted lists*
2. *Numbered lists*
3. *Definition lists*

In this chapter, we shall learn how to create such lists.

Building a bulleted list

We shall start with the simplest kind of list. It contains just the items without numbers. Each item is marked by a bullet.

Time for action – listing LaTeX packages

We shall create a list of packages that we got to know in the previous chapter:

1. Begin a new document and enter the following code:

```
\documentclass{article}
\begin{document}
\section*{Useful packages}
LaTeX provides several packages for designing the layout:
\begin{itemize}
  \item geometry
```

```
    \item typearea
    \item fancyhdr
    \item scrpage2
    \item setspace
\end{itemize}
\end{document}
```

2. **Typeset** and have a look at the output:

> ## Useful packages
>
> LaTeX provides several packages for designing the layout:
>
> - geometry
> - typearea
> - fancyhdr
> - scrpage2
> - setspace

What just happened?

It was not necessary to load any package. We began with a heading followed by some text. For the actual list, we used an environment called `itemize`. As we know about environments, `\begin{itemize}` starts it and `\end{itemize}` ends it. The command `\item` tells LaTeX that a new item to the list follows. Each item may contain text of any length and even paragraph breaks. Well, that's pretty easy, isn't it?

Nesting lists

When a list gets longer, we could make it clearer by dividing it. We just create lists in a list. It's advisable to use different bullets to keep the list levels apart easily. LaTeX does it for us automatically.

Time for action – listing packages by topic

We shall refine the package list by introducing categories:

1. Refine the aforementioned highlighted `itemize` environment of our example in the following way:

```
\begin{itemize}
  \item Page layout
  \begin{itemize}
```

```
  \item geometry
  \item typearea
\end{itemize}
\item Headers and footers
\begin{itemize}
  \item fancyhdr
  \item scrpage2
\end{itemize}
\item Line spacing
\begin{itemize}
  \item setspace
\end{itemize}
\end{itemize}
```

2. **Typeset** to see the new list:

- Page layout
  - geometry
  - typearea
- Headers and footers
  - fancyhdr
  - scrpage2
- Line spacing
  - setspace

What just happened?

We simply inserted another list inside the list. Up to four levels are possible, otherwise LaTeX would stop and print out the error message **! LaTeX Error: Too deeply nested.** As we saw, the first level is marked by a bullet, and the second by an en dash. A third level item would start with an asterisk symbol *. The fourth and last level would be marked by a centered dot.

Deeply nested lists can rarely be seen; such complicated structures might be hard to read. In such cases, it could be a good idea to revise the text structure or at least split the list.

Creating a numbered list

Bulleted lists are useful if the order of the items doesn't matter. However, if the order is important, we could organize the items by giving them numbers and creating a sorted list. That would allow a reader to follow our thoughts easily.

Time for action – writing a step-by-step tutorial

Let's prepare a tiny "how-to" about designing the page layout:

1. Start with a new document and enter the following code:

```
\documentclass{article}
\begin{document}
\begin{enumerate}
  \item State the paper size by an option to the document class
  \item Determine the margin dimensions using one of these
        packages:
  \begin{itemize}
    \item geometry
    \item typearea
  \end{itemize}
  \item Customize header and footer by one of these packages:
  \begin{itemize}
    \item fancyhdr
    \item scrpage2
  \end{itemize}
  \item Adjust the line spacing for the whole document
  \begin{itemize}
    \item by using the setspace package
    \item or by the command \verb|\linespread{factor}|
  \end{itemize}
\end{enumerate}
\end{document}
```

2. **Typeset** to generate the «how-to»:

1. State the paper size by an option to the document class

2. Determine the margin dimensions using one of these packages:

   - geometry
   - typearea

3. Customize header and footer by one of these packages:

   - fancyhdr
   - scrpage2

4. Adjust the line spacing for the whole document

   - by using the setspace package
   - or by the command \linespread{factor}

What just happened?

We used an **enumerate** environment. Except for the name, we use it just like the `itemize` environment; each list item is introduced by the command `\item`. Again, we nested two lists, but this time the lists are of a different kind. As we saw, that's no problem. Even though the unnumbered list is embedded within a numbered list, it's marked by bullets, because it's the first unnumbered level. Mixed nesting could go further than four levels, but four is the maximum for each kind and six in general.

The default numbering scheme for the `enumerate` environment is as follows:

First level:	1., 2., 3., 4., ...
Second level:	(a), (b), (c), (d), ...
Third level:	i., ii., iii., iv., ...
Fourth level:	A., B., C., D., ...

`\item` understands an optional argument; if you write `\item[text]`, then `text` will be printed instead of a number or a bullet. This way, you could use any numbering and any symbol for the bullet.

Customizing lists

The default appearance of lists is meaningful regarding spacing, indentation, and symbols. Nevertheless, it may be required to use another scheme for the enumeration, for the bullets, or to modify the line spacing or their indentation. There are packages helping us both to save space and to customize the symbols; let's start with the spacing.

Saving space with compact lists

A frequently arising question is how to reduce the space. LaTeX's lists are often regarded as being too spacious. We shall see how to implement that.

Time for action – shrinking our tutorial

We shall remove the white space around the list items and before and after the whole list as well:

1. In the previous example, load the package **paralist** and replace enumerate with `compactenum` and itemize with `compactitem`:

    ```
    \documentclass{article}
    \usepackage{paralist}
    \begin{document}
    ```

```
\begin{compactenum}
  \item State the paper size by an option to the document class
  \item Determine the margin dimensions using one of these
        packages:
  \begin{compactitem}
    \item geometry
    \item typearea
  \end{compactitem}
  \item Customize header and footer by one of these packages:
  \begin{compactitem}
    \item fancyhdr
    \item scrpage2
  \end{compactitem}
  \item Adjust the line spacing for the whole document
  \begin{compactitem}
    \item by using the setspace package
    \item or by the command \verb|\linespread{factor}|
  \end{compactitem}
\end{compactenum}
\end{document}
```

2. **Typeset** and compare the spacing:

> 1. State the paper size by an option to the document class
> 2. Determine the margin dimensions using one of these packages:
>   - geometry
>   - typearea
> 3. Customize header and footer by one of these packages:
>   - fancyhdr
>   - scrpage2
> 4. Adjust the line spacing for the whole document
>   - by using the setspace package
>   - or by the command `\linespread{factor}`

3. Now extend the highlighted list item for set space as follows:

```
\item by using the setspace package and one of its options:
  \begin{inparaenum}
  \item singlespacing
  \item onehalfspacing
  \item double spacing
  \end{inparaenum}
```

2. **Typeset** and look at the change in the line spacing subject:

> 4. Adjust the line spacing for the whole document
>   - by using the setspace package and one of its options: (a) singlespacing
>   (b) onehalfspacing (c) double spacing
>   - or by the command \linespread{factor}

What just happened?

The used package `paralist` provides several new list environments designed to be typeset within paragraphs or in a very compact look. We loaded this package and replaced the standard environments with their compact counterparts. In step 3, we used a new environment, where the items are enumerated but stay within the same paragraph.

For each standard environment, `paralist` adds three corresponding environments:

Numbered lists:

- `compactenum`: Compact version of the `enumerate` environment without any vertical space before or after the list or its items

- `inparaenum`: An enumerated list typeset within a paragraph

- `asparaenum`: Every list item is formatted like a separate common LaTeX paragraph, but numbered

Bulleted lists:

- `compactitem`: Compact version of the `itemize` environment like `compactenum`

- `inparaitem`: An itemized list typeset within a paragraph, rarely seen in print

- `asparaitem`: Like `asparaenum`, but with symbols instead of numbers

Choosing bullets and numbering format

To follow language specific habits or certain requirements, we might wish to enumerate by Roman numbers or alphabetically; parentheses or dots might be required. Some may prefer dashes instead of bullets. The package **enumitem** provides sophisticated features to implement such requirements.

Time for action – modifying lists using enumitem

Let's change the numbering scheme. We shall number alphabetically using circled letters. Furthermore, we will replace bullets by dashes:

1. We shall discard `paralist` and load the package `enumitem` instead. We will turn away from the compact environments returning to the standard list notation:

```
\documentclass{article}
\usepackage{enumitem}
\setlist{nolistsep}
\setitemize[1]{label=---}
\setenumerate[1]{label=\textcircled{\scriptsize\Alph*},
  font=\sffamily}
\begin{document}
\begin{enumerate}
  \item State the paper size by an option to the document class
  \item Determine the margin dimensions using one of these
packages:
  \begin{itemize}
    \item geometry
    \item typearea
  \end{itemize}
  \item Customize header and footer by one of these packages:
  \begin{itemize}
    \item fancyhdr
    \item scrpage2
  \end{itemize}
  \item Adjust the line spacing for the whole document
  \begin{itemize}
    \item by using the setspace package
    \item or by the command \verb|\linespread{factor}|
  \end{itemize}
\end{enumerate}
\end{document}
```

2. **Typeset** and see the output:

Ⓐ State the paper size by an option to the document class
Ⓑ Determine the margin dimensions using one of these packages:
 — geometry
 — typearea
Ⓒ Customize header and footer by one of these packages:
 — fancyhdr
 — scrpage2
Ⓓ Adjust the line spacing for the whole document
 — by using the setspace package
 — or by the command \linespread{factor}

3. Right above the highlighted line, insert the following lines:

```
\end{enumerate}
\subsubsection*{Tweaking the line spacing:}
\begin{enumerate}[resume*]
```

4. **Typeset** to see the change:

Ⓐ State the paper size by an option to the document class
Ⓑ Determine the margin dimensions using one of these packages:
 — geometry
 — typearea
Ⓒ Customize header and footer by one of these packages:
 — fancyhdr
 — scrpage2

Tweaking the line spacing:

Ⓓ Adjust the line spacing for the whole document
 — by using the setspace package
 — or by the command \linespread{factor}

What just happened?

We used the `enumitem` command to specify list properties. Let's take a closer look:

♦ `\setlist{nolistsep}`: `\setlist` sets properties valid for all types of lists. Here we specified `nolistsep` to achieve very compact lists analogous to the compact `paralist` environment.

♦ `\setitemize[1]{label=---}`: `\setitemize` modifies properties of bulleted lists. Here we chose an em dash as the label to get a leading wide dash.

- `\setenumerate[1]{label=\textcircled{\scriptsize\Alph*},font=\`
  `sffamily}`: `\setenumerate` sets properties valid for numbered lists. We used it
  to set a label and a font for the label. The command `\Alph*` stands for enumeration
  in capital letters.

All of those three commands allow arguments of the form `key=value`. Some useful
parameters are as follows:

Parameter	Meaning	Values	Example
`font`	Modifies the label font	Any font command	`font=\bfseries`
`label`	Sets the label for the current level	May contain `\arabic*`, `\alph*`, `\Alph*`, `\roman*`, `\Roman*`	`label=\emph\alph*)`
`label*`	Like label but appended to the current label	Like label	`label*=\arabic)`
`align`	Alignment of the label	`left` or `right`	`align=right`
`start`	Number of the first item	Integer	`start=10`
`resume,` `resume*`	Let's the counter continue from the previous lists value		`resume`
`noitemsep`	No extra space between items and paragraphs		`noitemsep`
`nolistsep`	No extra vertical spacing at all		`nolistsep`

These options may be set globally like `\setenumerate[level]{key=value list}`.
If the optional argument `level` is missing, this global command will apply to all levels.

Those options may be used locally like we did with `resume*`. Other examples are:

- `\begin{itemize}[noitemsep]` for a compact bulleted list

- `\begin{enumerate}[label=\Roman*.,start=3]` numbered by III., IV., ...

- `\begin{enumerate}[label=\alph*)],nolistsep]` for a very compact list
  numbered a), b), c), ...

The labeling commands would achieve a numbering as follows:

\arabic*	1, 2, 3, 4, …
\alph*	a, b, c, d, …
\Alph*	A, B, C, D, …
\roman*	i, ii, iii, iv, …
\Roman*	I, II, III, IV, …

The * has been added to distinguish those commands from LaTeX commands with the same name. Parentheses and punctuation may be used as wished. Later in the book, you will learn how to choose between thousands of symbols for labels and bullets.

There's even a short form: if you load enumitem with the option shortlabels, you may use a compact syntax like \begin{enumerate}[(i)], \begin{enumerate}[(1)] where 1, a, A, i, I stand for \arabic*, \alph*, \Alph*, \roman*, \Roman* respectively. This allows customization quickly and easily. However, consider using global commands to keep formatting consistent.

Suspending and continuing lists

In step 3 of our example, we interrupted the list. We continued writing normal text until we restarted the list by \begin{enumerate}[resume*]. The resume option tells enumitem to continue the list with the next number. The starred variant resume* does it with the same formatting like before. If you would like to complete the document, note that a \ subsubsection command should be preceded by a \subsection command. This should follow a \section command. Just using a lower-level heading without a parent heading could result in numbering like 0.0.1.

Producing a definition list

We shall proceed to the third kind of list, namely, definition lists, also called description lists. Every list item consists of a term followed by its description.

Time for action – explaining capabilities of packages

Now that we know some packages for creating lists, we shall write a short overview to show their capabilities. Let's choose some additional packages listed on `http://texcatalogue.sarovar.org`:

1. We will use a **description** environment. Create a document with the following code:

```
\documentclass{article}
\begin{document}
\begin{description}
  \item[paralist] provides compact lists and list versions that
can be used within paragraphs, helps to customize labels and
layout
  \item[enumitem] gives control over labels and lengths
    in all kind of lists
  \item[mdwlist] is useful to customize description lists, it
    even allows multi-line labels. It features compact lists and
    the capability to suspend and resume.
  \item[desclist] offers more flexibility in definition list
  \item[multenum] produces vertical enumeration in multiple
    columns
\end{description}
\end{document}
```

2. **Typeset** to get the definition list:

paralist provides compact lists and list versions that can be used within paragraphs, helps to customize labels and layout

enumitem gives control over labels and lenghts in all kind of lists

mdwlist is useful to customize description lists, it even allows multi-line labels. It features compact lists and the capability to suspend and resume.

desclist offers more flexibility in definition list

multenum produces vertical enumeration in multiple columns

What just happened?

We used the description environment like the other lists, except that we used the optional argument of \item. In the description environment, \item is defined such that the optional parameter will be typeset in the bold typeface.

The package paralist supports the description environment as well; there are the compactdesc, inparadesc, and asparadesc versions working analogous to the other lists.

The same is valid for enumitem: there's the global command \setdescription{format} working like \setitemize and \setenumerate. Furthermore, it also extends the description environment to accept optional formatting arguments of the form key=value, supporting the short form as well.

Have a go hero – adjusting the dimensions of lists

LaTeX's lists have a meaningful layout. However, there might be occasions when you would like to modify this layout, for instance, to change the margins or the item indentation. All layout dimensions are determined by LaTeX macros, so called **lengths**.

There's a package which is really great for visualizing layouts, which presents these length macros. It's called **layouts** and it has been written by Peter Wilson. Let's use it to examine LaTeX's list dimensions. We will use this small document:

```
\documentclass[12pt]{article}
\usepackage{layouts}
\begin{document}
\listdiagram
\end{document}
```

By simply typesetting it, we will get the following diagram:

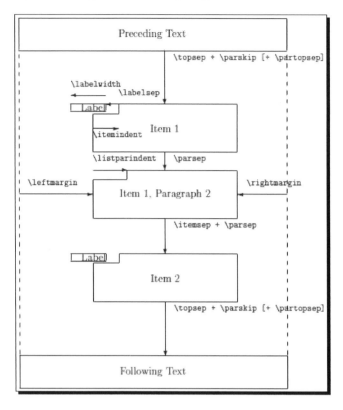

Isn't it fantastic? The `layouts` package can do even more, which you can read about in its documentation. For now, we stay on topic regarding lists.

Though there are LaTeX commands for customizing those lengths, for example, `\setlength{\labelwidth}{2cm}`, applying them to individual lists and certain nesting depths is hard. If you need to modify the list layout, the `enumitem` package comes handy again. Its commands like `\setlist` and its `key=value` interface may be used also for adjusting the values of the lengths you could see in the previous diagram.

For example, if we would like to remove the space between list items in the `description` environment and to reduce the left margin, we could load `enumitem` and write the following:

```
\setdescription{itemsep=0cm,parsep=0cm,leftmargin=0.5cm}
```

Note, we don't use the backslash for keys. Similarly, `\setitemize`, `\setenumerate`, and `\setlist` can be used for fine-tuning. Try assigning values by yourself, and test the effect on our examples. If you would like to learn more, have a look at the `enumitem` documentation.

Pop quiz

1. A list environment may be nested to up to how many levels?

   a. Two

   b. Three ✓

   c. Four

   d. Any number, just depending on the memory

2. All but one of these packages understand options in the form `key=value`. Which does not?

   a. `geometry`

   b. `paralist`

   c. `enumitem`

3. In which environment should `\item` be used with an optional argument?

   a. `itemize`

   b. `enumerate`

   c. `description`

   d. `inparaenum`

Summary

In this chapter, we got to know a new way to structure our text—lists. Specifically, we learned to create:

- Bulleted lists using the `itemize` environment

- Numbered lists using the `enumerate` environment

- Definition lists using the `description` environment

Furthermore, we worked with compact versions of such lists provided by the packages `paralist` and `enumitem`. Those packages allowed us to customize our lists at will.

You may regard those lists as an additional possibility to structure your text. Use it to clarify your ideas. Though you may design the layout of lists as you wish, it's highly recommended to use the same bullets and numbering scheme respectively for the same nesting level.

5
Creating Tables and Inserting Pictures

Scientific documents and others do not just contain plain text; they also present information and data in tables and use diagrams and drawings to visualize them. We shall become familiar with that.

In this chapter, we will learn how to perform the following:

- ◆ Lining up text and data in columns
- ◆ Typesetting complex tables
- ◆ Including pictures in our documents
- ◆ Adding captions to pictures and tables
- ◆ Controlling the placement of figures and tables

Let's tackle these tasks!

Writing in columns

Remember the time of the typewriter and early word processing software? When we needed to line up some text in columns, we could use tab stops. LaTeX provides a similar way to easily align text in columns, namely, the **tabbing** environment.

Time for action – lining up information using the tabbing environment

We would like to present a quick overview regarding LaTeX. We shall present one point on each line, aligned at words and double colons:

1. Begin a new document and open a `tabbing` environment:

    ```
    \documentclass{article}
    \begin{document}
    \begin{tabbing}
    ```

2. Write the text, set tab stops by `\=`, and end the line by `\\`:

    ```
    \emph{Info:} \= Software \= : \= \LaTeX \\
    ```

3. Add further lines, move to the next tab stop by `\>`, and again end lines by `\\`:

    ```
    \> Author \> : \> Leslie Lamport \\
    \> Website \> : \> www.latex-project.org
    ```

4. Close the `tabbing` environment and end the document:

    ```
    \end{tabbing}
    \end{document}
    ```

5. **Typeset** to get the output:

    ```
    Info: Software : LaTeX
          Author   : Leslie Lamport
          Website  : www.latex-project.org
    ```

What just happened?

The tabbing environment that we used begins a new line. We used three simple tags for markup:

*   `\=` sets a tab stop. We could put several tab stops on a line. If we use `\=` later, the next awaited tab stop would be reset to this position.

*   `\\` ends a row.

*   `\>` goes to the next tab stop. This could also mean to go backwards.

This way, we can quickly produce columns containing left-aligned text. If the rows of the tabbing environment would reach the end of a page, it could continue on the next page. What if a column is too long, running over the tab stop? Let's see how to solve that.

Time for action – lining up font commands

In *Chapter 2, Formatting Words, Lines, and Paragraphs*, we've got to know a lot of font commands and declarations. We saw a table containing those commands and example output. Now we shall create such a table ourselves:

1. Begin a new document, like the one in step 1 of our previous example, but define a command for setting the font of our header:

```
\documentclass{article}
\newcommand{\head}[1]{\textbf{#1}}
\begin{document}
\begin{tabbing}
```

2. Write the first row set tab stops by \= and use \> to move to the tab stops. Use the command \verb|...| to typeset the LaTeX commands:

```
\begin{tabbing}
Family \= \verb|\textrm{...}| \= \head{Declaration} \= \kill
  \> \head{Command} \> \head{Declaration} \> \head{Example}\\
Family \> \verb|\textrm{...}| \> \verb|\rmfamily|
  \> \rmfamily Example text\\
  \> \verb|\textsf{...}| \> \verb|\sffamily|
  \> \sffamily Example text\\
  \> \verb|\texttt{...}| \> \verb|\ttfamily|
  \> \ttfamily Example text
\end{tabbing}
```

3. **Typeset** and examine:

> **Type Command Declaration Example**
> Family\textrm{...\rmfamily   Example text

4. As we can see, the tab stops are too narrow. We shall correct it. Create a new head row containing the tab stops; this time, we will mark the line by \kill to hide that line. Use filler text to specify the width between the tab stops. Complete it with further font commands:

```
\begin{tabbing}
Family \= \verb|\textrm{...}| \= \head{Declaration} \= \kill
  \> \head{Command} \> \head{Declaration} \> \head{Example}\\
Family \> \verb|\textrm{...}| \> \verb|\rmfamily|
  \> \rmfamily Example text\\
  \> \verb|\textsf{...}| \> \verb|\sffamily|
  \> \sffamily Example text\\
  \> \verb|\texttt{...}| \> \verb|\ttfamily|
  \> \ttfamily Example text
\end{tabbing}
```

5. **Typeset** to get the result:

	Command	Declaration	Example
Family	\textrm{...}	\rmfamily	Example text
	\textsf{...}	\sffamily	Example text
	\texttt{...}	\ttfamily	Example text

What just happened?

After we noticed that our tab stops have been set too narrow, we constructed a new first row containing the tab stops. It consists of words representing the widest entries of each column. To hide this auxiliary row, we used the command \kill right at the end of the line; \kill at the end of a line causes this line to have no output.

Like in this example, the command \verb|code| typesets code "as it is", without interpreting commands within. Instead of |, any character may be chosen as the delimiter. \verb cannot be used in arguments of commands including \section and \footnote, and not in table heads.

For longer, **verbatim** text, use the environment with the same name: verbatim.

There are further useful commands:

- \+ at the end of a line causes each subsequent line to start at the first tab. Use it twice \+\+ to start at the second tab and so on.

- \- cancels a preceding \+; also using multiply has cumulative effect.

- \< at the beginning of a line cancels the effect of one previous \+ command for that line.

The mentioned commands already allow a good use of the tabbing environment. Even more commands can be found in the reference manual: http://texblog.net/help/latex/tabbing.html.

Inside tabbing environments, declarations are local to the current item. A following \=, \>, \\, or \kill command would stop the effect.

Tabbing environments cannot be nested.

Typesetting tables

We might need more complicated structures and formatting, like centering in columns, dividing lines, or even nested structures. LaTeX provides the **tabular** environment for typesetting simple and complex tables which can be nested.

Time for action – building a table of font family commands

We shall create a table like in the previous example, but this time, we would like to make all entries in a column horizontally centered to each other. We will also add some horizontal lines to mark the border and the header of the table:

1. Create a new document. Define a command for setting the font for the head row:

   ```
   \documentclass{article}
   \newcommand{\head}[1]{\textnormal{\textbf{#1}}}
   \begin{document}
   ```

2. Begin a `tabular` environment. As a mandatory argument, provide ccc standing for three centered columns:

   ```
   \begin{tabular}{ccc}
   ```

3. Write the table head row, write & to separate column entries, and \\ to end rows. Use \hline to insert horizontal lines:

   ```
   \hline
   \head{Command} & \head{Declaration} & \head{Output}\\
   \hline
   ```

4. Continue with the table body and end the environment and the document. For typesetting LaTeX commands, write \verb|\command|:

   ```
   \verb|\textrm| & \verb|\rmfamily| & \rmfamily Example text\\
   \verb|\textsf| & \verb|\sffamily| & \sffamily Example text\\
   \verb|\texttt| & \verb|\ttfamily| & \ttfamily Example text\\
   \hline
   \end{tabular}
   \end{document}
   ```

5. **Typeset** to see the table:

Command	Declaration	Output
\textrm	\rmfamily	Example text
\textsf	\sffamily	Example text
\texttt	\ttfamily	Example text

What just happened?

In the mandatory argument, we wrote a list of characters. Each character stands for a formatting option. As we used three characters, we've got three columns. c stands for centered alignment. Therefore, the entries of all columns have been centered.

Column entries are separated by &, while rows are terminated by \\. Don't end the last line by \\ unless you further wish to write a line below. It's also a good idea to align the ampersands in our source code to keep it readable.

Inside the entries, you may use ordinary text as well as LaTeX commands. As in the tabbing environment, declarations are local to the entry, like if each entry was surrounded by curly braces.

Furthermore, tabular has an optional alignment argument just like minipage. So, the complete definition is:

```
\begin{tabular}[position]{column specifiers}
row 1 col 1 entry & row 1 col 2 entry ... & row 1 col n entry\\
   ...
\end{tabular}
```

In the optional argument, t means alignment at the top row and b means alignment at the bottom row. The default is vertically centered alignment. This may come in handy if you would like to place two tables next to each other or within further text.

Drawing lines in tables

Within tabular, three types of lines may be used:

- \hline draws a horizontal line over the whole width of the table
- \cline{m-n} draws a horizontal line starting at the beginning of column m and ending at the end of column n
- \vline draws a vertical line over the full height and depth of the current row

Understanding formatting arguments

Of course, further formatting is possible. Have a look at this example table:

```
\begin{tabular}{|l|c|r|p{1.7cm}|}
  \hline
left & centered & right & a fully justified paragraph cell\\
\hline
  l & c & r & p\\
  \hline
\end{tabular}
```

This code would produce the following table:

left	centered	right	a fully justified paragraph cell
l	c	r	p

The options understood by the `tabular` environment are as follows:

- ◆ `l` for left alignment.
- ◆ `c` for centered alignment.
- ◆ `r` for right alignment.
- ◆ `p{width}` for a "paragraph" cell of a certain width. . If you place several p cells next to each other, they will be aligned at their top line. It's equivalent to using `\parbox[t]{width}` within a cell.
- ◆ `@{code}` inserts `code` instead of empty space before or after a column. This might also be some text or it could be left empty to avoid this space.
- ◆ `|` stands for a vertical line.
- ◆ `*{n}{options}` is equivalent to n copies of `options`, where n is a positive integer and `options` may consist of one or more column specifiers including `*` as well.

 It is very advisable to avoid vertical lines in tables. Lines should subtly support your information but not make reading difficult.

After loading the `array` package by `\usepackage{array}` you may use some options, such as:

- ◆ `m{width}` is similar to `\parbox{width}`: the base line is at the middle
- ◆ `b{width}` is like `\parbox[b]{width}`: the base line is at the bottom
- ◆ `!{code}` can be used like `|` but inserts `code` instead of a vertical line. In contrast to @{...}, the space between columns will not be suppressed.
- ◆ `>{code}` can be used before an `l`, `c`, `r`, `p`, `m`, or `b` option and inserts `code` right at the beginning of each entry of that column
- ◆ `<{code}` can be used after an `l`, `c`, `r`, `p`, `m`, or `b` option and inserts `code` at the end of the entry of that column

This example shows the effect of @{} and the alignment arguments p, m, and b:

```
\begin{tabular}{@{}lp{1.2cm}m{1.2cm}b{1.2cm}@{}}
  \hline
baseline & aligned at the top & aligned at the middle
& aligned at the bottom\\
  \hline
\end{tabular}
```

The output table is as follows:

			aligned at the bottom
baseline	aligned at the top	aligned at the middle	

Increasing the row height

You may have noticed that horizontal lines nearly touch the letters in the cells, especially capital letters. The array package introduces a length called \extrarowheight. If it has a positive value, this will be added to the height of every row of the table.

The next example, following the very first example of this chapter, shows how to extend the row height and shows the effect of the remaining array options:

```
\documentclass{article}
\usepackage{array}
\setlength{\extrarowheight}{4pt}
\begin{document}
\begin{tabular}{@{}>{\itshape}ll!{:}l<{.}@{}}
  \hline
  Info: & Software & \LaTeX\\
& Author & Leslie Lamport\\
& Website & www.latex-project.org\\
\hline
\end{tabular}
\end{document}
```

The output is as follows:

Info:	Software	:	LaTeX.
	Author	:	Leslie Lamport.
	Website	:	www.latex-project.org.

Here, `>{\itshape}` has been used to change the font of a row to italic. `>{}` is often used to insert an alignment declaration, but there's a pitfall: such declarations might change the internal meaning of `\\`, which is a shortcut for `\tabularnewline` within tables. But the array package offers a command to repair it; in such cases, just add `\arraybackslash`, for example:

```
\begin{tabular}{>{\centering\arraybackslash}p{5cm}}
```

Otherwise, the content of paragraph cells stated by p, m, or b will be fully justified.

After a specific row, you can add vertical space by the optional argument of `\\`, such as `\\[10pt]`.

You may even stretch a whole table: the macro `\arraystretch` contains a stretching factor with a default value of 1. Just redefine it. For example, `\renewcommand{\arraystretch}{1.5}` will increase the height of the rows by 50 percent. You could use it inside a group or an environment to keep the effect local.

Beautifying tables

Still our tables don't look as perfect as they look in good books. Especially, the lines and their distances to the text might need improvement. The **booktabs** package comes to the rescue; after loading it, you can enhance the quality of your tables by new line commands replacing `\hline` and `\cline`.

Time for action – adding nicer horizontal lines with the booktabs package

We shall use the new commands introduced by `booktabs`:

1. In the previous example, load the package `booktabs`:

    ```
    \usepackage{booktabs}
    ```

2. Use `\toprule`, `\midrule`, and `\bottomrule` instead of `\hline`. Specify a thickness as an optional argument:

    ```
    \begin{tabular}{ccc}
      \toprule[1.5pt]
      \head{Command} & \head{Declaration} & \head{Output}\\
      \midrule
      \verb|\textrm| & \verb|\rmfamily| & \rmfamily Example text\\
      \verb|\textsf| & \verb|\sffamily| & \sffamily Example text\\
      \verb|\texttt| & \verb|\ttfamily| & \ttfamily Example text\\
      \bottomrule[1.5pt]
    \end{tabular}
    ```

3. **Typeset** to see the difference:

Command	Declaration	Output
\textrm	\rmfamily	Example text
\textsf	\sffamily	Example text
\texttt	\ttfamily	Example text

What just happened?

British typesetters call a line a **rule**. The booktabs developer chose this terminology for the new commands. We used three of them. These are their definitions:

- \toprule [thickness] may be used to draw a horizontal line at the top of the table. If desired, a thickness may be specified, like 1pt or 0.5mm.

- \midrule [thickness] draws a horizontal dividing line between rows of a table.

- \bottomrule [thickness] draws a horizontal line to finish off a table.

- \cmidrule [thickness] (trim) {m-n} draws a horizontal line from column m to column n. (trim) is optional like thickness, it could be (l) or (r) to trim the line at its left or right end. Write (lr) to trim at both ends. Even adding {width}, like in (l{10pt}), is possible and specifies the trim width.

The package does not define vertical lines. They are not advisable anyway. The same applies to double rules. Neither vertical nor double rules are recommended. They are even widely considered to be bad typographic style.

Consider using \toprule and the other line commands without optional arguments—let's figure out how.

Have a go hero – adjusting lengths

We briefly introduced the command \setlength. Instead of specifying a line thickness by an optional argument to \toprule, \midrule, \cmidrule, or \bottomrule, always omit it. Instead, specify it once for your whole document by \setlength in the preamble.

These are the lengths that may be adjusted:

- \heavyrulewidth for the thickness of the top and bottom lines
- \lightrulewidth for the thickness of the middle lines by \midrule
- \cmidrulewidth for the thickness of \cmidrule
- \cmidrulekern for the trimming in \cmidrule
- \abovetopsep is the space above the top rule; the default is 0pt

- ◆ `\belowbottomsep` is the space below the bottom rule; the default is `0pt`
- ◆ `\aboverulesep` specifies the space above `\midrule`, `\cmidrule`, and `\bottomrule`
- ◆ `\belowrulesep` stands for the space below `\midrule`, `\cmidrule`, and `\toprule`

Try to change the thickness of the lines. The lengths already have reasoned values, but you may change them. So, the adjustment in your preamble would improve all tables in your document.

Spanning entries over multiple columns

Columns concerning the same subject might be grouped by a common header. In such a case, two cells in the header should be merged. The command `\multicolumn` does it for us.

Time for action – merging cells

Regarding our example table, commands and declarations are both **input**, whereas, the remaining column contains **output**. We shall emphasize that in our header:

1. In our example, insert another header row. Use `\multicolumn` to merge cells. Alter the column formatting argument and the middle rule. Changes are highlighted:

```
\begin{tabular}{@{}*3l@{}}
   \toprule[1.5pt]
   \multicolumn{2}{c}{\head{Input}} &
   \multicolumn{1}{c}{\head{Output}}\\
   \head{Command} & \head{Declaration} & \\
   \cmidrule(r){1-2}\cmidrule(l){3-3}
   \verb|\textrm| & \verb|\rmfamily| & \rmfamily Example text\\
   \verb|\textsf| & \verb|\sffamily| & \sffamily Example text\\
   \verb|\texttt| & \verb|\ttfamily| & \ttfamily Example text\\
   \bottomrule[1.5pt]
\end{tabular}
```

2. **Typeset** and see the output:

Input		Output
Command	Declaration	
\textrm	\rmfamily	Example text
\textsf	\sffamily	Example text
\texttt	\ttfamily	Example text

What just happened?

We used the command `\multicolumn` twice; once to merge two cells and surprisingly another time just for one cell. Let's first look at its definition:

```
\multicolumn{number of columns}{formatting options}{entry text}
```

The number of columns to be spanned may be a positive integer or just 1. The formatting options will be applied instead of the options specified in the tabular definition for this cell. We took advantage of this when we used `\multicolumn{1}{c}{...}`, overriding the l option of the column by a c option to get just this cell centered.

The other change we made concerns `\cmidrule`. We used it instead of `\midrule` together with the trimming argument to get a gap between the input and the output column.

Inserting code column-wise

There are many more font commands that we would like to add to the table. Writing `\verb|...|` in each cell is tiresome. We shall exploit the `>{...}` feature of the array package to define the formatting of the entries once for the column.

Time for action – using the array package

We shall modify the table definition to set our input columns in the typewriter font. At the same time, we will insert a column on the left, standing for our command type:

1. Extend the preamble of our example by defining a command `\normal`. It shall use `\multicolumn` to produce an l cell, no matter what the column formatting is:

```
\documentclass{article}
\usepackage{array}
\usepackage{booktabs}
\newcommand{\head}[1]{\textnormal{\textbf{#1}}}
\newcommand{\normal}[1]{\multicolumn{1}{l}{#1}}
\begin{document}
```

2. As `\verb` cannot be used in table headers, we shall use `\ttfamily`. Preceding it with `\textbackslash` is enough for our purposes. Use `>{...}` to insert it twice. Then add `<{Example text}` to the last column to save typing work:

```
\begin{tabular}{@{}l*2{>{\textbackslash\ttfamily}l}l%
<{Example text}@{}}
  \toprule[1.5pt]
& \multicolumn{2}{c}{\head{Input}} &
    \multicolumn{1}{c}{\head{Output}}\\
```

3. We'll use the `\normal` command to avoid the typewriter formatting in the header:

```
& \normal{\head{Command}} & \normal{\head{Declaration}}
& \normal{}\\
    \cmidrule(lr){2-3}\cmidrule(l){4-4}
```

4. Now we may continue listing the font command names:

```
Family & textrm&rmfamily & \rmfamily\\
& textsf & sffamily & \sffamily\\
& texttt & ttfamily & \ttfamily\\
    \bottomrule[1.5pt]
\end{tabular}
\end{document}
```

5. **Typeset** and look at the result:

	Input		Output
	Command	**Declaration**	
Family	\textrm	\rmfamily	Example text
	\textsf	\sffamily	Example text
	\texttt	\ttfamily	Example text

What just happened?

Using `>{\textbackslash\ttfamily}l` defines a left aligned row, where each entry is preceded by a backslash and by switching to typewriter font. We wrote `*2{...}` to define two columns of this style. Because the example text has been inserted according to our table definition with `<{...}`, we just had to put the declarations into the last column without the text.

Spanning entries over multiple rows

We already know how to span text over several columns. But what if text should cross over several rows? LaTeX doesn't define a command for it. However, the package **multirow** does.

Time for action – merging cells using the multirow package

Before we complement the font table, we would like to center the command type "Family" vertically, that is, span this cell over three columns. If we figured this out, we could use it later on:

1. In our previous example, additionally load `multirow`:

```
\usepackage{multirow}
```

2. Replace the word «Family»:

```
\multirow{3}{*}{Family} & textrm & rmfamily & \rmfamily & \\
```

3. Typeset to see the small change:

	Input		Output
	Command	Declaration	
	\textrm	\rmfamily	Example text
Family	\textsf	\sffamily	Example text
	\texttt	\ttfamily	Example text

What just happened?

We used the command `\multirow` to span three rows. Its definition is:

```
\multirow{number of rows}{width}{entry text}
```

The entry will span that number of rows from the row on which `\multirow` has been used. If the number is negative, it will span the rows above.

You can specify a width or just write * for the natural width. If a width has been specified, the text would be wrapped accordingly.

`multirow` understands further optional arguments for fine tuning. They are described in its documentation.

Adding captions to tables

Especially with longer text, we would like to add captions and numbers to our tables. Numbering the tables allows referring to them, whereas captions are informative, if the table is not exactly placed where we refer to it. LaTeX has built-in features to achieve that.

Time for action – adding a caption to our font table

Now it's time to complete our table. We shall list the remaining font commands. We'll use the first column to describe the category of the font commands: **Family**, **Weight**, **Shape**, and so on. Then we will add another column to show the effect of combining font commands.

To finish, we shall center the table and provide a number and a caption:

1. Put a **table** environment around our example table, use \centering inside, and insert a \caption command at the end of the table environment. Add more font commands and add another column at the right containing more examples:

```
\documentclass{article}
\usepackage{array}
\usepackage{booktabs}
\usepackage{multirow}
\newcommand{\head}[1]{\textnormal{\textbf{#1}}}
\newcommand{\normal}[1]{\multicolumn{1}{l}{#1}}
\pagestyle{empty}
\begin{document}
\begin{table}
\centering
\begin{tabular}{@{}l*2{>{\textbackslash\ttfamily}l}%
  l<{Example text}l@{}}
\toprule[1.5pt]
& \multicolumn{2}{c}{\head{Input}}
& \multicolumn{2}{c}{\head{Output}}\\
& \normal{\head{Command}} & \normal{\head{Declaration}}
& \normal{\head{Single use}} & \head{Combined}\\
  \cmidrule(lr){2-3}\cmidrule(l){4-5}
  \multirow{3}{*}{Family} & textrm & rmfamily & \rmfamily & \\
& textsf & sffamily & \sffamily& \\
& texttt & ttfamily & \ttfamily& \\
  \cmidrule(lr){2-3}\cmidrule(lr){4-4}
  \multirow{2}{1.1cm}{Weight} & textbf & bfseries & \bfseries
& \multirow{2}{1.8cm}{\sffamily\bfseries Bold and sans-serif} \\
& textmd & mdseries & \mdseries & \\
\cmidrule(lr){2-3}\cmidrule(lr){4-4}
\multirow{4}{*}{Shape} & textit & itshape & \itshape & \\
& textsl & slshape & \slshape &
  \multirow{2}{1.8cm}{\sffamily\slshape Slanted and sans-serif}\\
& textsc  & scshape & \scshape & \\
& textup & upshape & \upshape & \\
\cmidrule(lr){2-3}\cmidrule(lr){4-4}
Default & textnormal & normalfont & \normalfont & \\
\bottomrule[1.5pt]
\end{tabular}
\caption{\LaTeX\ font selection}
\end{table}
\end{document}
```

2. **Typeset** and our table is now ready:

	Input		Output	
	Command	Declaration	Single use	Combined
Family	\textrm	\rmfamily	Example text	
	\textsf	\sffamily	Example text	
	\texttt	\ttfamily	Example text	
Weight	\textbf	\bfseries	**Example text**	**Bold and**
	\textmd	\mdseries	Example text	**sans-serif**
Shape	\textit	\itshape	*Example text*	
	\textsl	\slshape	*Example text*	*Slanted and*
	\textsc	\scshape	EXAMPLE TEXT	*sans-serif*
	\textup	\upshape	Example text	
Default	\textnormal	\normalfont	Example text	

Table 1: LaTeX font selection

What just happened?

We put the `tabular` environment in a `table` environment. It's used in this way together with the `\caption` command:

```
\begin{table}[placement options]
table body
\caption{table title}
\end{table}
```

The `table` environment is a so-called **floating environment**. Unlike normal text, they might appear somewhere else other than what is defined by their position in the source code. The optional placement argument determines where the table might appear. However, LaTeX decides it. We shall discuss this at the end of this chapter together with the placement of graphics.

`\caption` understands an optional argument as well: if you write `\caption[short text]{long text}`, then `short text` will appear in a list of tables and `long text` in the document body. That's useful if you need very long descriptive captions.

Tables are automatically numbered.

Placing captions above

In typesetting, it's very common to place captions above the tables instead of below. This can be achieved by writing `\caption` before the table body. However, LaTeX expects caption to always be below, resulting in a cramped look to the table. There's too little space between the caption and the following table. You might wish to add some space, for instance, by entering `\vspace{10pt}` directly after a top caption.

Remember `booktabs`? If you begin tables with `\toprule`, just specify the length `\abovetopskip`, for example:

```
\setlength{\abovetopsep}{10pt}
```

By putting this line into your preamble, `10pt` space would be added below the caption and above the top line of the table.

Have a go hero – customizing captions

By default, the captions look like normal body text; there's no visual difference. Would you like to have a slight change in font size, a different formatting of the label, some margins or indentation, or any other customization? The **caption** package is the answer to most needs. By using a few options, you could enhance the visual appearance of all of your captions. Try:

```
\usepackage[font=small,labelfont=bf,margin=1cm]{caption}
```

This way, your captions will be smaller than normal text, the label with number will be bold, and it will not be as wide as normal text. The package offers a lot of features, both for document wide settings and fine-tuning. It's very well documented. So, have a look at its documentation.

Auto-fitting columns to the table width

`l`, `c`, and `r` columns have the width of their content. For `p` columns, you specify the width. This way, it's hard to find out the actual width of the table. Wouldn't it be a good idea to specify the table width and let LaTeX decide how wide the columns may be? The **tabularx** package allows that. Using it looks like:

```
\usepackage{tabularx}
...
\begin{tabularx}{width}{column specifiers}
...
\end{tabularx}
```

The new environment `tabularx` requires an additional argument: the width of the table. It introduces a new column type X. X columns behave like `p` columns, but they use all available space. One X column would take all of the available space. If you use several X columns, they would share the space equally. So you could write, for instance:

```
\begin{tabularx}{0.6\textwidth}{lcX}
```

This way you would get a table occupying 60 percent of the text width, a left aligned and a centered column as wide as their content, and a paragraph column as wide as possible until 60 percent is reached.

Though it's easy to use, the `tabularx` documentation gives further examples, informs about the derived types, and gives advice like this: don't let `\multicolumn` entries cross any X column.

There are two similar approaches:

◆ LaTeX provides a starred version of the `tabular` environment:

`\begin{tabular*}{width}[position]{column specifiers}`

The table is set to `width`, but by modifying the inter-column space. `tabularx` has been developed satisfying the need for a more useful way.

◆ The **tabulary** package provides another sophisticated `tabular` environment taking the total width. It's weighting each column width according to the natural width of the widest cell in the column.

Generating multi-page tables

All tabular environments we've got to know until now cannot cross page boundaries. The `tabbing` environment is an exception due to its different nature.

As tables might contain a lot of data, we need a solution. There are several packages:

◆ **longtable** provides an environment with the same name that's like a multi-page version of `tabular`. It provides commands to set table captions, continued captions, and special headers and footers when a page break occurs. It's probably the easiest way for multi-page tables and therefore the most popular. The package documentation describes all you need. In combination with the `booktabs` package, you will get very good results.

◆ **ltxtable** provides a combination of `longtable` and `tabularx`.

◆ **ltablex** is another approach to combine the features of `longtable` and `tabularx`.

◆ **supertabular** offers another multi-page extension of the internally used `tabular` environment, providing optional table tails and heads where page breaks occur.

◆ **xtab** extends `supertabular` and reduces some of its weaknesses.

◆ **stabular** implements a simple way to use page breaks in `tabular` without much ado.

Example tables and links to documentation can be found at `http://texblog.net/beginners-guide/tables/`.

Coloring tables

We didn't even color text yet, as this usually isn't what we do first with LaTeX. But of course, this can be done with text as well as with tables. For coloring text, use the **color** package or, better, the extension **xcolor**. For coloring tables, use the package **colortbl**. All can be combined by using:

```
\usepackage[table]{xcolor}
```

The package allows coloring columns, rows, single entries, and lines in many ways. The package documentation may tell you more.

Using landscape orientation

Very wide tables could be typeset in landscape orientation. The **rotating** package offers an environment called `sidewaystable` that you could use instead of the `table` environment. Both table and caption would be rotated +-90 degrees and placed on a separate page. The package provides further rotation-related environments and commands.

Aligning columns at the decimal point

Columns containing numbers are more readable when the entries are aligned at the decimal marker and perhaps at an exponent. Several packages support this:

- ◆ **siunitx** is primarily intended for typesetting values with units in a consistent way according to scientific conventions. However, it provides a tabular column type for such decimal alignment of numbers.

- ◆ **dcolumn** offers a column type for aligning at a comma, a period, or another single character.

- ◆ **rccol** defines a column type where numbers are "right-centered", that is, they are centered with respect to other entries but flushed right to each other. This way corresponding digits are aligned along the column.

In contrast to `dcolumn` and `rccol`, the `siunitx` package is very new and powerful.

Handling narrow columns

Text in very narrow columns might require special attention because justification is difficult if there's little space. Here's some advice:

- ◆ Have a look at the correct hyphenation. If necessary, improve it like we did in *Chapter 2*.

- TeX doesn't hyphenate the first word of a line, a box, or a table entry. So, a long word may cross the column boundary. To enable hyphenation, insert an empty word: write `\hspace{0pt}` directly at the beginning.

- Load `microtype` to improve justification, it shows the best effect in narrow columns.

- Full justification in `p` columns and the like may look bad because of big gaps. Consider using `>{\raggedright\arraybackslash}` for such columns.

- From the **ragged2e** package, using the command `\RaggedRight` can do even better and doesn't need `\arraybackslash`.

Pop quiz – tables

1. Which of these environments cannot cross page boundaries?

    a. `tabular`

    b. `longtable`

    c. `tabbing`

2. If you would like to format one entry different from the specification of its column, which command may be used?

    a. `>{...}`

    b. `@{...}`

    c. `\multirow`

    d. `\multicolumn`

Inserting pictures

Documents may not consist of just text and tables. You might wish to include pictures, diagrams, or drawings made with other programs. The **graphicx** package is dedicated to this.

Time for action – including a picture

We shall create a short document. Between two paragraphs, we would like to insert a picture. If there's no picture file available, we will use the **demo** mode of `graphicx`:

1. Begin a new document and load `babel` and `blindtext` to print some filler text:

    ```
    \documentclass[a5paper]{article}
    \usepackage[english]{babel}
    \usepackage{blindtext}
    \usepackage[demo]{graphicx}
    ```

```
\pagestyle{empty}
\begin{document}
\section{Including a picture}
\blindtext
```

2. Open a `figure` environment and declare `centering`:

```
\begin{figure}
\centering
```

3. Use the command `\includegraphics` with the filename as the argument:

`\includegraphics{test}`

4. Declare a caption, close the `figure` environment, and end the document with filler text:

```
\caption{Test figure}
\end{figure}
\blindtext
\end{document}
```

5. **Typeset** and have a look at the output:

Figure 1: Test figure

1   Including a picture

Hello, here is some text without a meaning. This text should show, how a printed text will look like at this place. If you read this text, you will get no information. Really? Is there no information? Is there a difference between this text and some nonsense like »Huardest gefburn«. Kjift – Never mind! A blind text like this gives you information about the selected font, how the letters are written and the impression of the look. This text should contain all letters of the alphabet and it should be written in of the original language. There is no need for a special contents, but the length of words should match to the language. Hello, here is some text without a meaning. This text should show, how a printed text will look like at this place. If you read this text, you will get no information. Really? Is there no information? Is there a difference between this text and some nonsense like »Huardest gefburn«. Kjift – Never mind! A blind

What just happened?

The most important command is \includegraphics. We specified a filename. This file would be loaded if it exists. Otherwise an error would occur. LaTeX supports the following file types:

- PNG, JPG, and PDF if you directly compile to PDF (**pdfLaTeX**)
- EPS if you compile to DVI and convert to PS and PDF (traditional LaTeX)

To clarify, PS means PostScript, EPS means Encapsulated PostScript, and DVI means Device Independent Format. The latter was the first output format to be supported by TeX. You definitely know the very popular picture formats PNG and JPG, often used for screenshots or photos.

You don't need to specify a filename extension, it will be automatically added. Put the file into the same directory as your document; otherwise specify a full or relative path name:

```
\includegraphics{appendix/figure1}
```

Don't use blanks in the filename or path! Blanks and special characters may cause problems with \includegraphics. If such symbols in filenames are required, load the package **grffile** to try to fix it. Also, in filenames, use slashes / instead of backslashes \, as the latter begin a LaTeX command.

Because we specified the demo option, graphicx doesn't require a file test.png or any other file; instead it's just printing a black filled rectangle. This is useful for testing or if you would like to discuss a LaTeX problem in an online forum, but don't wish to publish your pictures.

Go ahead; copy a picture of your choice into your document directory, give \includegraphics its filename, and compile. The picture will be embedded with its original size.

Scaling pictures

You may choose a different size. For this, let's look at the definition of includegraphics:

```
\includegraphics[key=value list]{file name}
```

The graphicx documentation lists all keys and possible values. Here are the most popular ones:

- width: The graphic would be resized to this width. Example: width= 0.9\textwidth.
- height: The graphic would be resized to this height. Example: height=3cm.
- scale: The graphic would be scaled by this factor. Example: scale=0.5.
- angle: The graphic would be turned by this angle. Example: angle=90.

There are options for clipping, but such post processing can be easily done with any graphics software.

Instead of turning a figure by 90 degrees, you could use the `sidewaysfigure` environment of the `rotating` package. It's analogous to `sidewaystable` that has been mentioned before.

Choosing the optimal file type

If you've got the final picture, well, just use this format and include it. However, if you are free to choose a file format, you could think about it for a moment.

`EPS` and `PDF` are both **vector graphics** format. They are scalable, also looking good at high resolution or if you zoom in. So, whenever possible, `PDF` (or `EPS`) should be preferred, for instance, when you export drawings or diagrams out of other office software. For such graphics, vector formats are common.

`PNG` and `JPG` are **bitmap** formats, also called **raster graphics**, commonly used for photos. If you zoom in, you would notice a loss of quality. `PNG` uses a lossless compression, whereas `JPG` pictures may lose quality when they are saved. So, if you make screenshots, use `PNG` or at least ensure that there's no loss compression if you choose `JPG`.

 Besides supporting vector graphics, both EPS and PDF may contain bitmap graphics. They are also called **container formats**.

There are a lot of tools to convert between graphic formats. These three are especially useful and included in both **TeX Live** and **MiKTeX**:

- **dvips** converts `DVI` files to the `PostScript` format
- **ps2pdf** converts `PostScript` files to `PDF`
- **epstopdf** converts `EPS` files to `PDF`, a package with the same name does it on-the-fly

These are command line tools. Some editors like **TeXnicCenter** use them to automate the way TEX => DVI => PS => PDF.

epstopdf is especially useful if you have to include Postscript pictures, but wish to benefit from **pdfLaTeX** features like font expansion and character protrusion accessible by `microtype`.

For further working with graphics, **ImageMagick** and **GIMP** are very capable open source programs.

Including whole pages

How can we include pictures wider or higher than the text area? `\includegraphics` could do it, but LaTeX would complain about width or size and might put it off to the next page. Oversized images and even whole pages can be included using the **pdfpages** package. It provides a command, `\includepdf`, which is able to include a complete page and even a multi-page PDF document at once. Despite its name and not even mentioned in its otherwise good documentation, it's capable of including PNG and JPG files, not just PDF.

`pdfpages` could also be used to resize several PDF pages and to arrange them on a single sheet.

Putting images behind the text

Do you need watermarks? Background images? Textboxes positioned at arbitrary positions on the page, preferably not interfering with the other text? The package **eso-pic** does it for you.

Another approach is offered by the **textpos** package, developed for placing boxes with text or graphics at absolute positions on a page.

Managing floating environments

When a page break occurs, normal text can be broken to continue on the next page. However, pictures cannot be divided. Simple tables cannot be split either. That's why LaTeX provides two **floating environments**, namely, `figure` and `table`. They are briefly called **floats**. Their content may float to a place where it's the optimum for the page layout. Let's figure out how to deal with it.

Time for action – letting a figure float

Both the `figure` and the `table` environment take an optional argument affecting the final placement of the figure or the table. We shall test the effect in our graphics example:

1. Go back to the previous example. This time, add the options `h` and `t`:

```
\begin{figure}[ht]
\centering
\includegraphics{test}
\caption{Test figure}
\end{figure}
```

2. **Typeset**, notice the change in the output.

3. Change the options into `!b`:

`\begin{figure}[!b]`

4. **Typeset**, the figure is now forced to float to the bottom. Compare both results:

1 Including a picture

Hello, here is some text without a meaning. This text should show, how a printed text will look like at this place. If you read this text, you will get no information. Really? Is there no information? Is there a difference between this text and some nonsense like »Huardest gefburn«. Kjift – Never mind! A blind text like this gives you information about the selected font, how the letters are written and the impression of the look. This text should contain all letters of the alphabet and it should be written in of the original language. There is no need for a special contents, but the length of words should match to the language. Hello, here is some text without a meaning. This text should

Figure 1: Test figure

show, how a printed text will look like at this place. If you read this text, you will get no information. Really? Is there no information? Is there a difference between this text and some nonsense like »Huardest gefburn«. Kjift – Never mind! A blind

1 Including a picture

Hello, here is some text without a meaning. This text should show, how a printed text will look like at this place. If you read this text, you will get no information. Really? Is there no information? Is there a difference between this text and some nonsense like »Huardest gefburn«. Kjift – Never mind! A blind text like this gives you information about the selected font, how the letters are written and the impression of the look. This text should contain all letters of the alphabet and it should be written in of the original language. There is no need for a special contents, but the length of words should match to the language. Hello, here is some text without a meaning. This text should show, how a printed text will look like at this place. If you read this text, you will get no information. Really? Is there no information? Is there a difference between this text and some nonsense like »Huardest gefburn«. Kjift – Never mind! A blind

Figure 1: Test figure

What just happened?

Just by adding some characters standing for placement options, we could force the figure to appear where we wanted it to.

Understanding float placement options

The optional argument of the `figure` and `table` environment tells LaTeX where it's allowed to place the figure or the table. Four letters stand for four possible places:

- ◆ `h` stands for **here**. The float may appear where it's been written in the source code.
- ◆ `t` stands for **top**. Placing at the top of a page is permitted.
- ◆ `b` stands for **bottom**. The float may appear at the bottom of a page.
- ◆ `p` stands for **page**. The float is allowed to appear on a separate page, where only floats may reside but no normal text.

A fifth option might come in handy:

♦   `!` tells LaTeX to try harder! Some constraints may be ignored, easing the placement.

If you don't specify any option, the float could be placed far away. New LaTeX users might be surprised. Specifying more options would help to place it as near as possible. The most flexible is using the placement `[!htbp]`, allowing a float everywhere. You still could consider removing a placement specifier if you don't like it.

Forcing the output of floats

If you would like to stop LaTeX from putting the floats, there's a way; the `\clearpage` command ends the current page and causes all already defined figures and tables to be printed out. You can use `\cleardoublepage` that does the same but in a two-sided layout it ensures that the next non-float page is a right-hand page. . If necessary, a blank page would be inserted.

Immediately ending the page might not be the best thing to do. It could leave a lot of empty space on the current page. The **afterpage** package offers a clever possibility; this package allows deferring the execution of `\clearpage` until the current page has ended:

```
\usepackage{afterpage}
. . .
body text
\afterpage{\clearpage}
```

Limiting floating

It may happen that tables and figures float far away, perhaps even into another section. The **placeins** package provides a useful command to restrict the floating. If you load `placeins` with `\usepackage{placeins}` and write `\FloatBarrier` somewhere in your document, no table or figure could float past it. This macro keeps floats in their place.

A very convenient way to prevent floats from crossing section boundaries is stating the section option:

```
\usepackage[section]{placeins}
```

This option causes an implicit `\FloatBarrier` to be used at the beginning of each section.

Two further options, namely, `above` and `below`, allow you to lower the restrictions, preventing floats from appearing above the start of the current section or below the start of the next section.

Figures don't float into the next chapter because `\chapter` implicitly uses `\clearpage`.

Avoiding floating at all

Would you like to place a float exactly where you want it? The obvious answer is: don't use a floating environment! Even a caption doesn't have the same importance if the table or figure is placed at the current point. However, if you really need a caption, you may use the \captionof command without a float. Both the **caption** package , KOMA-Script classes, and the tiny **capt-of** package provide that command:

```
\usepackage{capt-of}% or caption
...
\begin{center}
\begin{minipage}{\linewidth}%
\centering%
\includegraphics{test}%
\captionof{figure}{Test figure}%
\end{minipage}
\end{center}
```

The minipage keeps a picture and caption together. Furthermore, it's centered. Use \captionof within a group or environment like minipage or center. The definition is the same as \caption, except there is the additional argument specifying the float type:

```
\captionof{figure}[short text]{long text}
\captionof{table}[short text]{long text}
```

Be aware that the numbering could get wrong if you mix real floats and fixed figures or tables. As you don't benefit from LaTeX's positioning capabilities, you have to take care that pages are still properly filled.

The **float** package provides a convenient and consistent looking approach. It introduces the placement option H causing the float to appear right there:

```
\usepackage{float}
...
\begin{figure}[H]
\centering
\includegraphics{test}
\caption{Test figure}
\end{figure}
```

You may choose between these two options. If you wish to exploit further features of the float package, load it. Otherwise, consider using the one-liner capt-of. Perhaps not even that is necessary, assuming that you're already using the caption package or a KOMA-Script class.

Spanning figures and tables over text columns

There are starred forms of floats, namely, `figure*` and `table*`. In a two-column layout, they put the float into a single column. In one-column mode, there's no difference to the non-starred form.

Letting text flow around figures

Though it's a bit playful, you might wish to let text flow around a table or a figure. This can be achieved using the **wrapfig** package and its environments `wrapfigure` and `wraptable`.

Time for action – embedding a picture within text

We shall modify our picture embedding an example. We would like the picture to appear on the left side, accompanied by the body text on the right side:

1. In our example, additionally load the `wrapfig` package:

   ```
   \documentclass[a5paper]{article}
   \usepackage[english]{babel}
   \usepackage{blindtext}
   \usepackage[demo]{graphicx}
   \usepackage{wrapfig}
   \pagestyle{empty}
   \begin{document}
   ```

2. Begin an unnumbered section, place a `wrapfig` environment within some filler text:

   ```
   \section*{Text flowing around a picture}
   \blindtext
   \begin{wrapfigure}{l}{4.4cm}
   \includegraphics[width=4.4cm]{test}
   \caption{Test figure}
   \end{wrapfigure}
   \blindtext
   \end{document}
   ```

3. **Typeset** and look:

Text flowing around a picture

Hello, here is some text without a meaning. This text should show, how a printed text will look like at this place. If you read this text, you will get no information. Really? Is there no information? Is there a difference between this text and some nonsense like »Huardest gefburn«. Kjift – Never mind! A blind text like this gives you information about the selected font, how the letters are written and the impression of the look. This text should contain all letters of the alphabet and it should be written in of the original language. There is no need for a special contents, but the length of words should match to the language.

Hello, here is some text without a meaning. This text should show, how a printed text will look like at this place. If you read this text, you will get no information. Really? Is there no information? Is there a difference between this text and some nonsense like »Huardest gefburn«. Kjift – Never mind! A blind text like this gives you information about the selected font, how the letters are written

Figure 1: Test figure

and the impression of the look. This text should contain all letters of the alphabet and it should be written in of the original language. There is no need for a special contents, but the length of words should match to the language.

What just happened?

The `wrapfigure` environment understands parameters other than the `figure` environment. We used just two of them. If you need more, here's the complete definition:

```
\begin{wrapfigure}[number of lines]{placement}[overhang] {width}
```

The first optional argument states the number of wrapped text lines. If omitted, it would be automatically calculated from the height. `placement` can be one of the characters `r, l, i, o` for right, left, inner, or outer side or the corresponding uppercase letters `R, L, I, O` with the same meaning, but allowing the figure to float. Only one character for specifying the option is allowed. The other optional argument, `overhang`, may specify a width that the figure might stick into the margin. The final and mandatory argument gives the width of the figure.

The `wraptable` environment works analogous.

Breaking figures and tables into pieces

For grouping several sub figures or sub tables with captions within a single figure or table, there are several supporting packages you can choose from:

♦ **subfig** is a sophisticated package supporting inclusion of small figures and tables. It takes care of positioning, labeling, and captioning within single floats.

♦ **subcaption** is another package for this purpose and belongs to the `caption` package.

♦ **subfigure** is still available, but considered as obsolete since `subfig` has appeared.

Pop quiz – pictures and floats

1. This chapter listed all graphic formats supported by LaTeX. Now, identify from the following file types which is not directly supported by LaTeX!

   a. `jpg`

   b. `gif`

   c. `png`

   d. `eps`

   e. `pdf`

2. If you would like a figure or a table to float but to appear as near as possible to its source, which of the following float placement options would be appropriate?

   a. `h`

   b. `H`

   c. `htbp`

   d. `!htbp`

Summary

In this chapter, we have learned to create tables and figures, and how to place them within our document. Specifically, we dealt with:

♦ Putting text into columns

♦ Typesetting tables with captions

♦ Spanning columns and rows in tables

♦ Using packages to auto-fit columns and to create colored, landscape, and even multi-page tables

- Including pictures with captions
- Controlling and tuning placement of figures and tables

LaTeX is able to generate lists of tables and figures like a table of contents. We shall deal with such lists in *Chapter 7, Listing Contents and References*.

As our figures and tables are numbered, we can use these numbers to refer to them within the text. In the next chapter, we shall figure out how to do this, benefitting from LaTeX's cross-referencing capabilities.

6
Cross-Referencing

Our documents contain a lot of numbered things such as pages, sections, list items, figures, and tables. There's even more we have not covered yet. For instance, if you would like to write a mathematical text, you may number equations, theorems, definitions, and many more.

We number things not just to count them, but to refer to them in other places of our document. If you want to point the reader to the ninth figure in the third chapter, you might write "See figure 3.9". LaTeX automatically enumerates the figures for you. If you insert another figure, LaTeX will automatically adjust the numbering of all figures after it. But what's with the references?

LaTeX is able to take care of all of our cross-references. This is the subject of this chapter. We shall learn how to:

- ◆ Set labels that we shall use to refer to
- ◆ Refer to sections, footnotes, list items, tables, and more
- ◆ Refer to page numbers and ranges
- ◆ Make LaTeX refer verbosely to adjacent pages
- ◆ Automate naming of references
- ◆ Create references to external documents

Let's figure out how to do all this.

Setting labels and referencing

To be able to refer to a certain point, we have to mark it by a label. The name of that label will serve us afterwards.

Time for action – referencing items of a top list

We shall typeset a list of the most used packages for papers on the e-print archive site http://arXiv.org. Through the command \label, we will mark items that we can later refer to with the command \ref.

1. Create a new document with this code:

```
\documentclass{book}
\begin{document}
\chapter{Statistics}
\section{Most used packages on arXiv.org}\label{sec:packages}
The Top Five packages, used on arXiv.org\footnote{according
to the arXMLiv project\label{fn:project}}:
\begin{enumerate}
  \item graphicx
  \item amssymb \label{item:amssymb}
  \item amsmath \label{item:amsmath}
  \item epsfig
  \item amsfonts
\end{enumerate}
\chapter{Mathematics}
\emph{amsmath}, on position \ref{item:amsmath} of the top list
in section~\ref{sec:packages} on page~\pageref{sec:packages},
is indispensable to high-quality mathematical typesetting in
\LaTeX.\emph{amssymb}, on position \ref{item:amssymb},
provides a huge amount of math symbols.
See also the footnote on page~\pageref{fn:project}.
\end{document}
```

2. **Typeset** and have a look at the text on page 3:

> *amsmath*, on position ?? of the top list in section ?? on page ??, is indispensable to high-quality mathematical typesetting in LaTeX. *amssymb*, on position ??, provides a huge amount of math symbols. See also the footnote on page ??.

3. Do you see the question marks? The references are still missing! **Typeset** again and compare:

> *amsmath*, on position 3 of the top list in section 1.1 on page 1, is indispensable to high-quality mathematical typesetting in LaTeX. *amssymb*, on position 2, provides a huge amount of math symbols. See also the footnote on page 1.

What just happened?

We created cross-references with just three commands: `\label` marks the position, `\ref` prints the number of the element we refer to, and `\pageref` prints the page number of that element. Each command takes the name of the element as argument. Any name may be chosen by us.

We had to **Typeset** twice because LaTeX needs one run to produce the references that can be read in during the next compiler run. If LaTeX cannot resolve a reference, it prints two question marks instead.

Let's have a closer look.

Assigning a key

The command `\label{name}` assigns the current position to the key `name`. Specifically:

- If the `\label` command appeared in ordinary text, then the current sectional unit, like the chapter or the section, would be assigned.
- If the `\label` would be placed within a numbered environment, that environment would be assigned to the key.

So, we cannot mark a section within a table environment. To avoid any problem because of a possible unsuitable positioning, a good rule of thumb is to place the `\label` command right after the position we would like to mark. For instance, place it directly after the corresponding `\chapter` or after `\section`—not before, of course.

In the figure or table environments, `\caption` is responsible for the numbering. That's why `\label` has to be placed after `\caption`, not before. Therefore, typical floating environments look like the following:

```
\begin{figure}[htp]
\centering
\includegraphics{filename}
\caption{Test figure}\label{fig:name}
\end{figure}
```

Or as follows:

```
\begin{table}[hbp]
\centering
\caption{table descripion}\label{tab:name}
\begin{tabular}{cc}
...
\end{tabular}
\end{table}
```

A key may consist of letters, digits, or punctuation characters. Keys are case-sensitive.

If you write larger documents, the number of keys could become very high. Imagine, you have a section dealing with fonts and a font table—how to distinguish their keys? We could prefix them with the type of environment. It has become common practice to label figures with `fig:name`, tables with `tab:name`, sections with `sec:name`, and similar in other cases.

Referring to a key

Once a label has been set and given a name, we may refer to that name. For this, we use `\ref{name}`: this command prints the number that belongs to `name`. It could already be used before the corresponding `\label` command appears in your code.

Even though it's that simple, it's powerful. Each time we **Typeset** a document, LaTeX checks the keys and reassigns the numbers, responding to all changes. If LaTeX noticed that labels have been changed, it would inform you that a second **Typeset** run would be required to update the corresponding labels. If in doubt **Typeset** twice.

Referring to a page

The command `\pageref{name}` works analogous to `\ref`, except that it prints the corresponding page number.

Would all the references stay correct if we changed the section and page numbers? Let's put it to the test! Insert a section and a page break at the beginning:

```
\chapter{Statistics}
\section{Introduction}
\newpage
\section{Most used packages on arXiv.org}\label{sec:packages}
```

Typeset once. LaTeX will compile it, but it will show a message: *LaTeX Warning: Label(s) may have changed. Rerun to get cross-references right*. That's what we shall do! **Typeset** a second time, now all the numbers have been correctly adjusted:

> *amsmath*, on position 3 of the top list in section 1.2 on page 2, is indispensable to high-quality mathematical typesetting in LaTeX. *amssymb*, on position 2, provides a huge amount of math symbols. See also the footnote on page 2.

Using a reference together with the page number reference, you may write:

```
See figure~\ref{fig:name} on page~\pageref{fig:name}.
```

As you know how to define a command, you could make such referencing easier:

```
\newcommand{\fullref}[1]{\ref{#1} on page~\pageref{#1}}
...
See figure~\fullref{fig:name}.
```

This way, you would get a full reference like "See figure 4.2 on page 32". However, if the reference appears on the same page, like the figure, writing out the page number looks a bit odd. How can we avoid that? The **varioref** package provides a way.

Producing intelligent page references

The `varioref` package offers a command being able to add "on the preceding page", "on the following page", or on the page number to a reference, depending on the context.

Time for action – introducing variable references

We will use the `varioref` commands, `\vref` and `\vpageref`, to achieve enhanced reference texts:

1. Open our current example. Add the package `varioref` to your preamble:

```
\usepackage{varioref}
```

2. Edit the content of the second chapter:

```
\emph{amsmath}, on position \ref{item:amsmath} of the top list
in section~\vref{sec:packages}, is indispensable to high-quality
mathematical typesetting in \LaTeX. \emph{amssymb}, on position
\ref{item:amssymb}, provides a huge amount of math symbols.
See also the footnote \vpageref{fn:project}.
```

3. **Typeset** twice and look at the result:

> *amsmath*, on position 3 of the top list in section 1.2 on the facing page, is indispensable to high-quality mathematical typesetting in LaTeX. *amssymb*, on position 2, provides a huge amount of math symbols. See also the footnote on the preceding page.

What just happened?

The command \vref checked the distance to the referenced section. As it's on the facing page, that is, on the preceding page in a two-sided layout, it wrote "1.2 on the facing page". Similar for \vpageref, it refers to "the preceding page".

\vref{name} acts in the following way:

- If the reference and \label{name} are on the same page, it behaves exactly like \ref. The page number will not be printed.

- If the reference and the corresponding \label are on two successive pages, \vref prints the referred number and additionally "on the preceding page" or "on the following page", or "on the facing page". The latter will be chosen if the document is two-sided, that is, if \label and the reference fall onto a double-page spread.

- Otherwise it will print both \ref and \pageref.

\vpageref is equivalent to \pageref, but behaves like \vref concerning the page reference.

Even though varioref defines new commands, you may still use the common \ref and \pageref.

Fine-tuning page references

If label and reference are very close to each other, they would probably fall on the same page, but not necessarily. In such cases, we usually know if the label comes before or after the reference. It allows specifying an optional argument to \vpageref:

```
see the figure \vpageref[above]{fig:name}
```

This will print:

- "see the figure above" if the figure is on the same page
- "see the figure on the page before" if the figure is on the preceding page

Whereas, with the following:

```
see the footnote \vpageref[below]{fn:name}
```

This will print:

- ◆ "see the footnote below" if the footnote is on the same page
- ◆ "see the footnote on the following page" if the footnote is on the next page

In fact, \vpageref understands two optional arguments. The second optional argument would be used if the label and reference would fall on different pages. So, we could even write:

```
see the figure \vpageref[above figure][figure]{fig:name}
```

This would print:

- ◆ "see the above figure" if the figure is on the same page
- ◆ "see the figure on the page before" if the figure is on the preceding page

Actually, reversing the word order to "above figure" if necessary.

Sounds complicated? Well, your demands might increase over time, requiring more sophisticated features, so these features might come in handy some day.

Referring to page ranges

varioref offers two more commands:

- ◆ \vpagerefrange[opt]{key1}{key2}, where key1 and key2 denote a range (like a sequence of figures from fig:a to fig:c). If both labels fall onto the same page, the result is the same as with \vpageref. Otherwise, the output will be a range like "on pages 32-36". opt would be used if both labels fall onto the current page.
- ◆ \vpageref [opt]{key1}{key2}is analogous, but similar to \vref: see figures \vpageref{fig:a}{fig:c} may result in "see figures 4.2 to 4.4 on pages 36-37".

\vref, \vpageref, and \vpagerefrange have been implemented to remove any space to their left before they insert space of their own. For example, \vref inserts a nonbreakable space like we did before with ~. If this is not desired, use starred forms \vref*, \ vpageref*, or \vpagerefrange*.

More information regarding customization may be found in the package manual.

Using automatic reference names

Tired of writing `figure~\ref{fig:name}` and `table~\ref{fig:name}` again and again? Wouldn't it be great if LaTeX knew what type is meant by `\ref{name}` writing type and number? What if we desire to abbreviate, say, `fig.~\ref{fig:name}` in the whole document? The **cleverev** package eases the work: it automatically determines the type of cross-reference and the context in which it's used.

Basically, you could just use `\cref` instead of `\ref` or `\Cref` if you wish to capitalize. The corresponding range commands are `\crefrange` and `\Crefrange`.

Time for action – referring cleverly

We shall rewrite our first example using `cleveref`. To verify that the package acts cleverly, we consciously omit prefixes in key names to `\label` and `\cref`.

1. Modify our first example in this way:

```
\documentclass{book}
\usepackage{cleveref}
\crefname{enumi}{position}{positions}
\begin{document}
\chapter{Statistics}\label{stats}
\section{Most used packages on arXiv.org}\label{packages}
The Top Five packages, used on arXiv.org\footnote{according
to the arXMLiv project\label{project}}:
\begin{enumerate}
  \item graphicx
  \item amssymb \label{amssymb}
  \item amsmath \label{amsmath}
  \item epsfig
  \item amsfonts
\end{enumerate}
\begin{table}[tp]
  \centering
  (Identify obsolete packages on CTAN)
  \caption{Obsolete packages}\label{obsolete}
\end{table}
\chapter{Mathematics}
\emph{amsmath}, on \cref{amsmath} of the top list in
\cref{packages} of \cref{stats}, is indispensable to high-quality
Mathematical typesetting in \LaTeX. \emph{amssymb}, on
\cref{amssymb}, provides a huge amount of math symbols.
```

```
\Cref{obsolete} shows obsolete and outdated packages that
should be avoided. See also the \cref{project}.
\end{document}
```

2. **Typeset** twice and check the references for having the correct names:

> *amsmath*, on position 3 of the top list in section 1.1 of chapter 1, is indispensable to high-quality mathematical typesetting in LaTeX. *amssymb*, on position 2, provides a huge amount of math symbols. Table 1.1 shows obsolete and outdated packages that should be avoided. See also the footnote 1.

What just happened?

As we can see, we never needed to specify which object we refer to. \cref always chooses the right name and the correct number for us. That's really comfortable!

We used the command \crefname to tell cleveref which name it should use for enumerated items. The definition of \crefname is:

```
\crefname{type}{singular}{plural}
```

type may be one of chapter, section, figure, table, enumi, equation, theorem, or many other types we did not encounter yet. The singular version will be used for single references and the plural version for multiple. If you need capitalized versions, use \Crefname. So, a typical use may be:

```
\crefname{figure}{fig.}{figs.}
\Crefname{figure}{Fig.}{Figs.}
```

To sum up your benefits:

- ◆ You save much typing.
- ◆ You could use arbitrary labels. The package fancyref does a similar job but relies on prefixes like chap, fig, tab, and so on.
- ◆ If you decide to change wordings, it could be done easily by doing this once in the preamble, having the desired effect in the whole document.

However, it's recommended to use a prefix like fig: or sec: to distinguish the kind of referenced object; your code would become more understandable—it's common.

Combing cleveref and varioref

As `cleveref` fully supports `varioref`, you may use both to get the most out of them. `cleveref` redefines the commands of `varioref` to use `\cref` internally. So, you could use the good page referencing features of `varioref` together with the clever naming automatism!

Just load `varioref` before `cleveref`:

```
\usepackage{varioref}
\usepackage{cleveref}
```

Now, you may use `\vref`, `\cref`, `\ref`, or the other commands—whichever seems appropriate.

Referring to labels in other documents

If you write several related documents that refer to each other, you might want to use references to labels of another document. The package with the short name `xr` (standing for eXternal References) implements it. First load the package:

```
\usepackage{xr}
```

If you need to refer to sections or environments in an external document called, say, `doc.tex`, insert this command into your preamble:

```
\externaldocument{doc}
```

This enables you to additionally refer to anything that has been given a label in `doc.tex`. You may do this for several documents. If you need to avoid conflicts when an external document uses the same `\label` like the main document, declare a prefix using the optional argument of `\externaldocument`:

```
\externaldocument[D-]{doc}
```

This way, all references from `doc.tex` would be prefixed by `D-` and you could write `\ref{D-name}` to refer to `name` in `doc.tex`. Instead of `D-` you may choose any prefix that transforms your labels such that they become unique.

Have a go hero – turning references into hyperlinks

PDF documents offer bookmarks and hyperlink capabilities. How about exploiting that ourselves? There's an outstanding package offering hyperlink support; it's called **hyperref**. Try it: load `hyperref` right before `cleveref`. This order is important for the references to work. Even without any options or commands, your document will be hyperlinked as much as possible:

- All references become hyperlinks. Click any of those numbers to jump to the referred table, list item, section, or page.

- Each footnote marker is a hyperlink to the footnote text. Click it to jump down.

- If you insert `\tableofcontents`, you will get a bookmark list for the document, chapters, and sections listed in a navigation bar of you PDF reader.

`hyperref` can do even more for you: linking index entries to text passages, back-referencing of bibliography entries, and more. You can finely customize the behavior using options, for instance, choosing color or frames for hyperlinks. So, you could keep that valuable package in mind. In *Chapter 11, Enhancing Your Documents Further*, we shall return to this topic.

Pop quiz

1. For a reference to a table, at which position should the `\label` be placed?

    a. Before `\caption`

    b. After `\caption`

    c. After `\end{table}`

2. What should we do if we see two unexpected consecutive question marks in the output?

    a. Load the `hyperref` package.

    b. Look out for an undefined command. Check the syntax at that point.

    c. **Typeset** again. If the question marks stay, check the key to the reference at that point.

Summary

In this chapter, we learned how to reference chapters, sections, footnotes, and environments by their number or by the number of the corresponding page.

We even got to know some ways of clever and context dependent referencing.

In the next chapter, we shall deal with lists, which consist mainly of references: table of contents, lists of figures and tables, and bibliographies.

7

Listing Content and References

LaTeX makes it very easy to create lists for many purposes. For example, we've seen that just the simple command `\tableofcontents` *creates a nice looking table of contents. Let's just call it the TOC from now on. It simply takes the entries from the headings and from the numbers of the pages they fall on.*

In this chapter, we will perform the following:

◆ Decide which headings at which numbering level go to the TOC

◆ Create and customize a list of figures (LOF) and a list of tables (LOT)

◆ Insert arbitrary text and commands into the TOC and into other lists

◆ Cite books and create a bibliography

◆ Create an index

◆ Modify the headings for all those lists

We shall start with the content.

Customizing the table of contents

Besides just calling `\tableofcontents` to get a pre-designed list of content, LaTeX provides basic ways to modify it. Let's use some.

Time for action – refining an extensive table of contents

We shall build the frame of a document containing some headings. We will modify the automatically created table of contents to be finer and to contain additional entries.

In *Chapter 3, Designing Pages*, we saw the effect of \tableofcontents. The entries have been collected from the headings. We shall use this down to the subsubsection level.

Then we shall extend the TOC further. We will manually add entries for some headings:

1. Create a new document with the following code:

```
\documentclass{book}
\setcounter{tocdepth}{3}
\begin{document}
\tableofcontents
\part{First Part}
\chapter*{Preface}
\addcontentsline{toc}{chapter}{Preface}
\chapter{First main chapter}
\section{A section}
\section{Another section}
\subsection{A smaller section}
\subsubsection[Deeper level]{This section has an even deeper
level}
\chapter{Second main chapter}
\part{Second part}
\chapter{Third main chapter}
\appendix
\cleardoublepage
\addtocontents{toc}{\bigskip}
\addcontentsline{toc}{part}{Appendix}
\chapter{Glossary}
\chapter{Symbols}
\end{document}
```

2. **Typeset**. The first page will just show **Contents** but no entries.

3. **Typeset** a second time. Now the table of contents will be displayed:

Contents

What just happened?

We structured a document using several sectioning commands. In the first run, LaTeX read all of our sectioning commands and created a file with the extension `.toc`. This file contains the commands and the titles for all entries in the table of contents. During the first run, that file didn't exist yet, thus the TOC remained empty.

During the second run, the command `\tableofcontents` read the `.toc` file and printed the TOC.

In this example, we raised the depth of the TOC by one level. We added a chapter-like entry for the preface and inserted a part-like heading showing the beginning of the appendix, using `\addcontentsline`. Through `\addtocontents`, we inserted some space before the latter heading. Let's look at these commands in detail.

Adjusting the depth of the TOC

These are the standard sectioning commands and their so called TOC level:

Command	Level
\part	-1 (book and report class)
\chapter	0 (not available in article class)
\section	1
\subsection	2
\subsubsection	3
\paragraph	4
\subparagraph	5

In the book and in the report class, LaTeX creates TOC entries until level 2, in the article class until level 3. In a book, this means, for example, \subsubsection doesn't generate a TOC entry. There's a variable representing the level, namely, \tocdepth. It's an integer variable which we call a **counter**. To tell LaTeX to include subsubsections in the TOC, we would have to raise this counter. There are two basic ways to adjust a counter value:

- \setcounter{name}{n} specifies an integer value of n for the counter name
- \addtocounter{name}{n} adds the integer value of n to value of the counter name. n may be negative

Thus, the following command would ensure that even \subparagraph gives a TOC entry:

    \setcounter{tocdepth}{5}

Using \addcounter instead you may raise or lower the level without knowing its number.

 In contrast to commands, counter names don't begin with a backslash.

Shortening entries

As you have already learned in *Chapter 3*, you may choose a text for the TOC that's different to the heading in the body text. Each sectioning command understands an optional argument for the TOC entry, which is especially useful if you wish to use very long headings, but a shorter TOC entry would be sufficient. In our example, we did this by:

    \subsubsection[Deeper level]{This section has an even deeper level}

The body text shows the long heading while the TOC shows the short one. Running titles in the headings would use the short entry as well, as the space in headings is very limited.

Adding entries manually

Starred commands like `\chapter*` and `\section*` don't produce a TOC entry. In our example, we did that manually using this command:

```
\addcontentsline{file extension}{sectional unit}{text}
```

This command can be used in several contexts: the `file extension` may be:

- `toc` for the table of contents file
- `lof` for the list of figures file
- `lot` for the list of tables file

Or, any another extension of such a file type known to LaTeX.

The `sectional unit` determines the formatting of the entry. Specify `chapter` to create an entry that's formatted like normal chapter entries and similar for other sectional units like part, section, or subsection.

The third argument contains the `text` for the entry. This text may contain commands. Do you remember the `\protect` command? For a macro inside the entries, it's usually a good idea to write `\protect` right before it.

You may insert text or commands more directly with:

```
\addtocontents{file extension}{entry}
```

In contrary to `\addcontentsline`, the argument `entry` is written directly to the file without any additional formatting. You may choose any formatting you like.

This command may even be used for some customization, for example:

- `\addtocontents{toc}{\protect\enlargethispage{\baselineskip}}` extends the text height such that one additional line fits to the contents page.
- `\addtocontents{toc}{\protect\newpage}` causes a page break in the TOC. For instance, if the automatic page break happens after a chapter entry and before the following section entries, you might wish to force a page break already before the chapter entry.
- `\addtocontents{toc}{\protect\thispagestyle{fancy}}` changes the page style of the current TOC page to fancy. As the first page of a chapter is of plain style by default, the first page of the TOC would be plain as well, even if you specified `\pagestyle{fancy}`. This command overrides it.

Place such commands where they should be effective. To affect the first TOC page, place it at the beginning of your document. To cause a page break before a certain chapter, place it right before the corresponding `\chapter` call.

Creating and customizing lists of figures

As briefly mentioned in the previous chapter, the two commands for creating lists of figures and tables are `\listoffigures` and `\listoftables`. Depending on the class, they produce a fine list of all captions together with the figure respectively the table number and the corresponding page numbers. As with the TOC, all can be done automatically. However, we may use the same techniques, like with the TOC, to customize the other lists. Let's try that.

Time for action – creating a list of diagrams

Suppose all of our figures are diagrams. We shall avoid the term figure and we will typeset a list of diagrams:

1. Open our current example. Add these lines to your preamble:

   ```
   \renewcommand{\figurename}{Diagram}
   \renewcommand{\listfigurename}{List of Diagrams}
   ```

2. Right after `\tableofcontents`, add:

   ```
   \listoffigures
   ```

3. Add a diagram somewhere in Chapter 1:

   ```
   \begin{figure}
   \centering
   \fbox{Diagram placeholder}
   \caption{Enterprize Organizational Chart}
   \end{figure}
   ```

4. In the second part, in the third chapter, we'd like to add network design diagrams. Let's mark that in the LOF and let the diagrams follow:

   ```
   \addtocontents{lof}{Network Diagrams:}
   \begin{figure}
   \centering
   \fbox{Diagram placeholder}
   \caption{Network overview}
   \end{figure}
   \begin{figure}
   \centering
   ```

```
\fbox{Diagram placeholder}
\caption{WLAN Design}
\end{figure}
```

5. **Typeset** twice to get the document and the list:

List of Diagrams

What just happened?

We renamed the figures and the list heading by redefining LaTeX macros. At the end of the chapter, you will get a list of names used by LaTeX classes that you may redefine.

Like with the TOC, we used the command \addtocontents; this time to insert a bold heading into the .lof file where LaTeX collects the captions. It works similar to the TOC.

Creating a list of tables

You already know all you need to create and customize a list of tables! The file, where LaTeX collects the captions of the tables, has the extension .lot, and that's why the first argument of \addtocontents would be lot. Everything works analogous, like \listoftables, \tablename, and \listtablename.

Using packages for customization

Besides the described simple methods, there are packages providing sophisticated features for customizing the table of contents and the lists of figures and tables:

◆   **tocloft** gives extensive control over the typography of TOC, LOF, and LOT. You may even define new kinds of such lists.

◆   **titletoc** offers convenient handling of entries and is the companion to **titlesec**, a very good package for customizing sectioning headings.

- ◆ **multitoc** offers a layout in two or more columns using the **multicol** package.

- ◆ **minitoc** can create small TOCs for each part, chapter, or section.

- ◆ **tocbibind** can automatically add bibliography, index, TOC, LOF, and LOT to the table of contents. It's even capable of using numbered headings instead of the default unnumbered ones.

Let's continue with the announced index and the bibliography.

Generating an index

Extensive documents often contain an index. It is a list of words or phrases and page numbers pointing to where related material can be found in the document. In contrary to a full-text search feature, the index provides selective pointers to relevant information.

While it's our turn to identify and to mark the words for the index, LaTeX will collect this information and is able to typeset the index for us.

Time for action – marking words and building the index

Suppose our example would contain information about an enterprise and its structure and further about its network structure and design. We shall mark places in the text where these concepts occur. Finally, we will order LaTeX to typeset the index:

1. Go back to our example. In the preamble, load the **index** package and add the command to create the index:

   ```
   \usepackage{index}
   \makeindex
   ```

2. In the caption of our enterprise diagram, index this point with the keyword `enterprise`:

   ```
   \caption{\index{enterprise}Enterprise Organizational Chart}
   ```

3. In the third chapter, which contains our diagrams, index by the keyword `network`:

   ```
   \index{network}
   ```

4. Directly before `\end{document}`, create an entry for the index for the table of contents. To ensure that it shows the correct page number, end the page before:

   ```
   \clearpage
   \addcontentsline{toc}{chapter}{Index}
   ```

5. In the next line, order LaTeX to typeset the index:

```
\printindex
```

6. If you're using TeXworks, choose **MakeIndex** instead of **pdfLaTeX** in the drop-down box next to the typeset button. Then click typeset. If you use another editor, use its **MakeIndex** feature or type the following at the command prompt in the document directory:

```
makeindex documentname
```

7. Switch back to **pdfLaTeX**, **Typeset**, and look at the last page:

What just happened?

We loaded the `index` package, which improves LaTeX's built-in indexing capabilities. Alternatively, you could use the **makeidx** package which is part of standard LaTeX. The command \makeindex prepared the index. Both commands must be put into the preamble.

The command \index takes just one argument, namely, the word or the phrase to be indexed. This will be written to a file with the extension .idx. If you look into this file, you will find lines like the following:

```
\indexentry {enterprise}{9}
\indexentry {network}{15}
```

These stand for the index entries and the corresponding page numbers.

The external program **makeindex** takes that .idx file and produces an .ind file. The latter consists of LaTeX code for the index creation. Specifically, it contains the index list environment together with the items and looks like the following:

```
\begin{theindex}
\item enterprise, 9
\indexspace
\item network, 15
\end{theindex}
```

More complex indexes may contain subitems, page ranges, and references to other items. Let's see how to produce such an index.

Defining index entries and subentries

We already created simple index entries with:

```
\index{phrase}
```

Subentries are produced by specifying the main entry followed by the subentry, separated by an exclamation mark, for example:

```
\index{network!overview}
```

Also subentries may have subentries; just use another ! symbol, for example:

```
\index{enterprise!organization}
\index{enterprise!organization!sales}
\index{enterprise!organization!controlling}
\index{enterprise!organization!operation}
```

Up to three levels are possible.

Specifying page ranges

If several pages deal with the same concept, you may specify a page range for the index entry. Suffix the entry with |(where the range starts and add |) where it ends, as follows:

```
\index{network|(}
```

at the beginning of the network chapter and:

```
\index{network|)}
```

at the end of this chapter. This results in an entry of the form **Network, 15-17**.

Using symbols and macros in the index

`makeindex` sorts the entries alphabetically. If you would like to include symbols in the index, for example, Greek letters, chemical formulas, or math symbols, you could face the problem of integrating them into the sorting. For this purpose, \index understands a sort key. Use this key as prefix for the entry, separated by an @ symbol, for instance:

```
\index{Gamma@$\Gamma$}
```

Using macros for index entries is generally not really recommended. Macros would be sorted according to the macro name including the backslash, though it would be expanded when the index is typeset. Imagine, you've got a macro \group standing for **TeX Users Group**. If you write the following, then the entry **TeX Users Group** would be treated like **\group** in the sorting and won't appear among the entries beginning with **T**:

```
\index{\group}
```

However, you could repair such issues by adding a sort key:

```
\index{TeX@\group}
\index{schon@sch\"{o}n}
```

What if you wish to use the symbols |, @, and ! within index entries? Quote them by using a preceding ":

```
\index{exclamation ("!)!loud}
```

And don't worry, " itself may be used within verbatim text as follows:

```
\index{quote (\verb|""|)}
```

Referring to other index entries

Different words may stand for the same concept. For such cases, it's possible to add a cross-reference to the main phrase without a page number. Adding the code |see{entry list} achieves that, for example:

```
\index{network|see{WLAN}}
\index{WLAN}
```

As such references don't print a page number, their position in the text doesn't matter. You could collect them in one place of your document.

Fine-tuning page numbers

If an index entry refers to several pages, you might want to emphasize one page number to indicate it as the primary reference. You could define a command for emphasizing as follows:

```
\newcommand{\main}[1]{\emph{#1}}
```

And for the index entry, add a pipe symbol and the command name:

```
\index{WLAN|main}
```

Thus, the corresponding page number would be emphasized. Simply writing `\index{WLAN|emph}` or `\index{WLAN|texbf}` is possible as well. However, defining your own macro is more consistent—remember the concept of separating form and content.

Designing the index layout

If we extend our example document with the aforementioned example commands, `\printindex` gives us this layout, containing subentries, ranges, references, and emphasized entries:

Index

enterprise, 9
    organization, 9
       controlling, 11
       operation, 11
       sales, 9, 11

Γ, 15

network, 15–17
    overview, 15
    wireless, *see* WLAN

WLAN, *15*, 16

LaTeX provides some index styles called **latex** (the default), **gind**, **din**, and **iso**. To use another style, specify it using the `-s` option of the `makeindex` program, for example:

```
makeindex -s iso documentname
```

If you typeset after this call, the index layout would be changed to:

enterprise 9
    organization 9
       controlling 11
       operation 11
       sales 9, 11
Γ 15
network 15–17
    overview 15
    wireless .... *see* WLAN
WLAN *15*, 16

You could even define your own styles. To learn more about indexing and `makeindex`, use **texdoc** at the command prompt:

```
texdoc index
```

```
texdoc makeindex
```

 Though it seems natural to generate the index while writing the document, this might lead to inconsistencies in the index. It's recommendable first to finish writing and afterwards to work out what should appear in the index.

Creating a bibliography

Especially in scientific documents, a **list of references** or **bibliography** is very common. We shall work out how to typeset a bibliography and how to refer to its entries.

Time for action – citing texts and listing the references

Using LaTeX's standard features, we shall create a small list of references containing a book and an article by Donald E. Knuth, the creator of TeX. In our body text, we will refer to both:

1. Create a new document as follows:

```
\documentclass{article}
\begin{document}
\section*{Recommended texts}
To study \TeX\ in depth, see \cite{DK86}. For writing math texts,
see \cite{DK89}.
\begin{thebibliography}{8}
\bibitem{DK86} D.E. Knuth, \emph{The {\TeX}book}, 1986
\bibitem{DK89} D.E. Knuth, \emph{Typesetting Concrete
Mathematics}, 1989
\end{thebibliography}
\end{document}
```

2. **Typeset** and view the output:

> # Recommended texts
>
> To study TEX in depth, see [1]. For writing math texts, see [2].
>
> # References
>
> [1] D.E. Knuth, *The TEXbook*, 1986
>
> [2] D.E. Knuth, *Typesetting Concrete Mathematics*, 1989

What just happened?

We used an environment called **thebibliography** to typeset the list of references, which is similar to a description list as we've seen in *Chapter 4, Creating Lists*. Each item of this list has got a **key**. For citing in the body text, we referred to that key using the \cite command.

Let's look at these commands in detail.

Using the standard bibliography environment

LaTeX's standard environment for bibliographies has the following form:

```
\begin{thebibliography}{widest label}
\bibitem[label]{key} author, title, year etc.
\bibitem...

...
\end{thebibliography}
```

Each item is specified using the command \bibitem. This command requires a mandatory argument determining the key. We may simply refer to this key by \cite{key} or \cite{key1,key2}. \cite accepts an optional argument stating a page range, for example, \cite[p.\,18--20]{key}. You may choose a label by the optional argument of \bibitem. If no label has been given, LaTeX will number the items consecutively in square brackets, as we've seen.

Using labels, the environment could look as follows:

```
\begin{thebibliography}{Knuth89}
\bibitem[Knuth86]{DK86} D.E. Knuth, \emph{The {\TeX}book}, 1986
\bibitem[Knuth89]{DK89} D.E. Knuth, \emph{Typesetting Concrete
Mathematics}, 1989
\end{thebibliography}
```

And the output would then be as follows:

Recommended texts

To study TEX in depth, see [Knuth86]. For writing math texts, see [Knuth89].

References

[Knuth86] D.E. Knuth, *The TEXbook*, 1986

[Knuth89] D.E. Knuth, *Typesetting Concrete Mathematics*, 1989

As you can see, the output of `\cite` has been automatically adjusted to the new labels.

 The **cite** package offers compressed and sorted lists of numerical citations, like [2,4-6], and further formatting options for in-text citations.

The mandatory item of the environment should contain the widest label for the alignment of the items. So, for instance, if you have more than 9 but fewer than a 100 items, you may write two digits into the argument.

Using bibliography databases with BibTeX

Manually creating the bibliography is laborious. Especially, if you use references in several documents, it would be beneficial to use a database and let a program create the bibliography for you. This sounds more complicated than it really is. We will try this.

Time for action – creating and using a BibTeX database

We shall create a separate database file containing the references of our previous example. We will modify our example to use that database. To make this database usable, we have to call the external program **BibTeX**:

1. Create a new document. Begin with writing the entry for the TeXbook:

```
@book{DK86,
author = "D.E. Knuth",
title = "The {\TeX}book",
publisher = "Addison Wesley",
year = 1986
}
```

2. For the next entry, that is, the article, we will specify even more fields:

```
@article{DK89,
author = "D.E. Knuth",
title = "Typesetting Concrete Mathematics",
journal = "TUGboat",
volume = 10,
number = 1,
pages = "31--36",
month = apr,
year = 1989
}
```

3. Save the file and give it the name `tex.bib`. Open our example `tex` document and modify it as follows:

```
\documentclass{article}
\begin{document}
\section*{Recommended texts}
To study \TeX\ in depth, see \cite{DK86}. For writing math texts,
see \cite{DK89}.
\bibliographystyle{alpha}
\bibliography{tex}
\end{document}
```

4. **Typeset** one time with **pdfLaTeX**.

5. If you're using TeXworks, choose **BibTeX** instead of **pdfLaTeX,** present in the drop-down box next to the **Typeset** button, and then click on **Typeset**. If you write with another editor, use its **BibTeX** option or type at the command prompt in the document directory as follows:

```
bibtex documentname
```

6. **Typeset** twice with **pdfLaTeX**. Here's the result:

> ## Recommended texts
>
> To study TeX in depth, see [Knu86]. For writing math texts, see [Knu89].
>
> ## References
>
> [Knu86] D.E. Knuth. *The TeXbook*. Addison Wesley, 1986.
>
> [Knu89] D.E. Knuth. Typesetting concrete mathematics. *TUGboat*, 10(1):31-36, April 1989.

What just happened?

We created a text file containing all bibliography entries. In the next section, we shall look at its format in depth. In our document, we chose a style called **alpha**, which sorts entries according to the author's name and uses a shortcut consisting of author and year as label. Then we told LaTeX to load the bibliography file called `tex`. The extension `.bib` has been automatically added.

Afterwards, we called the external program `BibTeX`. This program knows from the example `.tex` file that `tex.bib` has to be translated. Thus out of this `.bib` file, it creates a `.bbl` file, which contains a LaTeX `thebibliography` environment and the final entries.

Finally, we had to **Typeset** twice, to ensure that all cross-references are correct.

Though we need some more steps to generate the bibliography, there are benefits: we don't need to fine-tune each entry. We can easily switch between styles. We can then reuse the `.bib` file.

So, let's look at the `.bib` file format. It supports various entry types like `book` and `article`. Furthermore, these entries contain fields like `author`, `title`, and `year`. Let's first look at the supported fields, and afterwards we shall talk about the different kinds of entries.

Looking at the BibTeX entry fields

Here's a list of the standard fields. Some fields are common, some are rarely used—we just list them in alphabetical order, following the `BibTeX` documentation:

address	Usually the address of the publisher. At least for small publishers, this information might be useful.
annote	An annotation, not used by the standard bibliography styles. Other styles or macros might use this.
author	The name(s) of the author(s).
booktitle	The title of a book, if you cite a part of that. For a book, use the `title` field instead.
chapter	A chapter number.
crossref	The key of the database entry being cross referenced.
edition	The edition (First, Second, and alike) of a book. Commonly it's capitalized.
editor	The name(s) of the editor(s).
howpublished	The way of publishing, especially if it's unusual. Capitalize the first word.
institution	Could be a sponsoring institution.
journal	A journal name; you may use common abbreviations.

key	Used for alphabetizing, cross-referencing, and labeling if the author information is missing. Don't confuse it with the key used in the `\cite` command which corresponds to the beginning of the entry.
month	The month in which the work was published or written if it's not yet published. Usually a three letter abbreviation is used.
note	Any additional useful information. Capitalize the first word.
number	The number of a journal or another kind of work in a series.
organization	Might be a sponsoring organization.
pages	A page number or range of page numbers, like 12-18 or 22+.
publisher	The name of the publisher.
school	Could be the name of the school where the document was written.
series	The name of a series of books or its number of a multi-volume set.
title	The title of the work.
type	The type of the publication.
volume	The volume of a journal or multi-volume book.
year	The year of the publication or the year when it was written if it hasn't been published yet. Commonly four numerals are used, such as 2010.

You may use any fields possibly supported by other styles and ignored by standard styles.

Referring to Internet resources

Today we often refer to online sources. To put Internet addresses into BibTeX fields, use the `\url` command of the `url` or `hyperref` package, for example, `howpublished = {\url{http://texblog.net}}`. Some styles offer a **url** field.

Understanding BibTeX entry types

Firstly, you decide which type of entry you want to add and then you fill in the fields. Different types may support different fields. Some fields are required, some are optional and may be omitted, and some are simply ignored.

Usually the name of the entry tells you its meaning. These are the standard entry types and their required and optional fields, according to the BibTeX reference:

Type	Required fields	Optional fields
article	author, title, journal, year	volume, number, pages, month, note
book	author or editor, title, publisher, year	volume or number, series, address, edition, month, note
booklet	title	author, howpublished, address, month, year, note
conference	author, title, booktitle, year	editor, volume or number, series, pages, address, month, organization, publisher, note
manual	title	author, organization, address, edition, month, year, note
mastersthesis	author, title, school, year	type, address, month, note
misc	none	author, title, howpublished, month, year, note
phdthesis	author, title, school, year	type, address, month, note
proceedings	title, year	editor, volume or number, series, address, month, organization, publisher, note
techreport	author, title, institution, year	type, number, address, month, note
unpublished	author, title, note	month, year

Have a look at the BibTeX reference for more details:

```
texdoc bibtex
```

If no other entry fits, choose **misc**. It doesn't matter if you use capitals or small letters; @ARTICLE is understood the same as @article. As the example showed, entries have the following form:

```
@entrytype{keyword,
fieldname = {field text},
fieldname = {field text},
...
}
```

Use braces around the `field text`. Straight quotes instead like in `"field text"` are supported as well. For numbers, you may omit the braces.

Some styles change the capitalization, which might lead to undesired lowercase letters. To protect letters or words from becoming lowercase, put additional braces around them. Preferably around a word instead of just the letter to keep ligatures and kerning improvement, that is, `{WAL}` looks better than `{W}AL` as TeX moves an A closer to a preceding W. Separating braces hampers TeX's micro-typographic improvements.

Choosing the bibliography style

Standard styles are as follows:

plain	Arabic numbers for the labels, sorted according to the names of the authors. The number is written in square brackets, which also appear with `\cite`.
unsrt	No sorting. All entries appear like they were cited in the text, otherwise it looks like `plain`.
alpha	Sorting is according to the names of the authors, the labels are shortcuts made of the authors name and the year of publication. Also here, square brackets are used.
abbrv	Like `plain`, but first names and other field entries are abbreviated.

The style should be chosen after `\begin{document}` and before `\bibliography`. You may write `\bibliographystyle` right before `\bibliography` to keep it together.

There are more styles available in TeX distributions and on the Internet. For instance, the **natbib** package provides styles and the capability to cite in a nice author-year scheme. This package further adds some fields, like ISBN, ISSN, and URL.

The package **biblatex** provides a complete reimplementation of the bibliographic features offered by **BibTeX** and LaTeX. Without learning the **BibTeX** language, you could create new styles just by using your LaTeX knowledge.

Listing references without citing

BibTeX takes only those references from the database that are cited in the text, and prints them out. However, you may specify keys for references, which should appear nevertheless the following for a single reference. Just write the following for a single reference:

    \nocite{key}

Or write the following to list the complete database

```
\nocite{*}
```

Changing the headings

Like in our diagram example, if you don't like the heading **Contents**, you could easily change it. The text of the heading is stored in the text macro \contentsname. So, just redefine it as follows:

```
\renewcommand{\contentsname}{Table of Contents}
```

Here's a list of all those headings:

List	Heading command	Default heading
Table of contents	\contentsname	**Contents**
List of figures	\listfigurename	**List of figures**
List of tables	\listtablename	**List of tables**
Bibliography	\bibname in book and report	**Bibliography** in book and report
	\refname in article	**References** in article
Index	\indexname	**Index**

Furthermore, as promised, here's a list of further macros for names used by LaTeX:

Name	Command	Default value
figure	\figurename	**Figure**
table	\tablename	**Table**
part	\partname	**Part**
chapter	\chaptername	**Chapter**
abstract	\abstractname	**Abstract**
appendix	\appendixname	**Appendix**

Not really surprising! Using name macros is especially useful when another language will be used. For instance, the **babel** package takes a language option and redefines all those name macros according to those languages.

However, they are also useful to choose abbreviations like **Fig.** or **Appendices** instead of **Appendix**.

Have a go hero – using natbib

Load the already mentioned `natbib` package and try its new styles **plainnat**, **abbrvnat**, and **unsrtnat**, for instance:

```
\usepackage{natbib}
\bibliographystyle{plainnat}
```

Our example would change as follows:

> ## Recommended texts
>
> To study TeX in depth, see Knuth [1986]. For writing math texts, see Knuth [1989].
>
> ## References
>
> D.E. Knuth. *The TeXbook*. Addison Wesley, 1986.
>
> D.E. Knuth. Typesetting concrete mathematics. *TUGboat*, 10(1):31–36, April 1989.

`natbib` reimplemented the `\cite` command and offers variations to it, with the main purpose of supporting author-year citations. It works with most other available styles. `natbib` introduces the citation command `\citet` for textual citations and the command `\citep` for parenthetical citations. There are starred variants printing the full author list, and optional arguments allow adding text before and after.

Check out the documentation if you would like to benefit from this fine package.

Pop quiz

1. Which of these commands should be used for adding unnumbered headings to the table of contents?

    a. `\addtocontents`

    b. `\addcontentsline`

    c. `\contentsname`

2. Which of the following indexing commands has to come before `\begin{document}`?

    a. `\index`

    b. `\printindex`

    c. `\makeindex`

3. Which command generates the bibliography?

    a. \bibliography

    b. \bibliographystyle

    c. \bibitem

Summary

In this chapter, we dealt with many kinds of lists. Specifically, we learned about:

- Generating and customizing the table of contents and lists of figures and tables
- Producing an index pointing to relevant information for keywords and phrases
- Creating bibliographies, both manually and using a bibliography database

These lists are intended to guide the reader to the information he's/she's looking for; they aren't just for listing and summarizing. That's why the headings of the list of figures and the list of tables usually don't appear in the TOC, as they commonly directly follow the TOC. Sometimes there's even the strange requirement to list the table of contents within itself. If you are not sure with a design or a requirement, have a look at a good book in your special field, to see how exemplary tables of contents, lists, and indexes might look.

In the next chapter, we shall look at scientific writing in depth.

8
Typing Math Formulas

Chapter 1, Getting started with LaTeX, claimed that LaTeX offers excellent quality for mathematical typesetting. Now it's time to prove this.

To make the most of LaTeX's capabilities, we shall learn how to perform the following:

◆ Writing basic formulas

◆ Embedding formulas within text and text within formulas

◆ Centering and numbering equations

◆ Aligning multi-line equations

◆ Typesetting math symbols such as roots, operators, Greek letters, and arrows

◆ Building fractions

◆ Stacking expressions

◆ Building matrices

That's a great undertaking—let's tackle it!

Writing basic formulas

LaTeX knows three general **modes**:

- The **paragraph mode**: The text is typeset as a sequence of words in lines, paragraphs, and pages. That's what we used until now.

- The **left-to-right mode**: The text is also considered to be a sequence of words, but LaTeX typesets it from left to right without breaking the line. For instance, the argument of \mbox will be typeset in this mode; that's why \mbox prevents hyphenation.

- The **math mode**: Letters are treated as math symbols. That's why they're typeset in italic shape, which is common for variables. A lot of symbols can be used, most of them exclusively in this mode. Such symbols are roots, sum signs, relation signs, math accents, arrows, and various delimiters like brackets and braces. Space characters between letters and symbols are ignored. Instead, the spacing depends on the type of symbols—distances to relation signs are different from distances to opening or closing delimiters. This mode is required for all math expressions.

Now we shall enter the math mode for the first time.

Time for action – discussing quadratic equations and roots

Our first small math text shall deal with the solutions of quadratic equations. We need to typeset formulas with constants, variables, superscripts for the square, and subscripts for the solutions. The solution itself needs a root symbol. Finally, we will use cross-references to formulas.

1. Start a new document. For now, we don't need any package:

   ```
   \documentclass{article}
   \begin{document}
   \section*{Quadratic equations}
   ```

2. State the quadratic equation with its conditions. Use an **equation** environment for it. Surround small pieces of math within text by \(... \):

   ```
   The quadratic equation
   \begin{equation}
     \label{quad}
     ax^2 + bx + c = 0,
   \end{equation}
   where \( a, b \) and \( c \) are constants and \( a \neq 0 \),
   has two solutions for the variable \( x \):
   ```

3. Use another equation for the solutions. The command for the square root is \sqrt. **The command for a fraction is** \frac:

```
\begin{equation}
  \label{root}
  x_{1,2} = \frac{-b \pm \sqrt{b^2-4ac}}{2a}.
\end{equation}
```

4. Let's introduce the discriminant and discuss the case zero. To get an unnumbered displayed equation, we surround the formula with \[... \]:

```
If the \emph{discrimimant} \( \Delta \) with
\[
  \Delta = b^2 - 4ac
\]
is zero, then the equation (\ref{quad}) has a double solution:
(\ref{root}) becomes
\[
  x = - \frac{b}{2a}.
\]
\end{document}
```

5. **Typeset** twice and look at the result:

Quadratic equations

The quadratic equation

$$ax^2 + bx + c = 0, \tag{1}$$

where a, b and c are constants and $a \neq 0$, has two solutions for the variable x:

$$x_{1,2} = \frac{-b \pm \sqrt{b^2 - 4ac}}{2a}. \tag{2}$$

If the *discrimimant* Δ with

$$\Delta = b^2 - 4ac$$

is zero, then the equation (1) has a double solution: (2) becomes

$$x = -\frac{b}{2a}.$$

What just happened?

Just as we said in Chapter 1, writing formulas also looks a lot like programming. However, this chapter will help you master it, and the results are worth the effort. The formulas have been built with commands: there are commands with arguments, like for roots and fractions, and simple commands for symbols, like for the Greek letter. Most symbols have to be within a math environment and don't simply work within normal text.

The equation environment created a displayed formula; that formula has been horizontally centered, some vertical space has been added before and after, further these formulas are consecutively numbered.

However, \ [... \] and \ (... \) are also, in truth, environments. Let's sort this out.

Embedding math expressions within text

LaTeX provides the math environment in-text formulas:

```
\begin{math}
expression
\end{math}
```

Since it's very laborious to write this environment for each small expression or symbol, LaTeX offers an alias that's doing the same:

```
\(
expression
\)
```

You may write it without line breaks, such as \(expression\).

A third way is by using a shortcut, coming from TeX:

```
$expression$
```

A disadvantage of the latter is that the commands for beginning and ending the math environment are the same, which may easily lead to errors. However, it's much easier to type, which may be the reason why it's still popular among LaTeX users.

 \(... \) might cause problems in moving arguments like in headings. To prevent any such problems, just load the package **fixltx2e**, which fixes this as well as other issues.

Displaying formulas

For displayed formulas, which have to be centered, LaTeX offers the **displaymath** environment:

```
\begin{displaymath}
expression
\end{displaymath}
```

The effect of this environment is that the paragraph will be ended, some vertical space follows, then the centered formula plus the following vertical space. As this math environment takes care of the spacing, don't leave empty lines before and after it! This would cause additional vertical space because of the superfluous paragraph breaks.

Also for this environment there's a shortcut. We already used it:

```
\[
expression
\]
```

In this case, putting the shortcuts \[and \] on separate lines commonly improves the readability as the formula is also kind of displayed in the source code.

There's also a TeX low level command:

```
$$
expression
$$
```

However, it's strongly recommended to use \[... \], because this LaTeX environment handles vertical spacing better.

For the rest of this chapter, all pieces of code use math mode. Either we explicitly use a math environment or we imagine that we are already in math mode, for short pieces of code.

Numbering equations

Equations and formulas in general may be numbered. However, this applies only to displayed formulas. The equation environment is responsible for this:

```
\begin{equation}
  \label{key}
  expression
\end{equation}
```

It looks similar to displaymath but numbered this time. The number will be displayed in parentheses on the right side of the equation.

Adding subscripts and superscripts

As exponents and indexes are frequently used, there are very short commands for typesetting them, for example, _ gives an index or subscript, ^ produces an exponent or superscript. Use braces to mark the concerned expression. So, the common forms are as follows:

```
{expression}_{subscript}
```

And:

```
{expression}^{superscript}
```

This may be nested. If you use subscripts and superscripts to the same expression, the order of ^ and _ is not important. In the case of single letters, numerals, or symbols, you can omit the braces. Let's look at an example:

```
\[ x_1^2 + x_2^2 = 1, \quad 2^{2^x} = 64 \]
```

$$x_1^2 + x_2^2 = 1, \quad 2^{2^x} = 64$$

Extracting roots

Our example contained a square root: \sqrt{value}. As there are roots of higher order, this command accepts an optional argument for the order. The complete definition is:

```
\sqrt[order]{value}
```

The size of the root symbol will be automatically adjusted to the height and the width of the value expression. Roots may be nested. Both can be seen in this example:

```
\sqrt[64]{x} = \sqrt{\sqrt{\sqrt{\sqrt{\sqrt{\sqrt{x}}}}}}
```

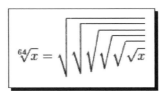

Writing fractions

Within text formulas, you may just write / to denote fractions, such as \((a+b)/2 \). For larger fractions, there's the \frac command:

```
\frac{numerator}{denumerator}
```

This command may also be used for in-text formulas. However, the line spacing could increase.

```
\[ \frac{n(n+1)}{2}, \quad \frac{\frac{\sqrt{x}+1}{2}-x}{y^2} \]
```

$$\frac{n(n+1)}{2}, \quad \frac{\frac{\sqrt{x}+1}{2}-x}{y^2}$$

Greek letters

Mathematicians like to use Greek letters, for instance, to denote constants. To get a lowercase Greek letter, just write the name with a backslash for the command. Here are the lowercase Greek letters with their corresponding LaTeX commands:

α \alpha	ζ \zeta	λ \lambda	π \pi	ϕ \phi
β \beta	η \eta	μ \mu	ρ \rho	χ \chi
γ \gamma	θ \theta	ν \nu	σ \sigma	ψ \psi
δ \delta	ι \iota	ξ \xi	τ \tau	ω \omega
ϵ \epsilon	κ \kappa	o o	υ \upsilon	

For some letters, variants are available:

ε \varepsilon	ϖ \varpi	ς \varsigma
ϑ \vartheta	ϱ \varrho	φ \varphi

As the omicron just looks like an o, there's no command for it. It's similar for most uppercase Greek letters, which are equal to Roman letters. The remaining uppercase Greek letters are produced as follows:

Γ \Gamma	Λ \Lambda	Σ \Sigma	Ψ \Psi
Δ \Delta	Ξ \Xi	Υ \Upsilon	Ω \Omega
Θ \Theta	Π \Pi	Φ \Phi	

For upright Greek letters, you may use the **upgreek** package.

Script letters

For the twenty-six uppercase letters A, B, C, ... , Z, there's a calligraphic shape, produced by \mathcal:

    \[\mathcal{A}, \mathcal{B}, \mathcal{C}, \ldots, \mathcal{Z} \]

$$A, B, C, \ldots, Z$$

 There are packages offering different calligraphic fonts, such as **zapfino** and **xits**.

Producing an ellipsis

You already know \ldots for a low ellipsis. It also works in math mode. We use the low ellipsis mainly between letters and commas. Between operation and relation symbols, a centered ellipsis is commonly used. Furthermore, a matrix may require a vertical ellipsis. Here's how all of them may be produced:

. .	: :	⋰ \ddots
· \cdot	... \ldots	⋮ \vdots
˙ \dot{}	⋯ \cdots	

Comparing in-line formulas to displayed formulas

Writing formulas in-line saves space and allows fluent explanations. This is recommendable for short math expressions within text.

Formulas in the displayed style are outstanding; they are centered and require more space. Furthermore, they can be numbered and you may refer to them using the \label and \ref techniques that you learned in *Chapter 5, Creating Tables and Inserting Pictures*.

Choose the style that is optimal for the readability of your text.

Changing the font, style, and size

In *Chapter 2, Formatting Words, Lines, and Paragraphs*, we learned how to modify the font of common text. There are further commands changing the font style in math mode:

Command	Used package	Example
\mathrm{...}		roman 123
\mathit{...}		*italic 123*
\mathsf{...}		sans − serif 123
\mathbb{...}	amsfonts	ABC
\mathbbm{...}	bbm	CRQZ1
\mathds{...}	dsfont	CRQZ1
\mathfrak{...}	eufrak	$\mathfrak{ABC}$ 123
\mathnormal{...}		*normal*

Though letters in math mode are italic, they are considered to be separate symbols, which results in a different spacing than that of an italic word. For instance, in math mode, fi may be the product of the variables f and i, but not the ligature fi. Compare:

```
\textit{Definition}, \(Definition\)
```

Definition, $Definition$

Also, \mathit treats the argument as text in italic math font. So, for text within formulas, use a text or math font command, or even better: use \text{...} of amsmath—we will return to this very soon.

If you wish to switch to bold typeface for a complete math expression, you can use the declaration \boldmath before the expression, that is, already outside math mode. The declaration \unboldmath switches back to the normal typeface. The latter has to be used outside math mode as well.

To make parts of a formula bold, you can switch to the left-to-right mode by \mbox and by using \boldmath in its argument.

Four **math styles** are available, determining the way of typesetting and the font size:

Style	Command	Meaning
display	\displaystyle	Default for letters and symbols in displayed formulas
text	\textstyle	Default for letters and symbols within in-text formulas
script	\scriptstyle	Smaller font size, used for subscripts and for superscripts
scriptscript	\scriptscriptstyle	Even smaller font size, for nested script style

The `textstyle` differs from the `displaystyle` in mainly two ways; in `textstyle`, variable sized symbols are smaller and subscripts and superscripts are usually placed beside the expression instead of below and above, respectively. Otherwise the font size is the same.

LaTeX switches the style automatically; if you write a simple exponent, it will be typeset in script style, that is, with a smaller font size.

You may force a desired style using one of the commands in the aforementioned table. This allows you, for instance, to:

- Type formulas within the text exactly like they would appear in a displayed formula: bigger fraction, bigger sum signs, further subscripts are set below, and superscripts are set above. Note, all of this increases the line spacing.
- Write exponents or indexes with bigger symbols.

Customizing displayed formulas

There are two options that modify the way the formulas are displayed:

`fleqn`	"left equation numbers"	This causes all displayed formulas to be aligned at the left margin.
`leqno`	"left equation numbers"	All numbered formulas would get the numbers on the left side instead of the right.

Often, formulas are not displayed just standalone. We may encounter situations where:

- A formula is too long to fit on one line
- Several formulas are listed row-by-row
- An equation shall be transformed step-by-step
- A chain of inequalities spans over more than one line
- Several formulas shall be aligned at relation symbols

We may also encounter similar situations, where we have to write multi-line formulas, often with some kind of alignment. The **amsmath** package offers specialized environments for nearly every such need.

Time for action – typesetting multi-line formulas

We shall use the `amsmath` package to experiment with a very long formula and with a system of equations:

1. Start a new document on an A6 paper and load the `amsmath` package.

```
\documentclass{article}
\usepackage[a6paper]{geometry}
\usepackage{amsmath}
\begin{document}
```

2. Use the `multline` environment to span a long equation over three lines. End the lines with\\:

```
\begin{multline}
\sum = a + b + c + d + e \\
    + f + g + h + i + j \\
    + k + l + m + n
\end{multline}
\end{document}
```

3. **Typeset** and look at the formula:

$$\sum = a + b + c + d + e \\ + f + g + h + i + j \\ + k + l + m + n \quad (1)$$

4. Now we handle a system of equations. Use the `gather` environment to add these equations. Again, end lines with \\:

```
\begin{gather}
  x + y + z = 0 \\
  y - z = 1
\end{gather}
```

5. **Typeset** and look at the equations:

$$x + y + z = 0 \quad (2)$$
$$y - z = 1 \quad (3)$$

6. Commonly, equation systems are aligned at the equal sign. Let's do this. Use the & symbol to mark the point that we wish to align:

```
\begin{align}
  x + y + z &= 0 \\
  y - z &= 1
\end{align}
```

7. **Typeset**; now the equations are aligned as desired:

$$x + y + z = 0 \qquad (4)$$
$$y - z = 1 \qquad (5)$$

What just happened?

Because we loaded the amsmath package, we have access to several multi-line math environments.

Each line in such an environment is ended by \\, except the last one. The alignment depends on the environment, as we've seen:

◆ **multline**: The first line is left-aligned, the last line right-aligned, and all other lines in between are centered

◆ **gather**: All lines are centered

◆ **align**: The lines are aligned at marked relation signs

Let's have a closer look.

Aligning multi-line equations

Here's a list of the amsmath multi-line environments:

Name	Meaning
multline	First line is left-aligned, last line is right-aligned, all others are centered.
gather	Each line is centered.
align	Use & to mark a symbol where the formulas shall be aligned. Use another & to end a column, if you need several aligned columns.
flalign	Similar to align with more than one column, but the columns are flushed to the left and the right margin, respectively.
alignat	Alignment at several places, each has to be marked by &.

Name	Meaning
split	Similar to align, but within another math environment, thus unnumbered.
aligned, gathered, alignedat	Used for an aligned block within a math environment. This can be displayed math or in-line math.

Numbering rows in multi-line formulas

In multi-line math environments, each line would be numbered like a normal equation. If you wish to suppress the numbering of a line, write \notag before the end of the line.

Use the starred variant like align*, or gather*, if you would like to avoid numbering completely.

Inserting text into formulas

To insert some text into a formula, standard LaTeX provides the \mbox command. amsmath offers further commands:

- ♦ \text{words} inserts text within a math formula. The size is adjusted according to the current math style, that is, \text produces smaller text within subscripts or superscripts.

- ♦ \intertext{text} suspends the formula, the text follows in a separate paragraph, then the multi-line formula is resumed, keeping the alignment. Use it for longer text.

These commands are the best choice, when you would like to use text within math environments.

Fine-tuning formulas

If we go beyond writing variables and basic math operators, we may need many symbols for special purposes: certain relation signs, unary and binary operators, function-like operators, sum and integral symbols and variants of the latter, arrows, and many more. LaTeX and additional packages offer thousands of symbols for many purposes. We shall have a look at some of them. But firstly, let's figure out how to write functions.

Using operators

Trigonometric functions, logarithm functions, and other analytic and algebraic functions are commonly written with upright Roman letters. Simply typing `log` would otherwise look like a product of the three variables, namely, l, o, and g. To ease the input, there are commands for many common functions or so called **operators**. Here's an alphabetical list of the predefined ones:

`\arccos, \arcsin, \arctan, \arg, \cos, \cosh, \cot, \coth, \scs, \deg, \det, \dim, \exp, \gcd, \hom, \inf, \ker, \lg, \lim, \liminf, \limsup, \ln, \log, \max, \min, \Pr, \sec, \sin, \sinh, \sup, \tan, \tanh`

The modulo function may be written in two ways, either by using `\bmod` for a binary relation or by using `\pmod{argument}` for a modulo expression in parentheses.

Some operators support subscripts which are set as follows:

`\[ \lim_{n=1, 2, \ldots} a_n, \qquad \max_{x<X} x \]`

$$\lim_{n=1,2,\ldots} a_n, \qquad \max_{x<X} x$$

Superscripts would be set above then.

Exploring the wealth of math symbols

Now, let's look at some math symbols and the commands for producing them. We shall cover many standard LaTeX symbols, some additional symbols are provided by the **latexsym** package. Even more symbols are accessible using, for instance, the **amssymb** package.

Binary operation symbols

Besides plus and minus, there are a few more operations:

Standard LaTeX			
II `\amalg`	∘ `\circ`	⊖ `\ominus`	⋆ `\star`
∗ `\ast`	∪ `\cup`	⊕ `\oplus`	× `\times`
○ `\bigcirc`	† `\dagger`	⊘ `\oslash`	◁ `\triangleleft`
▽ `\bigtriangledown`	‡ `\ddagger`	⊗ `\otimes`	▷ `\triangleright`
△ `\bigtriangleup`	⋄ `\diamond`	± `\pm`	⊎ `\uplus`
• `\bullet`	÷ `\div`	\ `\setminus`	∨ `\vee`
∩ `\cap`	∓ `\mp`	⊓ `\sqcap`	∧ `\wedge`
· `\cdot`	⊙ `\odot`	⊔ `\sqcup`	≀ `\wr`
latexsym			
⊴ `\unlhd`	⊵ `\unrhd`	▷ `\rhd`	◁ `\lhd`

Binary relation symbols

Values of expressions might be equal, but there are more possible relations, for example, they may be congruent, parallel, or they might stand in any other relation:

	Standard LaTeX		
$\approx$ \approx	$\equiv$ \equiv	$\prec$ \prec	$\succ$ \succ
$\asymp$ \asymp	$\frown$ \frown	$\preceq$ \preceq	$\succeq$ \succeq
$\bowtie$ \bowtie	$\mid$ \mid	$\propto$ \propto	$\vdash$ \vdash
$\cong$ \cong	$\models$ \models	$\sim$ \sim	
$\dashv$ \dashv	$\parallel$ \parallel	$\simeq$ \simeq	
$\doteq$ \doteq	$\perp$ \perp	$\smile$ \smile	

latexsym
$\bowtie$ \Join

Inequality relation symbols

If expressions are not equal, the inequality might be expressed in different ways:

$\geq$ \geq	$\gg$ \gg	$\leq$ \leq	$\ll$ \ll	$\neq$ \neq

Subset and superset symbols

For comparing sets and expressing relations between them, there are many symbols:

	Standard LaTeX	
$\sqsubseteq$ \sqsubseteq	$\subset$ \subset	$\supset$ \supset
$\sqsupseteq$ \sqsupseteq	$\subseteq$ \subseteq	$\supseteq$ \supseteq

latexsym	
$\sqsubset$ \sqsubset	$\sqsupset$ \sqsupset

Variable sized operators

For sums, products, and set operations, for example, we can use operator symbols which are variable in size: bigger in display style and smaller in text style.

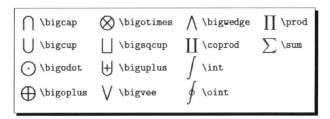

Arrows

Arrows are used for implications, maps, or descriptive expressions:

	Standard LaTeX	
↓ \downarrow	⟸ \Longleftarrow	⇒ \Rightarrow
⇓ \Downarrow	⟷ \longleftrightarrow	↘ \searrow
↩ \hookleftarrow	⟺ \Longleftrightarrow	↙ \swarrow
↪ \hookrightarrow	⟼ \longmapsto	↑ \uparrow
← \leftarrow	⟶ \longrightarrow	⇑ \Uparrow
⇐ \Leftarrow	⟹ \Longrightarrow	↕ \updownarrow
↔ \leftrightarrow	↦ \mapsto	⇕ \Updownarrow
⇔ \Leftrightarrow	↖ \nwarrow	
⟵ \longleftarrow	→ \rightarrow	

latexsym
↝ \leadsto

Harpoons

There are special arrows called harpoons:

↽ \leftharpoondown	⇁ \rightharpoondown	⇌ \rightleftharpoons
↼ \leftharpoonup	⇀ \rightharpoonup	

Symbols derived from letters

Some letter-like symbols are used in math:

Standard LaTeX				
⊥ \bot	∀ \forall	ɪ \imath	∋ \ni	⊤ \top
ℓ \ell	ℏ \hbar	∈ \in	∂ \partial	℘ \wp
∃ \exists	ℑ \Im	ȷ \jmath	ℜ \Re	

latexsym
℧ \mho

Variable sized delimiters

Also, delimiters such as parentheses, brackets, and braces can vary in size. If you write \left or \right before such a delimiter, its size will be automatically matched to the size of the inner expression. These size macros have to be used in pairs. To match a pair, if you don't wish to match a delimiter, use\left. or\right. to get an invisible delimiter.

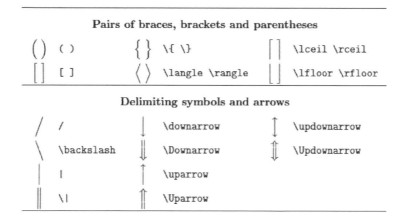

Pairs of braces, brackets and parentheses		
( ) ( )	{ } \{ \}	⌈ ⌉ \lceil \rceil
[ ] [ ]	⟨ ⟩ \langle \rangle	⌊ ⌋ \lfloor \rfloor

Delimiting symbols and arrows		
/ /	↓ \downarrow	↕ \updownarrow
\ \backslash	⇓ \Downarrow	⇕ \Updownarrow
			↑ \uparrow	
‖ |	⇑ \Uparrow	

Miscellaneous symbols

Here are more LaTeX symbols that do not match the mentioned categories:

Standard LaTeX			
ℵ \aleph	∅ \emptyset	∇ \nabla	♯ \sharp
∠ \angle	♭ \flat	♮ \natural	♠ \spadesuit
♣ \clubsuit	♡ \heartsuit	¬ \neg	√ \surd
◇ \diamondsuit	∞ \infty	′ \prime	△ \triangle

latexsym	
□ \Box	◇ \Diamond

"The Comprehensive LaTeX Symbol List" lists about 5000 symbols sorted in categories. If you need to search for a symbol, have a look at this document. As usual, with TeX Live, you could open this document by using the following at the command prompt:

```
texdoc symbols
```

You can find it on CTAN as well.

Writing units

If you use units in text, they should not look like variables: 'm' for meters should not look exactly like a variable m. Similarly, analogous 's' may stand for seconds, but not for a variable. A typographical convention is to use an upright font shape for units. Furthermore, it's common to use a thin space between the value and the dimension. So, for 10 meters, you may write `10\,\mathrm{m}`. However, this is very time-consuming. That's why several packages have been developed supporting correct and nice typesetting of units, for example, **units**, **fancyunits**, and **siunits**.

The most modern and comprehensive units package is **siunitx**, providing features of all the other packages and even more. It requires reading some documentation before use, but it's worth the effort.

Building math structures

Variables and constants are simple. But there are more complex objects, like binomial coefficients, vectors, and matrices. We shall figure out how to typeset such structures. Let's begin with simple arrays.

Creating arrays

For arranging math expressions within a surrounding expression, there's the **array** environment. We use it exactly like a `tabular` environment. However, it requires math mode and all of its entries are made using the math mode as well.

For example, by using variable sized parentheses around the array:

```
\[
  A = \left(
    \begin{array}{cc}
      a_{11} & a_{12} \\
      a_{21} & a_{22}
    \end{array}
  \right)
\]
```

$$A = \left(\begin{array}{cc} a_{11} & a_{12} \\ a_{21} & a_{22} \end{array} \right)$$

Writing binomial coefficients:

Binomial coefficients and matrices may be typeset using an array together with delimiters. However, the `amsmath` package provides shorter commands, for instance, `\binom` for binomial coefficients:

```
\binom{n}{k} = \frac{n!}{k!(n-k)!}
```

$$\binom{n}{k} = \frac{n!}{k!(n-k)!}$$

Typesetting matrices

As you might expect now of `amsmath`, there are many special matrix environments. A standard matrix can be typeset by the `pmatrix` environment:

```
\documentclass{article}
\usepackage{amsmath}
\begin{document}
\[
A = \begin{pmatrix}
a_{11} & a_{12} \\
a_{21} & a_{22}
```

```
\end{pmatrix}
\]
\end{document}
```

$$A = \begin{pmatrix} a_{11} & a_{12} \\ a_{21} & a_{22} \end{pmatrix}$$

You may notice that the parentheses are closer to the matrix entries than in the `array` example.

These are `amsmath`'s matrix environments:

Name	Delimiters of the matrix
matrix	without delimiters
pmatrix	parentheses ( )
bmatrix	square brackets [ ]
Bmatrix	braces { }
vmatrix	| |
Vmatrix	|| ||
smallmatrix	without delimiters, add them if needed, more compact

The compact `smallmatrix` environment is useful for matrices within running text.

Stacking expressions

Formulas may become complex: we might need to put one symbol above another one or above whole expressions, or we wish to put lines, braces, or dots above symbols. There are several ways.

Underlining and overlining

`\overline` puts a line above its argument, which may be nested:

```
s = \overline{AB}
```

$$s = \overline{AB}$$

The counterpart is `\underline`.

It doesn't have to be a line; braces are popular too. The commands are \underbrace and \overbrace. You may use subscripts and superscripts:

```
N = \underbrace{1 + 1 + \cdots + 1}_n
```

$$N = \underbrace{1 + 1 + \cdots + 1}_{n}$$

Setting accents

We've already seen accents in text mode. For the math mode, we need different commands. They may be applied to any letter. Here's the list of **math accents** using the lowercase letter 'a' as an example:

$\acute{a}$ \acute{a}	$\check{a}$ \check{a}	$\grave{a}$ \grave{a}	$\tilde{a}$ \tilde{a}
$\bar{a}$ \bar{a}	$\ddot{a}$ \ddot{a}	$\hat{a}$ \hat{a}	$\vec{a}$ \vec{a}
$\breve{a}$ \breve{a}	$\dot{a}$ \dot{a}	$\mathring{a}$ \mathring{a}	

Extensible	
$\widehat{abc}$ \widehat{abc}	$\widetilde{abc}$ \widetilde{abc}

The extensible ones are also called **wide accents**; they try to fit the width of their argument.

Putting a symbol above another

Besides the array environment, there are amsmath commands to directly stack expressions:

◆ \underset{expression below}{expression} puts an expression below another, using the subscript size below.

◆ \overset{expression above}{expression} puts an expression above another, using the subscript size above.

Writing theorems and definitions

LaTeX provides environment for theorems, definitions, and alike. Returning to our first example in this chapter, we could define a theorem environment by:

```
\newtheorem{thm}{Theorem}
```

Then, we declare a definition environment, using an optional argument stating an existing environment with which we would like to share the numbering:

```
\newtheorem{dfn}[thm]{Definition}
```

And in this simple way, we may use these environments:

```
\begin{dfn}
A quadratic equation is an equation of the form
\begin{equation}
  \label{quad}
ax^2 + bx + c = 0,
\end{equation}
where \( a, b \) and \( c \) are constants and \( a \neq 0 \).
\end{dfn}
\begin{thm}
A quadratic equation (\ref{quad}) has two solutions for the variable
\( x \):
\begin{equation}
  \label{root}
  x_{1,2} = \frac{-b \pm \sqrt{b^2-4ac}}{2a}.
\end{equation}
\end{thm}
```

In the output, such environments are numbered and labeled "Theorem" and "Definition", respectively. In *Chapter 10, Developing Large Documents*, when we are going to develop large documents, we will use this to create a complete document containing definitions, theorems, and lemmas.

There are two remarkable packages offering much more flexibility:

- **amsthm** provides several styles, allows fine customization, and includes a proof environment.
- **ntheorem** does similar work, but handles end marks in a better way.

If you would like to use such environments, have a look at their documentation, and compare the features to decide which package is the best for you.

Have a go hero – checking out the mathtools package

The **mathtools** package extends `amsmath`. If you need a certain feature and cannot find it, neither in standard LaTeX nor in `amsmath`, always look first at `mathtools`. Here are some of its features with examples:

- Tools for fine-tuning math typesetting, for example, compact styles:

$$2^{3^4} \quad \text{instead of} \quad 2^{3^4}$$

- Aligning limits of operators:

$$\liminf_{n \to \infty} \sup_{x^{n^2} \geq 0} x \quad \text{instead of} \quad \liminf_{n \to \infty} \sup_{x^{n^2} \geq 0} x$$

- Adjusting the width of operators:

$$x = \sum_{1 \leq i \leq j \leq n}^{\infty} x_{ij} \quad \text{instead of} \quad x = \sum_{1 \leq i \leq j \leq n}^{\infty} x_{ij}$$

- Better control over tags; modifying their appearance and showing only tags for equations that have been actually referenced

- Extensible symbols; more arrows and being able to automatically adjust their width, also extensible brackets and braces to be set under or over expressions

- New math environments for more flexible matrices, cases, improved multi-line formulas, and arrows between aligned formulas

- Less spacing for shorter inter text

- Declaration of paired delimiters

- Additional symbols such as a vertically centered colon, combinations of relation symbols with colons, shortcuts for auto-sized parentheses

- Techniques such as spreading lines in multi-line formulas, setting left sub- and superscripts, typesetting math within italic text, and producing multi-line fractions

Try to typeset these examples first without `mathtools`. You will notice some difficulties. Have a look into the documentation of this valuable package and find out which commands can be applied to achieve the aforementioned styles and alignments.

Pop quiz

1. Which environment produces a displayed formula?

   a. `\begin{math}` ... `\end{math}`

   b. `\[` ... `\]`

   c. `\(` ... `\)`

2. Which of these environments has to be used within math mode?

   a. `align`

   b. `aligned`

   c. `alignat`

3. The following commands may be used to insert text within math formulas. According to this chapter, which command would generally be the most appropriate?

   a. `\mbox`

   b. `\mathrm`

   c. `\textrm`

   d. `\text`

Summary

Now that we've got the necessary tools to write scientific texts, we are able to write complex math formulas, fine-tune math expressions, align and number equations, and access thousands of math symbols.

In the next chapter, we will not only deal further with math fonts, but also with fonts in general.

9
Using Fonts

The appearance of your text is significantly determined by the base font. You may choose a font that's especially clear and readable for a long piece of writing, or a fancy font for a greeting card. Your job application letter might use a very clear and serious font, whereas a mathematical article requires fonts with a lot of symbols and a text font that fits well with them.

Until now, we have been covering the logical properties of fonts. Though we always used the LaTeX standard font, we switched, for instance, from roman to sans-serif, or to typewriter, learned how to make text bold, italic, or slanted, but we never left the standard set of fonts.

In this chapter, we shall learn how to:

- ◆ Choose other sets of fonts for the whole document
- ◆ Load font packages for specific shapes

During this, we will also:

- ◆ See how to install additional fonts
- ◆ Look at various fonts and learn how to use them
- ◆ Speak about encoding of input text and of fonts in the output

Let's start discussing the encodings.

Preparing the encoding

Do you remember the ASCII code? All operating systems are able to understand it. However, when it comes to special characters like German umlauts or diacritics in general, currency symbols, and non-latin language characters, some systems work differently. We shall see how to deal with that.

Also, the output needs some kind of encoding. We shall figure out how to perfect that.

Time for action – directly using special characters

In a TeX document, we would like to use the German name of a street. It contains diacritics, so called umlauts. Let's check out how to make it work right.

1. Start a new document. Within a small parbox, write the text:

```
\documentclass{article}
\begin{document}
\parbox{3cm}{Meeting point: K\"onigsstra\ss e (King's Street)}
\end{document}
```

2. **Typeset** and have a first look:

```
Meeting        point:
Königsstraße
(King's Street)
```

3. Try **babel** instead! It provides shortcuts for German umlauts, if you state the ngerman option. Use "u for ü, a for ä, and s for ß":

```
\usepackage[ngerman]{babel}
...
\parbox{3cm}{Meeting point: K"onigsstra"se (King'sStreet)}
```

4. The output would be the same. Still the hyphenation remains as a problem: TeX cannot use hyphenation rules if macros are inside the words.

5. As babel is required for good hyphenation, we keep that. But we use **Unicode** encoding and another called **T1 font encoding**:

```
\documentclass{article}
\usepackage[ngerman]{babel}
\usepackage[utf8]{inputenc}
\usepackage[T1]{fontenc}
```

```
\begin{document}
\parbox{3cm}{Meeting point: Königsstraße (King's Street)}
\end{document}
```

6. **Typeset**. Now we've got the correct hyphenation:

> Meeting point: Kö-
> nigsstraße   (King's
> Street)

What just happened?

Firstly, using accent macros, or `babel` shortcut macros to construct diacritics, makes the TeX code less readable and hard to type. Furthermore, it creates a problem with hyphenation: for macros, hyphenation rules cannot be applied. That's why the justification has been so bad.

Two packages solve those problems:

- **inputenc** takes care of the input and translates special characters into TeX macros. It understands an option to mark the encoding. This depends on the editor and the operating system. As a rule of thumb: on Linux and Mac OS X, use `utf8`; on Windows, use `latin1`, except with TeXworks. Also, on Windows, TeXworks understands `utf8`, which is an implementation of Unicode.

- **fontenc** is responsible for the output encoding: TeX macros are translated into special characters. For instance, **ö** is no longer constructed of **o** and dots, but it's the glyph **ö** of the current font. Thus, hyphenation rules can be applied, the search feature of a PDF reader works with those characters, even copy and paste works fine. With standard encoding, copying and pasting **ö** would result in dots and an **o**.

> Unicode is an industry standard for text encoding, which hugely extends the ASCII code. Unicode supports more than 100,000 characters of many languages. It's become more and more supported by modern operating systems and editors.

To be able to benefit from those packages, you should know the encoding and you should use a font supporting the T1 encoding, also known as **Cork encoding**. Take it just as a name—we don't need to care further about encoding for now.

To see what happens with and without `fontenc`, use:

```
\showhyphens{Königsstraße}
```

Use it together with `babel` and `inputenc` and examine the log file. With standard font encoding, called `OT1`, you would read:

```
\OT1/cmr/m/n/10 K^^?onigsstra^^Ye
```

However, with T1 encoding, the log file would show:

```
\T1/cmr/m/n/10 Kö-nigs-straße
```

Installing additional fonts

TeX distributions usually install a lot of fonts. A package manager allows the installation of further fonts, like mpm with MiKTeX or tlmgr with TeX Live.

TeX Live includes only freely licensed fonts. Non-free fonts may be installed using a separate program. It's called **getnonfreefonts**. If it's not already installed with your version of TeX Live, you can download it from `http://www.tug.org/fonts/getnonfreefonts/`.

```
getnonfreefonts -l
```

This command lists all additionally available non-free fonts. If you wish to install a font, give its name as the argument or just type the following to install all available fonts:

```
getnonfreefonts -a
```

Type the following to get a brief documentation:

```
getnonfreefonts
```

`getnonfreefonts` would install the fonts in your TeX home directory. To make the fonts available for the complete local system, use `getnonfreefonts-sys` instead.

Progams ending with `-sys` work system wide. Further examples are: `updmap-sys`, which updates font map files, and `fmtutil-sys` for (re)creation of so-called format files. Such programs require administrator privileges, so run it as via sudo or as root on Linux or Mac OS X, on Windows use an administrator account if you ever need it. Normally the TeX distribution calls them automatically during installation and updates if required.

If you use T1 font encoding, which is strongly recommended, you might notice a decreased font quality. Don't worry this could happen if you don't have good T1 supporting standard fonts installed, thus bitmap fonts were used as replacement. It can be easily repaired by installing the **cm-super** package, which contains the European Computer Modern fonts, which are enhanced versions of the default Computer Modern fonts, with T1 support, in high quality. Alternatively, use one of the following fonts.

Choosing the main font

We shall explore some TeX fonts. To test fonts, we may use a **pangram**. This word has a Greek origin: "pan gramma" meaning "every letter". It stands for a sentence that uses every letter of the alphabet. Thus, a pangram is very convenient for displaying fonts.

Time for action – comparing Computer Modern to Latin Modern

We shall print out a very famous pangram phrase, once using the standard font Computer Modern and once using the Latin Modern font. Because Latin Modern is very similar to the standard font, but supports diacritics much better, while providing very high quality, it is widely considered that it will become the successor to the standard font. We will just compare serif and sans-serif typefaces:

1. Start a new document. Create a macro for the pangram plus numerals and use it:

   ```
   \documentclass{article}
   \newcommand{\pangram}[1][\rmfamily]{{#1 The quick brown fox jumps
   over the lazy dog. 1234567890}\par}
   \usepackage[T1]{fontenc}
   \begin{document}
   \large
   \pangram
   \pangram[\sffamily]
   \pangram[\ttfamily]
   \pangram[\itshape]
   \pangram[\slshape]
   \end{document}
   ```

2. **Typeset** and look at the font shapes:

   > The quick brown fox jumps over the lazy dog. 1234567890
   > The quick brown fox jumps over the lazy dog. 1234567890
   > The quick brown fox jumps over the lazy dog. 1234567890
   > *The quick brown fox jumps over the lazy dog. 1234567890*
   > *The quick brown fox jumps over the lazy dog. 1234567890*

3. Add this line to the preamble:

   ```
   \usepackage{lmodern}
   ```

4. **Typeset** again and compare:

> The quick brown fox jumps over the lazy dog. 1234567890
> The quick brown fox jumps over the lazy dog. 1234567890
> The quick brown fox jumps over the lazy dog.   1234567890
> *The quick brown fox jumps over the lazy dog. 1234567890*
> *The quick brown fox jumps over the lazy dog. 1234567890*

What just happened?

You might notice that the fonts are indeed looking the same. So, why use `lmodern`? Let's see.

Loading font packages

There are packages which provide fonts for all standards, shapes and weights, and more. Just load one to change all at once.

Latin Modern – a replacement for the standard font

Latin Modern has been designed to look like Computer Modern, but the encoding and manual fine-tuning has been improved. Latin Modern contains a huge amount of diacritic characters, whereas with Computer Modern such characters are built from letters and accents.

If you use `lmodern`, you don't need to install the big `cm-super` package anymore.

Kp-fonts – a full set of fonts

This font collection from the Johannes Kepler project provides Roman, sans-serif, and monospaced fonts as well as mathematics symbol fonts in different shapes and weights. Even bold extended and combinations like slanted Roman small caps are present.

Just load the package to use those fonts:

```
\usepackage{kpfonts}
```

The previous example will change to:

> The quick brown fox jumps over the lazy dog. 1234567890
> The quick brown fox jumps over the lazy dog. 1234567890
> The quick brown fox jumps over the lazy dog.   1234567890
> *The quick brown fox jumps over the lazy dog. 1234567890*
> *The quick brown fox jumps over the lazy dog. 1234567890*

Kp-fonts offers light versions with the same font metrics. They might look nice in print, but they aren't recommended for reading on screen.

To switch to the light font set, load the package with the option `light`:

```
\usepackage[light]{kpfonts}
```

The look will be different:

> The quick brown fox jumps over the lazy dog. 1234567890
> The quick brown fox jumps over the lazy dog. 1234567890
> The quick brown fox jumps over the lazy dog. 1234567890
> *The quick brown fox jumps over the lazy dog. 1234567890*
> *The quick brown fox jumps over the lazy dog. 1234567890*

Now let's look at specialized font packages.

Serif fonts

The standard serif font is called **Computer Modern Roman**. Latin Modern provides a very similar font, and you already know the Kp-fonts serif font. Further packages are specialized in serif fonts.

Times Roman

The package **mathptmx** defines a Times Roman text font. Additionally, it provides math support using suitable symbols of the standard Computer Modern symbol font together with Times Roman letters and more glyphs of further fonts. It supersedes the **times** package.

```
\usepackage{mathptmx}
```

> The quick brown fox jumps over the lazy dog. 1234567890

As you can see, Times is a very narrow font that's suitable for multi-column text like in newspapers, but not recommended for single-column text. Wide lines would be less readable.

The **txfonts** package is a good alternative, especially if you use Greek characters.

Charter

Charter is similar to Computer Modern, but a bit bolder:

```
\usepackage{charter}
```

> The quick brown fox jumps over the lazy dog. 1234567890

 For suitable math support, it's recommended to load the **mathdesign** package with the charter option: `\usepackage[charter]{mathdesign}`.

Palatino

The package `mathpazo` provides the Pazo math fonts, which are suitable for the Palatino text font. It may be loaded by:

```
\usepackage{mathpazo}
```

> The quick brown fox jumps over the lazy dog. 1234567890

Two options are recommended for `mathpazo`:

sc	"small caps"	Loads Palatino with "real" small caps instead of producing fake small caps by scaling capital letters.
osf	"old style figures"	Load Palatino with old style figures which would be used in text mode, not in math mode

Call `texdoc psnfss2e` to learn more. This opens the document *Using common PostScript fonts with LaTeX* by Walter Schmidt. Among others, it describes how to use `mathpazo` and `mathptmx`.

For Palatino, a slightly higher line spacing is recommended. So, a typical way to load Palatino together with Pazo is:

```
\usepackage[sc]{mathpazo}
\linespread{1.05}
```

Bookman

This is an old style serif font, provided by the **bookman** package:

```
\usepackage{bookman}
```

The quick brown fox jumps over the lazy dog. 1234567890

New Century Schoolbook

The **newcent** package provides this easy-to-read serif typeface:

```
\usepackage{newcent}
```

The quick brown fox jumps over the lazy dog. 1234567890

For a suitable math font, you might load the **fourier** math fonts: `\usepackage{fouriernc}`.

Concrete Roman

The Concrete font doesn't look well on screen, but offers a high quality in print. Just load the **concrete** package:

```
\usepackage{concrete}
```

The quick brown fox jumps over the lazy dog. 1234567890

Also for Concrete Roman, there's a matching math font package: `\usepackage{concmath}`.

Sans-serif fonts

We already talked about sans-serif fonts: they might be appropriate for headings, but many believe that running text with traditional serifs is much more readable.

If required, the main body font could be made sans-serif by `\renewcommand{\familydefault}{\sfdefault}`.

Helvetica

The classical sans-serif font Helvetica is simple and clean. You probably know a descendant: Arial.

```
\usepackage{helvet}
```

> The quick brown fox jumps over the lazy dog. 1234567890

Use the option `scaled` if the font looks too big, especially when used together with a serif font. For instance, if you also use `times` or `mathptmx`, you might write:

```
\usepackage[scaled=0.92]{helvet}
```

Bera Sans

Another nice sans-serif font is offered by **berasans**. It has been derived from Frutiger.

```
\usepackage{berasans}
```

> The quick brown fox jumps over the lazy dog. 1234567890

Computer Modern Bright

CM Bright has been derived from Computer Modern Sans Serif. The package **cmbright** provides this font together with a lighter typewriter font and a sans-serif math font.

```
\usepackage{cmbright}
```

> The quick brown fox jumps over the lazy dog. 1234567890

Kurier

Kurier is a bit different; look at the letter **g**:

```
\usepackage{kurier}
```

> The quick brown fox jumps over the lazy dog. 1234567890

Typewriter fonts

Typewriter, a.k.a. monospaced, fonts are widely used for source codes. We've seen it already.

Courier

Courier is a very wide running typewriter font, provided by the package with the same name.

```
\usepackage{courier}
```

```
The quick brown fox jumps over the lazy dog.  1234567890
```

Inconsolata

Inconsolata is a very nice monospaced font designed for source code listings. It's very readable and not as wide as Courier.

```
\usepackage{inconsolata}
```

```
The quick brown fox jumps over the lazy dog. 1234567890
```

Bera Mono

Bera Mono is another font of the Bera family, consisting of Bera Serif, Bera Sans, and Bera Mono. Originally, they had been developed under the name Bitstream Vera.

```
\usepackage{beramono}
```

```
The quick brown fox jumps over the lazy dog.  1234567890
```

Exploring the world of LaTeX fonts

Probably the best place to browse LaTeX fonts is **The LaTeX Font Catalogue**.
Visit `http://www.tug.dk/FontCatalogue/`:

The LaTeX Font Catalogue

[FRONT PAGE] [SERIF FONTS] [SANS SERIF FONTS] [TYPEWRITER FONTS] [CALLIGRAPHICAL AND HANDWRITTEN FONTS]
[UNCIAL FONTS] [BLACKLETTER FONTS] [OTHER FONTS] [FONTS WITH MATH SUPPORT] [ALL FONTS, BY CATEGORY]
[ALL FONTS, ALPHABETICALLY] [ABOUT THE LaTeX FONT CATALOGUE] [PACKAGES THAT PROVIDE MATH SUPPORT]

Calligraphical and Handwritten fonts

Augie
The quick brown fox jumps over the sleazy dog

Auriocus Kalligraphicus
The quick brown fox jumps over the sleazy dog

BrushScriptX-Italic
The quick brown fox jumps over the sleazy dog

Calligra
The quick brown fox jumps over the sleazy dog

French Cursive
The quick brown fox jumps over the sleazy dog

JD
The quick brown fox jumps over the sleazy dog

Jana Skrivana
The quick brown fox jumps over the sleazy dog

Lateinische Ausgangsschrift
The quick brown fox jumps over the sleazy dog

Lukas Svatba
The quick brown fox jumps over the sleazy dog

Österreichische Schulschrift
The quick brown fox jumps over the 'razy dog

PV Script
The quick brown fox jumps over the sleazy dog

Schwell
The quick brown fox jumps over the sleazy dog

Just choose a category, click on a font to see some examples, usage, and sources.

Pop quiz

1. Which package allows us to type ä, ü, ü, ß, and other such characters directly in the editor?

   a. `babel`

   b. `inputenc`

   c. `fontenc`

2. All but one of the following packages improves full justification. Which one does not?

   a. `babel`

   b. `microtype`

   c. `inputenc`

   d. `fontenc`

Summary

Now we are able to use different body text fonts. Our documents doesn't need to look like standard LaTeX writings anymore.

We learned about:

♦ Specifying the encoding for source and output

♦ Installing and choosing font sets and specific fonts

You probably know Truetype fonts: though they generally offer lower quality, there's a lot, and they may be used with **XeTeX**, **XeLaTeX**, **LuaTeX**, and **LuaLaTeX**. These compilers even support the OpenType font standard. All these compilers are supported by TeX Live and TeXworks as well which are enhanced versions of TeX, LaTeX respectively.

Now let's go back to LaTeX; we shall learn how to develop and manage bigger documents in the next chapter.

10

Developing Large Documents

The first chapter of this book claimed that LaTeX handles large documents easily. When you create extensive documents, you will notice that LaTeX keeps on doing its job reliably. For the computer, it doesn't matter how the source code is formatted. But for you, as the developer, it's important to keep your source document manageable. After all, it may consist of hundreds of pages with thousands of lines, possibly containing a lot of external pictures.

In this chapter, we shall learn how to:

- ◆ Split a document into several files
- ◆ Input and reuse pieces of code
- ◆ Swap out document-wide settings
- ◆ Compile just a part of a document
- ◆ Create a main document built upon sub-files

A bigger document requires a more complex structure, so we shall figure out how to:

- ◆ Design a title page
- ◆ Use Roman page numbers in the front matter
- ◆ Add a back matter without sectioning numbers

We will work it out while developing a book, using separate files for the preamble and for each chapter.

Bigger documents require more work, so we shall find out how to:

- ◆ Work more effective using templates
- ◆ Acquire and evaluate templates

That's a big step forward on the way to writing a thesis, a book, or an extensive report. Let's go on with it.

Splitting the input

Divide and conquer—this could be our motto now. We shall figure out how to break down a document into several sub-documents. Thus, while we are writing, we will be able to manage a huge project consisting of many chapters in separate files.

Firstly, we shall separate settings and body text by swapping out the preamble. Secondly, we shall write chapters in separate files and include them afterwards.

Time for action – swapping out preamble and chapter contents

We begin to write an extensive document about equations and equation systems. The result should be in the style of a thesis or a book. We can use the last example in *Chapter 8, TypingMath Formulas*, where we dealt with theorems concerning equations.

1. Create a new document. Inside this, load all the packages and specify the options, like we did in our preambles before. Use all the beneficial packages that we already learned about:

```
\usepackage[english]{babel}
\usepackage[utf8]{inputenc}
\usepackage[T1]{fontenc}
\usepackage{lmodern}
\usepackage{microtype}
\usepackage{natbib}
\usepackage{tocbibind}
\usepackage{amsmath}
\usepackage{amsthm}
\newtheorem{thm}{Theorem}[chapter]
\newtheorem{lem}[thm]{Lemma}
\theoremstyle{definition}
\newtheorem{dfn}[thm]{Definition}
```

2. Save this document under the name preamble.tex.

3. Start another new document and copy the contents of the chapter `Equations` in the theorem example of Chapter 8 into it:

```
\chapter{Equations}
\section{Quadratic equations}
\begin{dfn}
A quadratic equation is an equation of the form
\begin{equation}
  \label{quad}
  ax^2 + bx + c = 0
\end{equation}
where \( a, b \) and \( c \) are constants and \( a \neq 0 \).
\end{dfn}
```

4. Save this document under the name `chapter1.tex`.

5. Create another document for the next chapter, write something, and save it as `chapter2.tex`:

```
\chapter{Equation Systems}
\section{Linear Systems}
...
\section{Non-linear Systems}
...
```

6. Now we shall construct the top-level document. Create another file called `equations.tex`. This one starts with the `documentclass` and lists the preamble and the chapters for inclusion:

```
\documentclass{book}
\input{preamble}
\begin{document}
\tableofcontents
\include{chapter1}
\include{chapter2}
\end{document}
```

7. **Typeset** the document twice. Remember, this action is necessary to get the table of contents. For now, check the contents, to see if everything is in its place:

Contents

What just happened?

We constructed a top-level document that we called `equations.tex`. It's tempting to just call it `main.tex` or something similar. However, as this filename determines the name of the resulting PDF document, we chose a meaningful name.

This is the framework of our project. It's an ordinary LaTeX document, but we reduced it as much as possible and used two commands to import external `.tex` files:

- `\input` reads in another file, just as if it had been typed in.
- `\include` also reads in an external file, but automatically inserts `\clearpage` before and after.

The latter offers more to you, so let's have a closer look—we shall treat the simpler command first.

Including small pieces of code

The simplest command to read in a file is:

```
\input{filename}
```

When LaTeX encounters this command, it reads in the file with the name `filename` exactly as if its contents have been typed at that point. Accordingly, all commands in this file would be processed by the LaTeX compiler. You can even nest `\input`—this command may be used inside an included file.

If the filename doesn't have an extension, the extension `.tex` will be added automatically, thus `filename.tex` would be inserted. You may also specify a path, relative or absolute. As a backslash begins a command, use slashes / instead of backslashes \ in paths, also in Windows.

> Using relative path names makes moving and copying of a project easier.

Use `\input` if you wish to put your preamble into a separate file. Besides keeping your root document clean, a separate preamble can easily be copied and adjusted for use in another document.

However, simply splitting and inputting is not yet considered document management. For instance, though you could comment out selected `\input` lines for partial compilation, the numbering of pages, sections, and so on may be ruined, and cross-referencing to omitted document parts would fail.

There's a better way—so let's look at the other command.

Including bigger parts of a document

When it comes to including one or more pages, this command proves to be useful:

```
\include{filename}
```

The argument is treated the same way as `\input`. However, there are some important differences:

1. `\include` implicitly starts new pages.`\include{filename}` behaves like:

    ```
    \clearpage
    \include{filename}
    \clearpage
    ```

2. This makes it useful for page ranges such as chapters or sections. One consequence is that you may use `\include` only after `\begin{document}`.

3. `\include` cannot be nested. You could still use `\input` within included documents, though it might not be a good idea to complicate the structure further.

4. Most importantly, `\include` supports a mechanism of choosing which parts of the document you wish to compile—so we come to another command, namely, `\includeonly`.

Let's see how the latter command works.

Compiling parts of a document

Such a partial document, which is intended for \input or \include, cannot be compiled standalone: you need a root document that specifies the document class.

However, once you swapped out parts of the document using \include, while compiling your root document, you may specify which parts are actually included by this command:

```
\includeonly{file list}
```

The argument may be a comma-separated list of filenames. If a file, name.tex, is not specified within this argument, \include{name} would not insert this file but just behave like \clearpage instead. This allows excluding chunks or whole chapters from compiling. If you work on a huge document, this speeds up compilation if you choose to include just your current chapter while keeping the labels and references of the excluded chapter this way.

You may notice that LaTeX produces an .aux file for each included .tex file. LaTeX still reads in all those .aux files containing information such as chapter and page numbers. Of course, the included files need to be **Typeset** at least once. This way, cross-referencing the numbering of pages, chapters, sections, and so on will remain intact even if you temporarily exclude the chapters.

Try it out—add the following:

```
\includeonly{chapter2}
```

Add it to your preamble in equation.tex and compile. The result will be just the second chapter keeping the correct numbering.

You can use \include without \includeonly. Finally, when you finish your work, just comment the latter command out to typeset your complete document.

Creating front and back matter

In contrast to reports, books often begin with introductory material such as copyright information, a foreword, acknowledgements, or a dedication. This part, including the title page and the table of contents, is called the **front matter**.

At the end, a book might include an afterword and supporting material like a bibliography, and an index. This part is called the **back matter**.

The book class and some other classes like scrbook and memoir support this kind of sectioning directly. Often, desired consequences of this sectioning are differences in the numbering of pages and chapters. Let's see how it works.

Time for action – adding a dedication and an appendix

Our book shall begin with a dedication. The front matter shall consist of the table of contents, lists of tables and figures, and a dedication. All the pages of the front matter shall be numbered with Roman letters. Finally, we add an appendix providing supplementary proofs which we like to present outside the main chapters:

1. Create a file `dedication.tex`:

   ```
   \chapter{Dedication}
   This book is dedicated to one of the greatest mathematicians of
   all time: Carl Friedrich Gauss. Without him, this book wouldn't
   have been possible.
   ```

2. Create a file `proofs.tex`:

   ```
   \chapter{Proofs}
   ...
   ```

3. Extend the main file `equation.tex` by the highlighted lines:

   ```
   \documentclass{book}
   \input{preamble}
   \begin{document}
   \frontmatter
   \include{dedication}
   \tableofcontents
   \listoftables
   \listoffigures
   \mainmatter
   \include{chapter1}
   \include{chapter2}
   \backmatter
   \include{proofs}
   \nocite{*}
   \bibliographystyle{plainnat}
   \bibliography{tex}
   \end{document}
   ```

4. As you can see in the last highlighted line, we re-used the file `tex.bib` from *Chapter 7, Listing Contents and References*. **Typeset**, run **BibTeX**, and **Typeset** again. Check out the numbering within the table of contents:

Contents

What just happened?

We saw that the page number of the contents page has been typeset in Roman numbers. This applies to all front matter pages. Further, all the chapters in front and back matter are unnumbered even though we did not use the starred command `\chapter*`.

The three commands `\frontmatter`, `\mainmatter`, and `\backmatter` are responsible. They modified both the page and chapter numbering in the following way:

`\frontmatter`	Pages are numbered with lowercase Roman numbers.
	Chapters generate a table of contents entry but don't get a number.
`\mainmatter`	Pages are numbered with Arabic numbers.
	Chapters are numbered and produce a table of contents entry.

| `\backmatter` | Pages are numbered with Arabic numbers. |
| | Chapters generate a table of contents entry but don't get a number. |

Besides that, `\frontmatter` and `\mainmatter` call `\cleardoublepage`. `\backmatter` calls `\cleardoublepage` in openright mode, that is, if chapters start on right hand pages, otherwise it's using just \clearpage.

Like the `book` class, the classes `scrbook` and `memoir` provide the same command with very similar behavior.

Designing a title page

A good looking title page can quickly be created using `\maketitle` as we did in *Chapter 2, Formatting Words, Lines, and Paragraphs*. Document classes usually offer this command to generate a suitable pre-formatted title page. Alternatively, you could use a `titlepage` environment to freely design its layout. So, let's design a nice title page for our book of equations.

Time for action – creating a title page

In Chapter 2, we have already used some formatting commands such as `\centering` and font size and shape commands such as `\Huge` and `\bfseries` to format a title. We shall do it similarly within a `titlepage` environment:

1. Create a file `title.tex` with the following content:

```
\begin{titlepage}
\raggedleft
{\Large The Author\\[1in]}
{\large The Big Book of\\}
{\Huge\scshape Equations\\[.2in]}
{\large Packed with hundreds of examples and solutions\\}
\vfill
{\itshape 2011, Publishing company}
\end{titlepage}
```

2. Our final book shall have A5 format, and so shall the title page. Therefore, let's add that to the preamble:

```
\usepackage[a5paper]{geometry}
```

3. **Typeset**. Now we've got a title page:

The Author

The Big Book of

EQUATIONS

Packed with hundreds of examples and solutions

2011, Publishing company

What just happened?

The titlepage environment typesets its contents on a separate page. Though this title page will be numbered like any other page, the page number won't be printed on that page.

Within this environment, we used some basic LaTeX font commands to modify the font size and shape. By grouping with curly braces, we limited those commands. Line breaks like \\[.2in] just cause some more space before the following line. \vfill inserts an elastic vertical space which stretches as much as possible such that the page is filled. This way we put the last line off to the end of the page.

Note, this page has the same page dimensions as the other pages in the document. That means, in a double-sided book it's a right-hand page. Thus, you may notice unequal left and right margins, which might look undesirable especially, if your title is in the center. But the explanation is simple: this title page is intended to be an inner title, not the cover page. The inner title page is of course a right-hand page.

A cover page is a different thing. This should be one-side and thus it should have equa̲
and right margins. A cover page is often produced as a stand-alone document, printed ̲
separately. For a electronic document, you may use the **pdfpages** package or a tool like
pdfjam to merge PDF documents.

> The **titling** package offers features to create sophisticated title pages. To
> get some ideas how title pages may be designed, you could have a look at
> *Some Examples of Title Pages* by Peter Wilson, available from `texdoc`
> `titlepages` and at `http://ctan.org/pkg/titlepages`.

Working with templates

When we start to develop a document, we specify the document class, choose meaningful
packages and options, and create a frame for the contents. To repeat these steps for each
document would be too laborious.

If we plan to write several documents of the same type, we may create a **template**.
This could be a `.tex` file containing:

- ◆ Declaration of a suitable document class together with a set of meaningful options
- ◆ Routinely-used packages and packages which are most eligible for our document type
- ◆ A predefined layout for header, footer, and body of the text
- ◆ Self-made macros to ease our work
- ◆ A framework of sectioning commands, where we fill in the headings and the body text
- ◆ Or a framework containing `\include` or `\input` commands, for which we create the body text chunks later on.

While we improve our LaTeX knowledge, such templates might grow and become better
and more sophisticated. Many users publish their elaborate templates on the Internet.
Many universities, institutes, journals, and publishers do the same, offering templates for
documents such as thesis, papers, journal articles, and books, meeting their requirements.

You will find a collection of templates, arranged by document type such as thesis,
reports, letters, and presentations, accompanied by sample output, in a template
gallery at `http://texblog.net/latex/templates`.

You may download a template and start to fill in your text. Alternatively, you could start a
document with a pre-defined template offered by your editor. Let's try that.

Time for action – starting with a template

LaTeX editors often provide templates to start with. TeXworks offers some as well. So we shall test this feature, let's take one, open it, modify it, and **Typeset**:

1. In the TeXworks main menu, click on **File** and then on **New from template**. A window will open allowing you to choose a template:

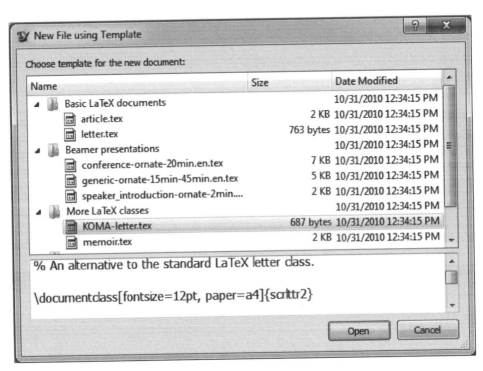

2. In the lower part of the window, you can read the template's source. Here's an example of KOMA-Script (KOMA-letter.tex):

```
% !TEX TS-program = pdflatex
% !TEX encoding = UTF-8 Unicode
% An alternative to the standard LaTeX letter class.
\documentclass[fontsize=12pt, paper=a4]{scrlttr2}
% Don't forget to read the KOMA-Script documentation, scrguien.pdf
\usepackage[utf8]{inputenc}
\setkomavar{fromname}{} % your name
\setkomavar{fromaddress}{Address \\ of \\ Sender}
\setkomavar{signature}{} % printed after the \closing
```

```
\renewcommand{\raggedsignature}{\raggedright} % make the signature
ragged right

\setkomavar{subject}{} % subject of the letter

\begin{document}
\begin{letter}{Name and \\ Address \\ of \\ Recipient}

\opening{}  % eg. Hello

\closing{} %eg. Regards

\end{letter}
\end{document}
```

3. Click on **Open**. Fill in the gaps and edit the filler text of the example:

```
\documentclass[fontsize=12pt, paper=a4]{scrlttr2}
\usepackage[utf8]{inputenc}
\setkomavar{fromname}{My name} % your name
\setkomavar{fromaddress}{Street, City}
\setkomavar{signature}{Name} % printed after the \closing
\setkomavar{subject}{Invoice 1/2011} % subject of the letter
\setkomavar{place}{Place}
\setkomavar{date}{January 1, 2011 }
\begin{document}
\begin{letter}{Customer Name\\ Street No. X \\ City \\ Zipcode}

\opening{To whom it may concern}  % eg. Hello

Text follows \ldots
\bigskip

\closing{With kind regards} %eg. Regards

\end{letter}
\end{document}
```

4. **Typeset**. Have a look at our test letter:

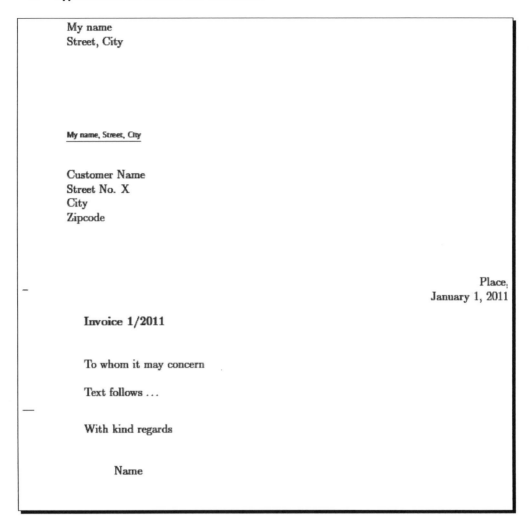

What just happened?

That was easy! We just opened the template and modified the filler texts. Reading the KOMA-Script documentation, we can learn that the command \setkomavar is used for specifying values for template parameters such as name, address, and subject. We used that to declare the date and the place as well.

Once we have written our personal data into this template, we may save that for later use instead of typing our address for each letter.

The KOMA-Script documentation (`texdoc scrguien`) describes the features of this letter class well. Using this, you would be able to create your personal professional-looking letter template for business use.

Imagine putting a job application letter created with the LaTeX layout and fonts together with microtype next to an application letter produced with some other word processing software—which one will use to create a better impression!

Have a go hero – evaluating and enhancing templates

While looking for LaTeX templates, code, and tips on the internet, you will find a lot of information and code. This code might be outdated and this information might be obsolete.

When you develop your own template, you probably would like to be sure to use the best packages, options, and solutions available today. How can you be sure?

Both questions can be answered by studying **l2tabu**. This is the common shortcut for *An essential guide to LaTeX2e usage*, a document focusing on obsolete commands and packages, which also demonstrates the most common and severe mistakes that LaTeX user's tend to make. As LaTeX has developed over many years, some packages and techniques are still available and described in online resources, but it may not be recommendable any more. Read this guide. It will help you to evaluate templates and code found on the Internet, but also to ensure that you produce optimal code yourself.

Just type:

```
texdoc l2tabuen
```

At the command prompt or visit `http://ctan.org/pkg/l2tabu`.

 To test a template, you may use the **blindtext** package and its command `\Blinddocument`. This command generates dummy content for a big document, which would demonstrate the output quality of a template. This package is required to load `babel`. If you don't like that, you may use the **lipsum** package instead.

Pop quiz

1. Which of these commands can be used both in the preamble and body text?

   a. `\input`

   b. `\include`

   c. `\includeonly`

2. All but one of the following commands may cause a page break. Which is the one that doesn't?

   a. `\include`

   b. `\input`

   c. `\mainmatter`

   d. `\begin{titlepage}`

Summary

The techniques we learned in this chapter will help us to develop and maintain bigger projects. Though enthusiastic users prefer LaTeX also to write small documents, many people learn LaTeX because they plan to write longer texts. However, splitting documents and the use of templates are useful as well for small writings such as letters—just think of header, footer, address fields, and so on.

In this chapter, we dealt with:

- Creating and managing large documents consisting of several files
- Structuring documents with front matter and back matter
- Designing a separate title page
- Using, creating, and evaluating templates

Now that we're able to develop and handle large documents, we shall see how to improve them further.

11

Enhancing Your Documents Further

By now, you're capable of writing structured documents in fine typographical quality. You are able to meet high expectations for classic publications such as books, journal articles, or a university thesis.

What about presentations? They are usually more colorful than prints. Perhaps you would like to publish your documents online? Such electronic documents or e-books usually require some kind of navigation.

This chapter shall provide us with tools for such enhancements. We shall figure out how to perform the following:

- ◆ Adding hyperlinks to the table of contents, lists of figures and tables, and to any cross-reference
- ◆ Creating bookmarks for a navigation bar
- ◆ Designing headings
- ◆ Using color with LaTeX

Let's implement this by using packages that are dedicated to these subjects.

Using hyperlinks and bookmarks

There's a sophisticated package called **hyperref**, which does nearly all basic hyper-linking automatically. That's great! Let's check it out.

Time for action – adding hyperlinks

We shall load the `hyperref` package and inspect its effect:

1. Open the file `preamble.tex`, which we used in the previous chapter. At its end, add this line:

   `\usepackage{hyperref}`

2. Save this document under the same name.

3. Open our book of equations from the previous chapter; we called it `equations.tex`.

4. **Typeset** the document twice without making any changes. Let's see how the document now appears!

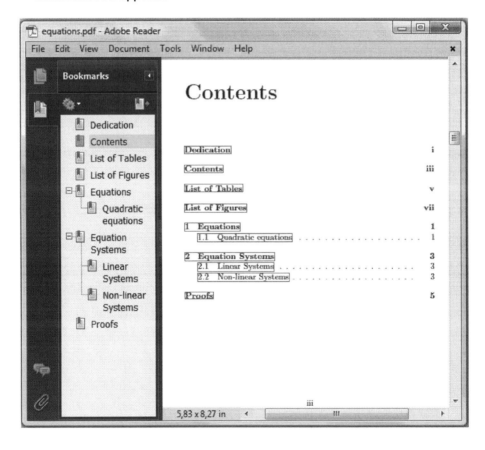

5. The **Chapter 1** looks like the following screenshot:

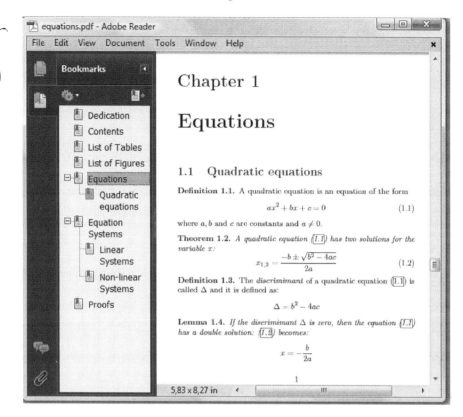

What just happened?

By just loading the `hyperref` package, our document has significantly changed:

- We got a bookmark bar, which allows us to easily navigate through the document.
- Each entry in the table of contents has become a hyperlink to the beginning of the corresponding chapter respectively. Hyperlinks are marked by red frames.
- All cross-references have become hyperlinks.

This is a great improvement for electronic versions of our documents! The print version would not be affected—neither the bookmarks nor those red frames would be printed.

If you don't like the default look of the hyperlinks, it can easily be changed by editing the options to `hyperref`. Let's try this.

Time for action – customizing the hyperlink appearance

We shall pass options to `hyperref` affecting the way hyperlinks are emphasized:

1. Open the file `preamble.tex` again. This time, specify the options for `hyperref`:

    `\usepackage[colorlinks=true,linkcolor=red]{hyperref}`

2. Save this document, go to the main document `equations.tex`, and compile it twice. The table of contents is changed:

Contents

What just happened?

Instead of frames, we now got a red color for emphasized links. The color can be seen in a printed document.

`hyperref` offers ways to set up the options. The first one we used is:

`\usepackage[key=value list]{hyperref}`

Alternatively, we could just write `\usepackage{hyperref}` and set the options afterwards:

`\hypersetup{key=value list}`

Our example would do the same with:

```
\hypersetup{colorlinks=true,linkcolor=red}
```

These methods may be combined. Here's a selection of especially useful options:

Option	Type	Default	Effect
draft	boolean	false	Turns off all hypertext options
final	boolean	true	Turns all hypertext options on
debug	boolean	false	Prints extra diagnostic messages into the log file
raiselinks	boolean	true	Fits the height of links to the real size of objects such as text or graphics
breaklinks	boolean	false	Links may be broken across lines (true by default with pdftex)
pageanchor	boolean	true	Gives pages implicit anchors, needed for the index
backref	boolean	false	Adds back links to bibliography items
hyperindex	boolean	true	Links page numbers in the index, the pageanchor option should be set
hyperfootnotes	boolean	true	Converts footnote markers into hyperlinks
linktocpage	boolean	false	In TOC, LOF and LOT page numbers would be linked instead of the text
colorlinks	boolean	false	Writes links and anchors in color, depending on the type of link such as page references, URLs, file references, and citations
linkcolor	color	red	Color for internal links
anchorcolor	color	black	Color for anchor texts
citecolor	color	green	Color for citations of bibliography items
filecolor	color	cyan	Color for links to local files
urlcolor	color	magenta	Color for URLs
frenchlinks	boolean	false	Uses small caps for links instead of color
bookmarks	boolean	true	Writes bookmarks for the Acrobat Reader
bookmarksopen	boolean	false	Shows all bookmarks in an expanded view
bookmarksnumbered	boolean	false	Includes the section number in bookmarks
pdfstartpage	text	1	Specifies which page would be shown when the PDF file is opened

There are many more options for customizing link borders, PDF page size, anchors, bookmark appearance, and PDF page display style. The `hyperref` documentation lists them all. Have a look at it—it's a really valuable document! Many PDF and hypertext-related questions in web forums just arise because users did not know that they have already got an extensive manual on their own hard disk, namely, `texdoc hyperref`.

`hyperref` supports more than just **pdfLaTeX**, which most users choose today. If you, for instance, use XeTeX, you may give the `xetex` option to `hyperref`. If you typeset to DVI and use `dvips` to convert to Postscript and to PDF afterwards, use the `dvips` option. There are more than a dozen of such driver options; you can read about those backend drivers in the manual. If no driver is specified, the `hypertex` driver would be used, which is, in most times, the appropriate driver.

Some text options allow us to specify the metadata of PDF files, such as the author name, title, and keywords. This information is shown if you inspect the document properties with the PDF reader. Even more beneficial, Internet search engines are able to find and classify your PDF document according to this meta information. If you publish on the Internet, this improves the chances of the readers finding your publication!

Time for action – editing PDF metadata

We shall add PDF metadata to our book of equations. Besides choosing sensible keywords, we will set the title and the author's name. During development, why not choose the great mathematician to whom we dedicated our book. So, let's do it!

1. Open the file `preamble.tex` and add the following lines:

```
\hypersetup{pdfauthor={Carl Friedrich Gauss},
    pdftitle={The Big Book of Equations},
    pdfsubject={Solving Equations and Equation Systems},
    pdfkeywords={equations,mathematics}}
```

2. Save that file. Go to the main document `equations.tex` and **Typeset**. Let's inspect the document properties! So, if you use the Acrobat Reader, click on the **File** menu and then **Properties**:

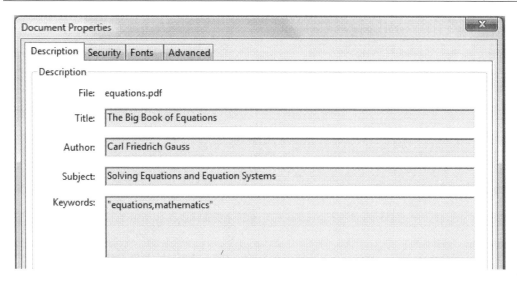

What just happened?

Well, that was easy. We provided all document properties by using the `hyperref` option. We just had to take care to enclose each entry in curly braces.

The most commonly used meta-information options are:

Option	PDF meta-information field
`pdftitle`	Sets the title
`pdfauthor`	Sets the author
`pdfsubject`	Sets the subject
`pdfcreator`	Sets the creator
`pdfproducer`	Sets the producer
`pdfkeywords`	Sets the keywords

As `hyperref` redefines many commands of other packages in order to add hyperlink functionality, it has to be loaded after those packages. A good rule of thumb is to load the package as the last package in your preamble. A few packages are exceptions to that rule, namely, `algorithm`, `amsrefs`, `bookmark`, `chappg`, `cleveref`, `glossaries`, `hypernat`, `linguex`, `sidecap`, and `tabularx` are known to be exceptions.

Creating hyperlinks manually

As `hyperref` already creates links for nearly all kinds of references, it's rarely necessary to create links by oneself. But of course, it's possible. `hyperref` provides user commands for that:

- ◆ `\href{URL}{text}` makes `text` to a hyperlink, which points to the URL address
- ◆ `\url{URL}` prints the URL and links it
- ◆ `\nolinkurl{URL}` prints the URL without linking it
- ◆ `\hyperref{label}{text}` changes `text` to a hyperlink, which links to the place where the label has been set, thus to the same place `\ref{label}` would point to
- ◆ `\hypertarget{name}{text}` creates a target `name` for potential hyperlinks with `text` as the anchor
- ◆ `\hyperlink{name}{text}` makes `text` to a hyperlink, which points to the target `name`

Sometimes you might need just an anchor, for instance, if you use `\addcontentsline`, which creates a hyperlinked TOC entry, but there hasn't been a sectioning command setting the anchor. The TOC entry would point to the previously set anchor, thus to the wrong place! The command `\phantomsection` comes to the rescue; it's just setting an anchor like `\hypertarget{}{}` would do. It's mostly used this way for creating a TOC entry for the bibliography while linking to the correct page as follows:

```
\cleardoublepage
\phantomsection
\addcontentsline{toc}{chapter}{\bibname}
\bibliography{name}
```

This tiny command has been the answer to a lot of questions on online forums. Well, not everybody reads manuals.

Creating bookmarks manually

Your bookmark panel might already be full of chapter and section entries. But what if you wish to add bookmarks by yourself? That's been foreseen.

`\pdfbookmark[level]{text}{name}` creates a bookmark with `text` at the optionally specified `level`. The default level is 0. Treat `name` just as `\label`; it should be unique because it stands for the internal anchor.

You can also create bookmarks relative to the current level:

- ◆ `\currentpdfbookmark{text}{name}` puts a bookmark at the current level
- ◆ `\belowpdfbookmark{text}{name}` creates a bookmark one level deeper
- ◆ `\subpdfbookmark{text}{name}` increases the level and creates a bookmark at that deeper level

The `bookmarks` package offers more features for customizing bookmarks. Moreover, it requires just one compiler run in contrary to `hyperref`; thus its use is recommended.

Math formulas and special symbols in bookmarks

Due to PDF restrictions, math and special symbols cannot be used in PDF bookmarks. This might cause a problem, for instance, in sectioning commands with math symbols in their title or font commands which would be passed to the bookmark. There's a solution though:

```
\texorpdfstring{string with TeX code}{text string}
```

It returns the argument depending on the context to avoid such problems. It can be used like this:

```
\section{The equation \texorpdfstring{$y=x^2$}{y=x\texttwosuperior}}
```

That may come handy sooner than you might guess.

If you load hyperref with `unicode` option, you could use Unicode characters in bookmarks, such as in `\section{\texorpdfstring{$\gamma$}{\textgamma} radiation}`.

Benefitting from other packages

There's a huge amount of LaTeX packages. For nearly every possible task, somebody has written a package either solving or supporting it. Nearly all packages are stored on CTAN. But how can we find what we need? Let's have a look at an online catalogue.

Time for action – visiting the TeX Catalogue Online

We shall browse for PDF-related packages in the online catalogue to find something that's useful for us:

1. Open your favorite Internet browser and go to the address `http://texcatalogue.sarovar.org/`:

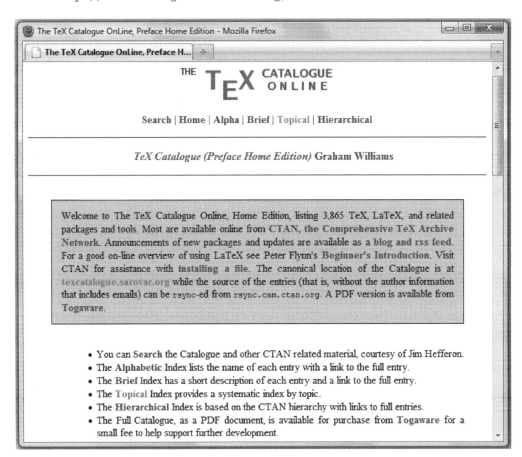

2. We can see different indexes. The systematic topical index is often the most useful when you're looking for some subject, So, let's click on **Topical**. We get a huge list. In the overview, click on **Creating PDF documents**. Then it scrolls down to that category:

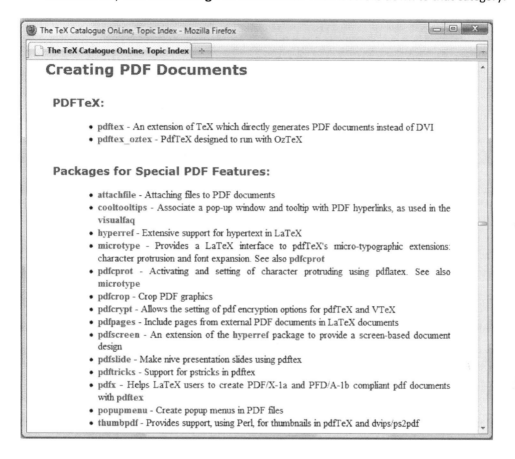

3. Well, we found some packages! **cooltooltips** sounds fancy, so let's click it:

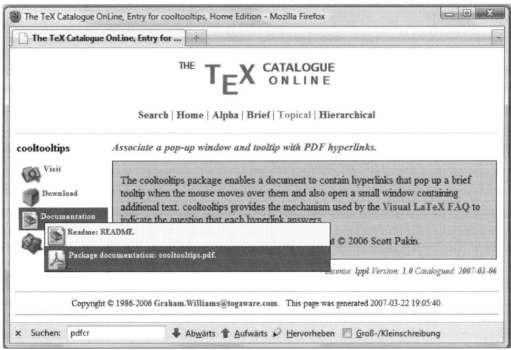

4. Now we may read the brief description and open the documentation to learn more about that package.

What just happened?

The TeX Catalogue is a really valuable source. Its category view is especially useful if you are looking for a package but don't know its exact name. It's also an easy way to locate and download documentation if texdoc doesn't work for you.

So, you found `cooltooltips`, and now you can enhance your PDF document by mouse-over effects and pop-ups.

If the package you desire is not yet on your computer, then you need to install it.

Time for action – installing a LaTeX package

The pretty new `biblatex` package is often not yet installed. So, let's catch up on it!

1. Go to the **Start** menu and look for the **TeX Live Manager**:

2. Launch the **TeX Live Manager** with a mouse click:

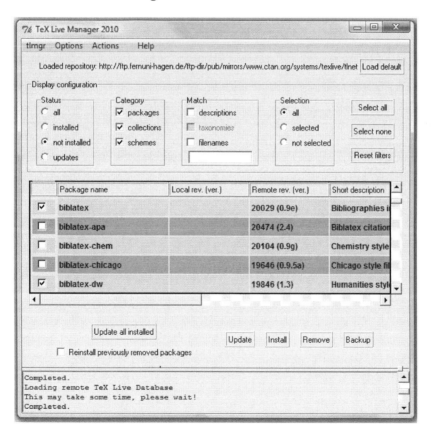

If you installed TeX Live on Linux or without a **Start** menu group, you may start the **TeX Live Manager** at the command prompt. The name of the executable file is **tlmgr**. So, type `tlmgr -help` to get a summary of the available options and actions.

3. In the menu, click on **tlmgr** and then **Load default net repository** to get the most recent repository. The status bar at the bottom will inform you about the success.

4. Choose the package you desire! Perhaps filter the **Status** to make it easier. Then click on **Install**. Done!

What just happened?

Though you could just download packages to your computer, it's very recommendable to use a package manager instead. That's what we did! With TeX Live, use the **TeX Live Manager** a.k.a. **tlmgr**, and with MiKTeX, use the **MiKTeX package manager** a.k.a. **mpm**. If you use Linux and installed TeX Live using your operating system's repositories instead of **tlmgr**, then use your OS package manager for adding LaTeX packages; this might be **Synaptic**, **aptitude**, **apt-get**, **YaST**, **rpm**, or any other, depending on your kind of Linux distribution—you will know it for sure if you use Linux.

Package managers are usually easy to handle: choose, install, or update plus some further useful features. A manual installation could be hard, at least if a package consists of more than a `.sty` file—there might be documented source files needing compilation or various font files requiring some know-how regarding the TeX filesystem structure. The **UK TeX FAQ**, listed among the online resources in the last chapter, offers detailed information about package installation.

Use a package manager, if available, so that you are on the safe side.

Designing headings

In *Chapter 2, Formatting Words, Lines, and Paragraphs*, we encountered the problem of customizing headings. There has to be a consistent way to modify the font of the headings, their spacing, and their numbering for the whole document. Fortunately, there's a handy package for that, it's called **titlesec**. We shall use it now.

Time for action – designing chapter and section headings

We return to our example that we used in this chapter. Our goal is to create centered headings. The font size should be smaller, further we reduce the space above and below. Finally, we switch to a sans serif font which is a good choice for bold headings:

1. Open the file `preamble.tex` which we already used in this chapter. Insert this line to load the `titlesec` package:

```
\usepackage{titlesec}
```

2. Add this command to specify layout and font of the chapter headings:

```
\titleformat{\chapter}[display]
  {\normalfont\sffamily\Large\bfseries\centering}
  {\chaptertitlename\ \thechapter}{0pt}{\Huge}
```

3. Now define the section heading by calling `\titleformat` again:

```
\titleformat{\section}
  {\normalfont\sffamily\large\bfseries\centering}
  {\thesection}{1em}{}
```

4. Add this line to adjust the chapter headings spacing:

```
\titlespacing*{\chapter}{0pt}{30pt}{20pt}
```

5. Save `preamble.tex` and **Typeset** the main document `equation.tex`. Let's see how the headings have changed:

Chapter 1

Equations

1.1   Quadratic equations

Definition 1.1. A quadratic equation is an equation of the form

$$ax^2 + bx + c = 0 \qquad (1.1)$$

where a, b and c are constants and $a \neq 0$.

What just happened?

We loaded the package `titlesec`, which provides a comprehensive interface for customizing headings, of parts, chapters, sections, and even smaller sectioning parts down to subparagraphs.

In step 2 we chose displayed style, which means that numbering and actual title use separate lines. Firstly, we used `\normalfont` to switch to the base font, to be on the safe side. By `\sffamily` we switched to sans-serif font, chose size and weight and finally declared that the complete heading shall be centered. In step 3 we did this very similar, we just omitted `[display]` to get number and title on the same line.

To understand the remaining arguments, have a look at the `\titleformat` definition:

```
\titleformat{cmd}[shape]{format}{label}{sep}{before}[after]
```

The meaning of the arguments is as follows:

- cmd stands for the sectioning command we redefine, that is, `\part`, `\chapter`, `\section`, `\subsection`, `\subsubsection`, `\paragraph`, or `\subparagraph`

- shape specifies the paragraph shape. The effect of the possible values is:
  - display puts the label into a separate paragraph
  - hang creates a hanging label like in standard sections and is the default option
  - runin produces a run-in title like `\paragraph` does by default
  - leftmargin sets the title into the left margin
  - rightmargin puts the title into the right margin
  - drop wraps the text around the title, requires care to avoid overlapping
  - wrap works like drop but adjusts the space for the title to match the longest text line
  - frame works like display and additionally frames the title

- format may contains commands which will be applied to label and text of the title.
- label prints the label, that is, the number.
- sep is a length which specifies the separation between label and title text. With display option, it's the vertical separation, with frame option it means the distance between text and frame, otherwise it's the horizontal separation between label and title.

- ◆ `before` can contain code which comes before the title body. The last command of it is allowed to take an argument, which should then be the title text.
- ◆ `after` can contain code which comes after the title body.

That's a lot of options! Have a look at the `titlesec` documentation to learn even more.

We used the `titlesec` command `\chaptertitlename`, which is `\chaptername` by default, that is, it defaults to `Chapter`. In an appendix, it changes to `\appendixname`.

By the remaining command we customized the spacing of all chapter headings:

`\titlespacing*{cmd}{left}{beforesep}{aftersep}[right]`

- ◆ `left` works differently depending on the shape: with drop, `leftmargin` and `rightmargin` it's the title width. With `wrap`, it's the maximum width. With `runin`, it sets the indentation before the title. Otherwise it increases the left margin. If negative, it decreases, which means overhanging into the margin.
- ◆ `beforesep` sets the vertical space before the title.
- ◆ `aftersep` sets the separation between title and text. With `hang`, `block`, and `display`, it's has a vertical meaning. With `runin`, `drop`, `wrap`, `leftmargin`, and `rightmargin`, it's a horizontal width. Again, it may be a negative value.
- ◆ `right` increases the right margin when `hang`, `block` or `display` shape is used.

If you use the star, the indentation of the following paragraph would be removed as you know of sections. With drop, wrap and run-in the starred version has no meaning.

In our example, we avoided the indentation of the paragraph which follows a chapter heading, and we specified a space of 30 pt before the heading and 20 pt after it. That's less than before, standard classes use 50 pt above chapter headings.

It's very recommendable to read the `titlesec` documentation to get the most out of it. In its appendix, it shows how the headings in standard classes would be defined by `\titleformat` and `\titlesec`. That's a great point to start off by copying these definitions and beginning to modify them.

Using sans-serif headings is very common today. They don't have such a heavy and ancient appearance like bold serif headings. However, serif text offers the best readability for body test. Now it's up to you to choose—you've got the tools!

Coloring your document

We could enhance our texts further by colors. We didn't deal with it yet, because most people use LaTeX for writing serious books and articles, or letters where too much color may harm the appearance. But why not try something fancy? For instance, diagrams and tables in presentations are often colorful.

We just need to load the **color** package:

```
\usepackage{color}
```

From now on, we have to use a command to set the text color:

- ♦ `\color{name}` is a declaration that switches to the color `name`. Just try `\color{blue}`.
- ♦ `\textcolor{name}{text}` is the corresponding command form, coloring just `text`. That's like `{\color{name}}`, not new for you.

The package offers the command `\definecolor`. Use this to mix your own colors. You may read it in the documentation of the `color` package or of the `graphicx` package, if needed.

But much better is to use the **xcolor** package, which extends the color facilities. It offers a lot of readily mixed colors; you just need to call it by its name and it has powerful capabilities regarding color definition. If only for the huge color samples table, look at the package documentation.

Have a go hero – creating colorful tables

Now you're able to do everything with the color you like. Now think of diagrams in financial journals or tables of sports tournaments using rounded corners, shading, and fading. Is LaTeX capable of that? Yes, it is!

The following presentation slide has been created with LaTeX— can you believe it?

Rank	Distribution	Hits	
1	Ubuntu	2114	▼
2	Fedora	1451	▲
3	Mint	1297	–
4	OpenSUSE	1228	▲
5	Debian	910	▼
6	Mandriva	907	▲
7	PCLinuxOS	764	▲
8	Puppy	738	▲
9	Sabayon	671	▲
10	Arch	625	▼

Linux distribution ranking, 26th August 2009

Data by DistroWatch.com, spanning over the last 6 months, hits per day.

The code for this presentation can be found on `http://texblog.net` and in the book's example archive.

Optionally, you can have a look at this differently designed table, before we come to its source code:

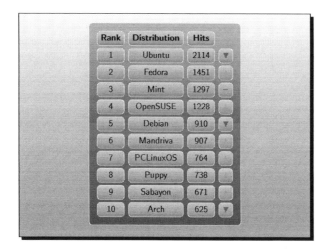

The document is not very long, but it contains some new subjects:

```
\documentclass[svgnames]{beamer}
\setbeamertemplate{background canvas}[vertical shading]%
[top=blue!1,bottom=blue!30]
\setbeamertemplate{navigation symbols}{}
\usepackage{tikz}
\usetikzlibrary{matrix}
\newcommand{\up}{\textcolor{YellowGreen}{$\blacktriangle$}}
\newcommand{\down}{\textcolor{Red}{$\blacktriangledown$}}
\newcommand{\const}{\textcolor{darkgray}{\textbf{--}}}
\newcommand{\head}[1]{\textbf{#1}}
\newenvironment{matrixtable}[4]{%
\begin{tikzpicture}[matrix of nodes/.style={
execute at begin cell=\node\bgroup\strut,
execute at end cell=\egroup;}]
\matrix (m) [matrix of nodes,top color=blue!20,
bottom color=blue!80,draw=white,
nodes={draw,top color=blue!10,bottom color=blue!35,
draw,innersep=2pt,minimum height=3.1ex},
columnsep=1ex,row sep=0.6ex,inner sep=2ex,
roundedcorners,column 1/.style={minimum width=#1},
column 2/.style={minimum width=#2},
column 3/.style={minimum width=#3},
column 4/.style={minimum width=#4}]}%
{;\end{tikzpicture}}
\begin{document}
\begin{frame}[fragile,bg=lightgray]
\begin{center}
\begin{matrixtable}{1.2cm}{2.4cm}{1.2cm}{0.6cm}{
\head{Rank} & \head{Distribution} & \head{Hits} & \\
1 & Ubuntu & 2114 & \down \\
2 & Fedora & 1451 & \up \\
3 & Mint & 1297 & \const \\
4 &OpenSUSE& 1228 & \up \\
5 &Debian& 910 & \down \\
6 &Mandriva& 907 & \up \\
7 &PCLinuxOS& 764 & \up \\
8 & Puppy & 738 & \up \\
9 & Sabayon & 671 & \up \\
10 & Arch & 625 & \down \\
}
\end{matrixtable}
\end{center}
\end{frame}
\end{document}
```

Indeed, this looks a bit different than what we've done before. However, as you are a hero, you may check out the magic behind it! We used the following:

- The **beamer** class—this is a feature-rich presentation class for producing slides. It offers many predesigned colorful themes. More can be found on the Internet. There's a user's guide with many examples on more than 200 pages—and it's probably already on your hard drive! texdoc, you know.

- The **xcolor** package—the `beamer` class loads it implicitly, so we did not have to do this. We just gave beamer the `svgnames` option to pass it along to `xcolor`, which provides us with a color naming scheme.

- The **TikZ** package—that's a jewel! `TikZ` is an enormously capable package for creating graphics. Our small example just used a tiny feature of it: a matrix of nodes. The manual is twice as large as the `beamer` documentation. However, this benefits you—a free book about producing graphics with LaTeX. You can learn to create diagrams, charts, plots, trees, and arbitrary graphics using coordinates, nodes, shapes, layers, transparency, shadings, transformations, and shadings.

That's heavy stuff. But check it out—you will see that there's more in the LaTeX world than dry scientific or technical texts!

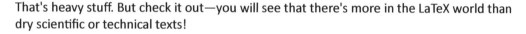

Pop quiz

1. By which command could you create an anchor, to which a hyperlink can point?

   a. `\href`

   b. `\hyperlink`

   c. `\hyperref`

   d. `\hypertarget`

   e. `\hypersetup`

2. According to the text, which characters are allowed in bookmarks?

   a. only letters

   b. only letters and numbers

   c. only letters and Unicode characters including numbers

   d. letters and math symbols without line breaks

Summary

This chapter started with easy and comfortable hyper-linking and ended with an outlook to a very powerful graphic package, namely, `TikZ`.

By reading this chapter, we are now capable of:

- Enhancing our document with a hypertext structure
- Designing visually different styles for different types of links
- Providing a navigation bar for the reader by adding bookmarks
- Editing the PDF metadata
- Designing font and layout of headings
- Adding color to our texts

Now that we've got most of the tools we need for successful writing, what's ahead is specialized advanced classes and packages. However, this won't be difficult for you. Since you have mastered the fundamental LaTeX challenges, you're now able to use any other package together with reading its documentation. The vast majority of classes and packages are very well documented. And there are no secrets—everything is open source.

During our work, we may encounter errors and warnings. That's common, also for advanced LaTeX users. The following chapter will prepare us for troubleshooting.

12
Troubleshooting

During typesetting, it may happen that LaTeX prints out warning messages. It's even possible that LaTeX doesn't produce the desired output but shows error messages instead. That's absolutely normal and can be caused, for example, by small typos in command names or by unbalanced braces. Even professional LaTeX typesetters have to deal with errors—they just know how to do it efficiently.

Don't worry too much about the potential errors—let LaTeX check it for you. Then you just need to do the corrections at the places pointed out by LaTeX.

This chapter prepares us to:

◆ Understand error messages and to fix them

◆ Deal with warnings

◆ Use all the information LaTeX produces during typesetting

Let's first tackle the error handling.

Understanding and fixing errors

If the LaTeX typesetting engine encounters a problem, it will issue an error message. This is informative and it's intended to help you. So, read the messages carefully. Besides the line number, where the error occurred, a diagnostic message is also provided.

Concentrate on the very first error message. If you continue typesetting, further errors might be just a consequence of the first one that confused the compiler.

Time for action – interpreting and fixing an error

Let's create a tiny test document. For sure you know those "Hello world!" printing programs—we shall write one in LaTeX. Though we are used to the uncommon capitalization used in the words TeX and LaTeX, we will now try if \Latex works as well.

1. Create a new document containing these lines:

```
\documentclass{article}
\begin{document}
\Latex\ says: Hello world!
\end{document}
```

2. **Typeset**. LaTeX will stop and print out the following message:

! Undefined control sequence.

l.3 \Latex

\ says: Hello world!

3. Click on the cancel icon in the upper-left corner of TeXworks to stop typesetting. Go to line 3, correct \Latex into \LaTeX and **Typeset** again. Now LaTeX produces output without an error:

> LaTeX says: Hello world!

What just happened?

LaTeX commands are case-sensitive. Because we did not respect that, LaTeX had to deal with a macro called \Latex, which is just unknown. As a command is also called a **control sequence**, we got the error **Undefined control sequence**.

If TeX encounters an error, it stops typesetting and asks for user input. You could press the *Enter* key to continue typesetting though or cancel and correct the error immediately.

Let's analyze the three parts of the error output:

◆ An error message begins with an exclamation mark, which is followed by a short description of the problem.

◆ Then LaTeX prints out the number of the input line where the error was raised and the part of the line until the problem occurred.

◆ After a line break, the remaining part of the input line is printed out.

So you are not on your own without a clue! LaTeX tells you exactly:

- The kind of error
- The exact location of the error

Most editors show you the line number or allow jumping to the line number you enter. As you are now at the problematic place, you only need to know why LaTeX complains—if you don't see it yourself immediately. Leslie Lamport's LaTeX book and documentation lists error messages alphabetically together with some background information. You may choose that for look-up.

We shall now have a closer look at frequent TeX and LaTeX error messages. In this book, let's do that by topic.

Using commands and environments

Command names might easily be misspelled or just misused. Let's check out LaTeX's common complaints.

- **Undefined control sequence**: As in our example, TeX stumbled across an unknown command name. There are two possible reasons:
  - The command name might be misspelled. In that case, you just need to correct it and restart the typesetting.
  - The command name is correct, but it's defined by a package you didn't load. Add a `\usepackage` command to your preamble, which loads that package.

- **Environment undefined**: That's similar to **Undefined control sequence**, but this time you began an environment which is unknown. Again, this may be caused by misspelling or by a missing package—you know how to correct it.

- **Command already defined**: This happens when you create a command with a name that's already used, for example, with `\newcommand` or `\newenvironment`. Just choose a different name. If you really would like to override that command, use `\renewcommand` or `\renewenvironment` instead.

- **Missing control sequence inserted**: A control sequence has been expected but didn't appear. A common cause is using `\newcommand`, `\renewcommand`, or `\providecommand`, but not specifying a command name as its first argument.

- **\verb illegal in command argument**: The `\verb` command for producing verbatim text is a delicate one; it cannot be used within arguments of commands or environments. The **examplep** package offers commands for using verbatim text in such places.

Writing math formulas

The most frequent mistake is forgetting to enter math mode. The first of the following errors would be raised then:

- **Missing $ inserted**: There are a lot of commands which may only be used in math mode. Just think of symbols; most of them require math mode. If TeX is not in math mode, but encounters such a symbol, it stops and prints out that error. Usually it can be repaired by inserting that missing $, possibly several. Remember that you cannot use paragraph breaks inside a math expression. This means that blank lines within a math expression are illegal; the math mode has to be ended before the blank line.

- **Command invalid in math mode**: Some commands are not applicable within math formulas. In that case, use the command outside the math mode.

- **Double subscript, double superscript**: Two subsequent subscripts, superscripts respectively such as in `$a_n_1$` cannot be typeset. To correct that, group by braces, like in `$a_{n_1}$` or `$a_{n_{1}}$`.

- **Bad math environment delimiter**: This can be a consequence of illegally nesting math mode. You must not start math mode if you are already inside math mode, for example, don't use \ [within an `equation` environment. Similarly, you must not end the math mode before you started it. Ensure that your math mode delimiters match and that braces are balanced.

Handling the preamble and document body

The preamble is intended for document-wide settings like class, packages, options, and command definitions. After the preamble has ended, output may be produced in the document body. If these rules are broken, one of the following errors would occur:

- **Missing \begin{document}**: It seems to be obvious; you might have forgotten the command `\begin{document}`. But the error may occur even if you did not forget that! In that case, there may be a problem in the preamble. Specifically, if a character or a command within the preamble produces output, that error would be raised. Just remember: output is not allowed before `\begin{document}`.

- **Can be used only in preamble**: This error message belongs to a command which is only allowed to be used in the preamble, not after `\begin{document}`. Move that command upwards into your preamble, or remove it. For example, `\usepackage` can only be used in the preamble.

♦ **Option clash for package**: An option clash happens if you load a package twice but with different options. If you did that, it's usually better to reduce it to one `\usepackage` call with the desired options. But the cause might be hidden. Imagine that a class or a package implicitly loads a certain package together with some options. If you want to load the package too but with different options, there's a problem!

> You could try to fix an option clash by omitting reloading the package while specifying the desired options to the document class. Remember, class options are inherited by packages. Some packages and classes even offer commands to set options after loading. For example, the `hyperref` package provides `\hypersetup{options}`, and similarly the `caption` package offers `\captionsetup`. KOMA classes support such late options and are described in their manual.

Working with files

The most common errors regarding files are mistakes in filename or path. Then the first of the following errors would be raised:

♦ **File not found**: LaTeX tried to open a file that doesn't exist. Possibly you:

   ❑ Used `\include` or `\input` to include a `.tex` file but a file with the specified name doesn't exist

   ❑ Tried to use a non-existing package or misspelled the package's name. Packages can be recognized by the file extension `.sty`.

   ❑ Used a document class that doesn't exist or just has a different name. Class files have the extension `.cls`.

   Well, just correct the filename in your input document or rename the file.

♦ **\include cannot be nested**: We learned in *Chapter 10, Developing Large Documents*, that we cannot use `\include` within files that are being included by themselves. Instead, use `\input` within such files.

Creating tables and arrays

Admittedly, `tabular` and `array` environments don't have the simplest syntax. Those & and \\ might easily be misplaced, which causes LaTeX to complain. Further, we have to be careful with the formatting arguments. Let's start with the arguments to the environment:

- **Illegal character in array arg**: In the argument to a `tabular` or an `array` environment, you may specify the column formatting. You line up characters such as `l`, `c`, `r`, `p`, `@`, and width arguments such as `{1cm}`. If you use any character that doesn't have such a meaning, LaTeX will tell you that. The same applies to the formatting argument of `\multicolumn`.

- **Missing p-arg in array arg**: A bit more specific than the previous message, it tells us that the width argument to the `p` option is missing. Supplement the `p` with a width such as `{1cm}` or change the `p` into another option such as `l`, `c`, or `r`.

- **Missing @-exp in array arg**: That's similar to the error; the expression after the `@` option is missing. You just need to add it, in curly braces, or remove the `@` option.

Now we shall take a look at the potential error messages concerning the table body.

- **Misplaced alignment tab character &**: As you know, the ampersand character has the special meaning of separating columns in a row of a tabular or array environment. If you accidentally use it in normal text, this error will appear. Type `\&` if you desire an ampersand symbol in the output.

- **Extra alignment tab has been changed to \cr**: This happens if you use more separation characters & than the defined columns. For example, the \\ ending a row could have been forgotten.

Working with lists

Lists follow a certain structure and cannot be endlessly nested. At some point, LaTeX would complain:

- **Too deeply nested**: As mentioned in *Chapter 4*, *Creating Lists*, you can nest four levels of a list. If you mix list types, you could go up to six. But if you go further than what LaTeX accepts, you would get this error message.

Think over if you really need a deep nesting. If this is the case, you could consider using sectioning commands like `\paragraph` or `\subsubsection` for outer levels.

Working with floating figures and tables

In *Chapter 5*, *Creating Tables and Inserting Pictures*, we learned about inserting figures and tables, and how to adjust their placement. If you use a lot of figures or tables, you might encounter the following error:

- **Too many unprocessed floats**: If you use many floating objects and LaTeX saves them because it doesn't find an appropriate place, LaTeX's room for that might get full, so this error appears. There might even be just one non-fitting float blocking those who follow. It may be solved as follows:

    - By adding placement options to the figure and table environment respectively, thus lowering their placement requirements.

    - By inserting a \clearpage to flush out the floats at a suitable place, or perhaps even cleverer: \afterpage{clearpage} with the **afterpage** package.

General syntax errors

Just like with any markup or programming language, LaTeX's documents have to follow a syntax. For example, braces and delimiters have to match. If there's a mistake, LaTeX would point to it:

- **Missing { inserted, missing } inserted**: Though it reads its like caused by unbalanced braces, it may be because of a confusion of TeX, which could be caused before the place where the error occurred. Well, check the used syntax thoroughly.

- **Extra }, or forgotten $**: This time there's a problem with unbalanced braces, or math mode delimiters don't match correctly. You need to correct the matching.

- **There's no line here to end**: Using \\ or \newline between paragraphs in vertical mode, is not meaningful and causes this error. Don't try to get more vertical space by writing \\. Use \vspace instead or other skip commands like \bigskip, \medskip, or \smallskip. For instance, a blank line may be produced by \vspace{\baselineskip}.

 Sometimes, the cause of the error might be a bit hidden to the user: TeX might be in vertical mode when you don't expect it to be. In such cases, you could force the \\ to work if you write \leavevmode directly before it. Inserting some whitespace before, like using ~ , works too.

Handling warnings

Warning messages are just for your information. They don't need to point to a serious problem, but often it's a good idea to read these tips carefully and to act accordingly. This may improve your document.

Time for action – emphasizing on a sans-serif font

We shall write our complete document using a sans-serif font. As we did not yet see how emphasizing without serifs looks, we will try that:

1. Take our "Hello world!" example and modify it this way:

```
\documentclass{article}
\renewcommand{\familydefault}{\sfdefault}
\begin{document}
\emph{Hello world!}
\end{document}
```

2. **Typeset**. LaTeX will print out a warning:

   LaTeX Font Warning: Font shape `OT1/cmss/m/it' in size <10> not available

   (Font) Font shape `OT1/cmss/m/sl' tried instead on input line 4.

3. Check the output:

   Hello world!

What just happened?

The macro `\familydefault` stands for the default font family which shall be used in the LaTeX document. For this macro, we specified the value `\sfdefault`, which means the default sans-serif font. This means simply that sans-serif is now default, no matter which font has been chosen. As you can imagine, other possible values are `\rmdefault` and `\ttdefault`. By changing `\familydefault`, we don't have to write `\sffamily` again and again.

But then we emphasized our text and got a warning! The message means that simply there's no Computer Modern Sans Serif font (**cmss**) in **OT1** encoding (just standard), in medium weight (**m**) and italic shape (**it**) in **10pt** size. Further, LaTeX told us how it tried to repair that; instead of italic it chose a slanted shape. That's not too bad; at least it looks similar and the output is produced.

This is basically what happens when warnings occur: LaTeX informs about a potential problem or disadvantage, but it tries to choose the best alternative and continues typesetting. It's not uncommon that a longer document produces dozens of warnings, most often dealing with horizontal or vertical justification.

Often, it doesn't hurt if you ignore warnings, which don't seem very serious. Though following them up is a good habit. Who desires to have a perfect document, fixes all warnings. This way you cannot overlook a potential real problem.

Let's have a look at very common warning messages, what they mean, and how we could fix them.

Justifying text

These warnings are the most frequently occurring:

- **Overfull \hbox**: A line is too long and doesn't fit to the text width. This may result in text extending past the margin. This may be caused by hyphenation problems, which can be fixed by using \hyphenation, as you already learned, or by inserting \-. You could break the line manually or polish your words otherwise.

- **Underfull \hbox**: The opposite to the previous warning; a line is not wide enough to fit to the text width. This could be caused by \linebreak, if there's not enough text on the line. Also, \\ or \newline may cause it, such as \\\\.

- **Overfull \vbox**: The page is too long because TeX could not break it accordingly. The text might hang out past the bottom margin.

- **Underfull \vbox**: There's not enough text on the page. TeX had to break the page too early.

In *Chapter 2, Formatting Words, Lines, and Paragraphs*, we learned how to improve the justification, reducing such warnings. Remember, already loading the microtype package may help a bit.

> The declaration \sloppy switches to a pretty relaxed typesetting, thus avoiding many such warnings. It's counterpart is \fuzzy, switching back to the default behavior. If you ever use \sloppy, maybe in a kind of emergency, it's better to keep it local by grouping or use the respective environment—\begin{sloppypar} ... \end{sloppypar}. Additionally, check out recommendations and alternatives regarding \sloppy in l2tabu, which has been mentioned in *Chapter 10*.

Referencing

Many warnings deal with referencing. Common mistakes are missing label or cite keys or keys that have been used twice. Sometimes LaTeX just tells you that another typeset run is required.

- **Label multiply defined**: `\label` or `\bibitem` has been used with a label name that's already been used. Make label names unique.

- **There were multiply-defined labels**: Like the previous warning, but after processing the complete document; a label has been defined by two `\label` commands.

- **Labels may have changed. Rerun to get cross-references right**: Just typeset again to let LaTeX correct the referencing.

- **Reference ... on page ... undefined**: `\ref` or `\pageref` has been used without a corresponding `\label` definition. Insert a `\label` command at a suitable place.

- **Citation ... on page ... undefined**: A `\cite` command did not have a corresponding `\bibitem` command.

- **There were undefined references or citations**: Summarizing after processing—any `\ref` or `\cite` command did not have a corresponding `\label` or `\bibitem` command.

 Whenever you get warnings regarding referencing, it's a good idea to simply rerun typesetting. Often, such warnings then disappear, because LaTeX couldn't resolve all references in the first run itself.

Choosing fonts

We already encountered the first of the following warnings in our example:

- **Font shape ... in size <...> not available**: You chose a font that's not available. This may be a result of combining font commands that results in a non-existing font. Also, it could just be of an unavailable size. LaTeX would choose a different font or size and inform you about that choice in detail.

- **Some font shapes were not available, defaults substituted**: LaTeX prints this after processing the entire document if any of the chosen fonts had been unavailable.

Placing figures and tables

We already encountered the first of the following warnings in our example:

- **Float too large for page**: A figure or table is too large to fit the page. It would be output, but on an oversize page.

◆ **h float specifier changed to ht**: If you specified an h option to a floating figure or table which doesn't fit there, it would be placed on top of the next page and that warning would be issued. The same can occur for !h and !ht.

Customizing the document class

A warning may be issued if you use an illegal class option:

◆ **Unused global option(s):** You specified an option to \documentclass, which is unknown to the class and to any loaded package. This could be, for example, a base font size which is not supported. Just check the option which LaTeX complains about.

Also packages may print out warnings if they foresee any problem. All these warnings are intended to help you in designing your document.

Avoiding obsolete classes and packages

At the end of *Chapter 10*, we talked about the dangers of outdated information. LaTeX exists since decades, and so do tutorials, examples, packages, and templates. Many are totally outdated and some even refer to the old LaTeX standard 2.09, where even document classes didn't exist. In *Chapter 10*, we pointed to the definitive guide l2tabu that comes to the rescue.

Many problems just occur because of the use of obsolete packages. For example, some that aren't maintained any more may conflict with newer packages. Often, you just need to find the recommended successor of an obsolete package and use that.

Here's a short list for helping you in that matter:

Obsolete packages	Recommended successors
a4, a4wide, anysize	geometry, typearea
backrefx	backref
bitfield	bytefield
caption2	caption
dinat	natdin
doublespace	setspace
dropping	lettrine
eps, epsfig	graphicx

Obsolete packages	Recommended successors
euler	eulervm
eurotex	inputenx
fancyheadings	fancyhdr
floatfig	floatflt
glossary	glossaries
here	float
isolatin, isolatin1	inputenc
mathpple	mathpazo
mathptm	mathptmx
nthm	ntheorem
palatino	mathpazo
picinpar	floatflt, picins, wrapfig
prosper, HA-prosper	powerdot, beamer
ps4pdf	pst-pdf
raggedr	ragged2e
scrlettr	scrlttr2
scrpage	scrpage2
seminar	powerdot, beamer
subfigure	subfig, subcaption
t1enc	fontenc
times	mathptmx
utopia	fourier
vmargin	geometry, typearea

That's not set in stone. Of course, you may still use the so-called obsolete packages. They may work well even today. But check out their description on their CTAN package home page; usually there are comments regarding up-to-dateness and related packages.

An up-to-date version of that list can also be found on `http://texblog.net/packages`. There's an ongoing discussion at `http://mrunix.de` on the creation and maintenance of such a list.

General troubleshooting

There may be situations where we cannot solve a problem simply by reading and acting on warnings or error messages. Imagine a mysterious error, an untraceable error location, irresolvable references, or just unclear messages from classes or packages.

Locating the cause by the line number which LaTeX printed out or by knowing what we've done since the previous typesetting run, usually helps. Once a problematic line or chunk is located, it could be removed or fixed. Otherwise, it might become difficult.

Here are the general first steps we might go through then:

♦ *Compile several times.* This may be necessary for correct referencing, positioning of floating figures, and creation of table of contents, bibliography, and lists of tables and figures.

♦ *Check the order in which you load the packages.* Some packages, like `hyperref`, don't work well if loaded before or after certain packages. You may just swap some lines to correct or to test that.

♦ *Remove auxiliary files.* If anything strange happens, it's sometimes a good idea to remove all files created by LaTeX during typesetting. These files have the same name as the main document but have extensions such as `.aux`, `.toc`, `.lot`, `.lof`, `.bbl`, `.idx`, or `.nav`, just to name some examples.

If the problem persists, we could try to isolate the cause.

1. Create a copy of your document. If necessary, copy the complete folder. From now on, work on the copy.

2. Remove a part of the document which probably is not involved in the problem.

3. **Typeset,** to ensure that the problem persists. If this is the case, go back to step 2. If the problem is gone, you isolated the problem within the part you just removed. In this latter case, restore the deleted part, you may delete other parts.

4. After some repetitions, you located the problem. If you didn't already, reduce the number of loaded packages, repeating step 2 and typesetting.

5. You end up with a really tiny but complete example document which reproduces the error.

Removing or rewriting that identified part of your document could help. What if you really want to use that part and would like to fix that error? Now that your problem can be shown with such a very small example code, you could post that problem to an online LaTeX forum and ask for help.

Have a go hero – examining LaTeX's log files

You are not dependent on just the errors and warnings that your editor shows to you! LaTeX keeps track of any information, each warning, and every error. All of these will be collected in a file with the same name like your document but carrying the extension `.log`. This is an ordinary text file and may be opened with any editor, including your LaTeX editor.

For instance, the log file for our second example looks like the following:

```
This is pdfTeX, Version 3.1415926-1.40.10 (Web2C 2009)
(format=pdflatex 2010.6.25) 20JAN 2011 23:16
entering extended mode
%&-line parsing enabled.
**helloworld.tex
(./helloworld.tex
LaTeX2e <2009/09/24>
Babel <v3.81> and hyphenation patterns for english, ... loaded.
(c:/texlive/2009/texmf-dist/tex/latex/base/article.cls
Document Class: article 2007/10/19 v1.4h Standard LaTeX document class
(c:/texlive/2009/texmf-dist/tex/latex/base/size10.clo
File: size10.clo 2007/10/19 v1.4h Standard LaTeX file (size option)
)
\c@part=\count79
\c@section=\count80
\c@subsection=\count81
\c@subsubsection=\count82
\c@paragraph=\count83
\c@subparagraph=\count84
\c@figure=\count85
\c@table=\count86
\abovecaptionskip=\skip41
\belowcaptionskip=\skip42
\bibindent=\dimen102
) (./warning.aux)
\openout1 = `warning.aux'.
LaTeX Font Info: Checking defaults for OML/cmm/m/it on input line 3.
LaTeX Font Info: ... okay on input line 3.
...
```

```
LaTeX Font Warning: Font shape `OT1/cmss/m/it' in size <10> not
available
(Font) Font shape `OT1/cmss/m/sl' tried instead on input line 4.
[1
{c:/Users/guest/.texlive2009/texmf-var/fonts/map/pdftex/updmap/pdftex.
map}]
(./helloworld.aux) )
Output written on helloworld.pdf (1 page, 17376 bytes).
```

Check out the log files of some documents you produced until now. The information therein makes a very technical impression, but this might help you a lot in troubleshooting.

Pop quiz – troubleshooting

1. If you get several error messages during one typesetting run, which one is the most important, according to the text?

   a. The first

   b. The last

   c. All error messages should be dealt with before another typesetting run

2. Which it the extension of the file containing errors, warnings, and information?

   a. aux

   b. toc

   c. log

   d. lof

Summary

This chapter prepared us to solve problems that might occur.

Specifically, we have learned about:

◆ Locating and fixing errors

◆ Understanding warning messages

◆ Analyzing LaTeX's typesetting log

Correcting errors is absolutely necessary. Dealing with warnings is a valuable bonus.

If you encounter any problem which you aren't able to solve on your own, don't hesitate to ask for help on a LaTeX Internet forum. You've got the tools within this chapter, and also:

◆ You know how to create a tiny but complete example which demonstrates the problem

◆ You are able to report an error message

◆ You know about the log file and could provide its information

For LaTeX friends online, it's often an easy task to use this information in solving your problem, and definitely a lot of LaTeX enthusiasts have fun in helping other LaTeX users.

The next chapter will point the way to LaTeX web forums and also to many other online resources.

13

Using Online Resources

There's a vast amount of LaTeX information and material on the Internet, and it has grown over many years. Today, thanks to the virtues of free and open source software, a huge TeX community exists, sharing knowledge and expertise.

On the Internet, you can find:

◆ Software archives offering nearly all LaTeX material available

◆ Web forums, where LaTeX users talk about problems and solutions

◆ Homepages of user groups, TeX distributions, and free editors

◆ Blogs of individual LaTeX users

◆ LaTeX mailing lists you may subscribe to

As you know how to navigate through the World Wide Web, this chapter does not contain practical examples. Instead, let's take a walk through the Internet.

Web forums, discussion boards, and Q&A sites

Before we proceed to software archives and homepages, let's go where the online world takes place!

Usenet groups

It all began with the Usenet. Around 1980, a long time before the World Wide Web was born, this discussion network emerged. It consists of many thousands of groups, so-called newsgroups, each dedicated to a certain subject. Not to our surprise, there's a TeX newsgroup!

comp.text.tex

`http://groups.google.com/group/comp.text.tex/topics`

The easiest way is just to access this URL hosted by Google. Just browse it using its web interface. Alternatively, you could install a Usenet reader program and connect to a Usenet web server. At this point, you should familiarize yourself better with Usenet. A great starting point is its Wikipedia entry at `http://en.wikipedia.org/wiki/Usenet`. There you would find an introduction, links to necessary software, and further reading.

comp.text.tex is the classic TeX discussion board. Then and now, there are distinguished experts reading and posting messages. You can search and browse an archive reaching back over more than 20 years.

Newsgroups in other languages

If you understand the language, you could check out the German or French Usenet TeX groups:

`http://groups.google.de/group/de.comp.text.tex/topics`

`http://groups.google.de/group/fr.comp.text.tex/topics`

Web forums

During the last few years, web forums emerged. They offer an easier and more user-friendly access to discussion groups. Initially, LaTeX has been the topic in sub forums of more general computer forums, among other software. After LaTeX became more and more popular, websites dedicated to it have been founded.

LaTeX-Community.org

`http://www.latex-community.org/`

In January 2007, the originator of the LaTeX editor TeXnicCenter—Sven Wiegand, founded the web forum **LaTeX Community**. This site has been the first forum with the single topic LaTeX. It is split into many sub forums, each dealing with a certain LaTeX topic, such as Math and Science or Fonts and Character Sets, with a certain LaTeX distribution or a specific LaTeX editor.

Today it's supplemented by a news section and a know-how section containing articles and essays of the community.

The author of this book supports the fellow community members as a moderator on that site.

Participating is as easy as in any other web forum. You don't need to register for reading, as it's freely available. Just for writing, you need to register once, choosing a login name and a password. Then you may ask questions yourself or support other users who turned there looking for help.

Questions are very welcome! They are the foundation of the site. You may increase the chance of receiving helpful answers by:

- Choosing a meaningful header
- Describing your problem clearly
- Quoting the error or warning messages you've got
- Including a code example, which allows others to reproduce the problem

The latter is the optimal approach. There's even a website explaining why and how at `http://www.minimalbeispiel.de`, in English and German. Once a problem could be reproduced, it's nearly solved, even if it seems to be difficult at first sight. Experienced users who are familiar with the source code of the LaTeX kernel and packages can explain how something works and are able to create solutions for nearly any problem.

TeX and LaTeX on Stack Exchange

`http://tex.stackexchange.com/`

There are question and answer sites, which are different to classical web forums. While in the web forums, people talk and discuss, these Q&A sites have a simpler structure. There's a question, followed by answers. There's no discussion, besides comments.

Time for action – asking a question online

Is there anything you wanted to know about LaTeX? Did you encounter any serious problem you could not solve? Then post a question on `http://tex.stackexchange.com/`:

1. Visit `http://tex.stackexchange.com`:

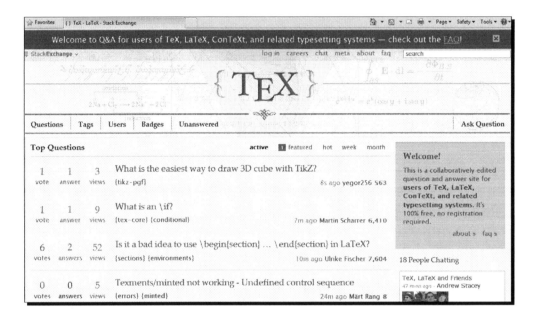

2. In the upper-right corner, click on **Ask Question**:

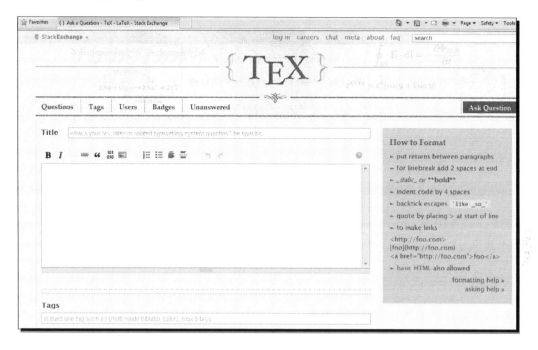

3. Fill out the **Title** field and type in your question, and choose some meaningful keywords for the **Tags** field. When you are done, click on **Post Your Question**. The final question will look like the following:

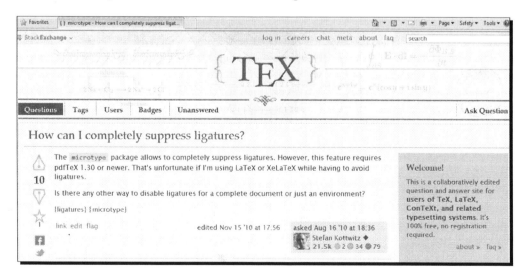

What just happened?

That wasn't really hard! Besides editing our question we:

 ◆ Chose a meaningful title to get readers interested in checking out our question

 ◆ Specified some keywords, so called **tags**, which are used to filter the site's contents

Stack Exchange is a network of free, community-driven Q&A sites. The TeX site, often briefly called TeX.SE, was founded in 2010 specifically for users of TeX and LaTeX.

You don't have to register to post questions and answers—you could simply start off just as we saw! Like in the LaTeX Community web forum, nearly all questions will be answered, because on this site also, TeX users are happy to share their expertise with everybody. It's extremely rare that a question would not get a satisfactory answer. Until now, that happened only with very unclear questions without details which nobody could answer at all. If you think of the advice aforementioned regarding formulating good questions, this won't happen to you.

This TeX Q&A site is developed to an easily accessible knowledge base, because:

 ◆ Questions are **tagged**. For each question, one or more tags should be chosen, describing the subject. For example, if your question is about a problem with \label and \ref for equations, choose the tags **cross-referencing** and **equations**. This makes it easy to find answers to certain subjects. Specialized experts watch their favorite tags.

 ◆ Answers are **voted** on. Users vote helpful and meaningful answers up, while misinformation is voted down. This way, the best answer floats to the top. So you don't have to read through an entire multi-page thread to find the best solution, like it's necessary in classical web forums.

Both tagging and voting enhance the information access. They may be used for sorting and refining search results.

There's another concept called **reputation**. You don't need to care about that, but perhaps you would like to know what it means. Users who post good questions and useful answers earn reputation points depending on the votes on their questions and answers. A certain amount of reputation points allows going beyond simply asking and answering, for example:

 ◆ You can leave comments

 ◆ You can create new tags or retag questions

 ◆ Advertising is reduced

 ◆ You are able to edit other users posts

 ◆ You could even have access to moderation tools

The reputation is a rough measurement for the user status in the community. A user with high reputation is so trusted by the community that we can be sure he/she would act carefully. Thus, the site is community-moderated and shows aspects of a collaborative Wiki.

The site offers a list of frequently asked questions that explain all the details—check it out. Such lists are common, so let's have a look at LaTeX-specific lists next.

Frequently Asked Questions

Now you know where to ask for help. However, during the long existence of online LaTeX communities, the probability that another user has had the same problem like you is very high! There's a bunch of questions which appear again and again. If you post such a question, the community member might point you to a **FAQ**. This is an abbreviation for "Frequently Asked Questions" and refers to a list of such questions that also contains answers to them.

UK TeX FAQ

```
http://www.tex.ac.uk/cgi-bin/texfaq2html?introduction=yes
```

This is a FAQ site maintained by the UK TeX Users' Group, especially by Robin Fairbairns. It is regularly posted to **comp.text.tex**. It contains several hundred frequently asked questions and well-thought answers. They are sorted by topic, and that list is still growing and is continuously being improved.

Visual LaTeX FAQ

```
http://www.ctan.org/tex-archive/help/Catalogue/entries/visualfaq.html
```

This is a very different approach: the Visual FAQ is a PDF document containing hundreds of text and graphic elements, such as tables, figures, lists, footnotes, and math formulas: thirty pages full of samples. At all these objects, key positions are marked and hyperlinked. Just click on any marked object and you will be lead to the corresponding UK TeX FAQ entry. Take a look—it's a fancy interface.

MacTeX FAQ

```
http://tug.org/mactex/faq/
```

Are you a Mac user? Then this FAQ is made for you. It covers installation and use of the MacTeX LaTeX distribution and the popular Mac LaTeX editor TeXShop.

AMS-Math FAQ

`http://www.ams.org/tex/amsmath-faq.html`

As you know, `amsmath` is the most recommended math package. There's a list of questions and answers to `amsmath` and `AMS` classes and packages on the website of the American Mathematical Society.

LaTeX Picture FAQ

`http://ctan.org/pkg/l2picfaq`

As a lot of questions are about including pictures, this How-to has been developed. It deals, for example, with the various image file formats, conversion tools, picture manipulation, and placement of floating figures. The document contains a lot of small code examples and is a very useful small resource for a LaTeX beginner.

As it originates in a German LaTeX forum, `http://mrunix.de`, it's been written in German. It has been translated into English, but the translation is not yet published on CTAN.

Mailing lists

Now we come again to a classic media: electronic mailing lists. They are both used for announcements and for discussion. If you subscribe to such a list, you will receive announcements and discussion contributions by other subscribers. You could silently receive and read all the messages, and you could send e-mails to the list address which would then be sent to all other subscribers. Now you know you should read an FAQ before.

Today many people prefer easier accessible media, such as web forums. However, these lists still exist and might be as long as e-mail is popular.

texhax

`http://tug.org/mailman/listinfo/texhax`

This is a list for general TeX discussion, a companion to **comp.text.tex**, established in the 1980s. It has hundreds of subscribers and there are many experts among them.

tex-live

`http://tug.org/mailman/listinfo/tex-live`

The name says it all: it deals with the TeX Live collection. If you installed this software distribution, you might be interested in subscribing to get the latest news and to read and write about issues with it.

texworks

`http://tug.org/mailman/listinfo/texworks`

This list supports the user of the LaTeX editor—TeXworks, that we used in the first chapter. If you decided to use that editor later on and you are interested in the latest builds, tricks, scripts, and news, you may subscribe.

List collections

Aforementioned were some especially useful examples matching the software used in this book. There's a lot more that you can find here:

- ◆ `http://tug.org/mailman/listinfo` : More than 50 mailing lists for TeX and LaTeX-specific subjects such as bibliographies, hyphenation, PostScript, pdfTeX, and development.

- ◆ `http://gmane.org/lists.php` : A collection of mailing lists; some of them are (La)TeX related.

TeX user groups as well as developers of LaTeX editors and other software often provide mailing lists, especially for announcements. You can read about that on their homepages. We shall now look at some of them.

TeX user group sites

TeX user groups are organizations for people interested in TeX and LaTeX. They provide support for their members, but also for TeX and LaTeX users in general.

TUG – the TeX users group

`http://www.tug.org/`

That's a big institution. It was founded in 1980 and has always had a great influence on the development and popularity of TeX. Their homepage is a portal to the TeX world with links to support, documentation, and software.

The LaTeX project

`http://www.latex-project.org/`

The LaTeX3 project team maintains the LaTeX 2e standard and develops the next version of LaTeX, called LaTeX3. This website informs about their work and about LaTeX in general.

UK TUG – TeX in the United Kingdom

`http://uk.tug.org/`

This user group supports and promotes TeX in the UK. Also this site is a good starting point to explore TeX resources but specifically those offered by the UK TUG.

Local user groups

`http://www.tug.org/usergroups.html`

`http://www.ntg.nl/lug/`

These pages list local TeX user groups from many countries in the world. Their websites often contain material in national languages and further information on the TeX world.

Homepages of LaTeX software and editors

Like most software manufacturers and distributors, free and open source software projects offer information on their homepages.

LaTeX distributions

Today there are two big LaTeX distributions, both very modern and comprehensive, plus some descendants:

- ◆ **TeX Live:** `http://tug.org/texlive/` is a cross-platform LaTeX software collection. It runs on Windows, Mac OS X, Linux, and Unix.
- ◆ **MiKTeX:** `http://www.miktex.org/` is a very user-friendly and popular LaTeX distribution specifically for the Windows operating system.
- ◆ **proTeXt:** `http://www.tug.org/protext/` is a MiKTeX-based distribution for Windows that especially focuses on easy installation.
- ◆ **MacTeX:** `http://www.tug.org/mactex/` is derived from TeX Live and has been customized specifically for Mac OS X.

LaTeX editors

There are many LaTeX editors available, from easy-to-use to complex and professional.

Cross-platform

These editors support many systems including Windows, Mac OS X, Linux, and Unix:

- **TeXworks**: `http://tug.org/texworks/` is light-weight and comfortable.

- **Texmaker**: `http://www.xm1math.net/texmaker/` offers many features.

- **TexmakerX**: `http://texmakerx.sourceforge.net/` is derived from Texmaker and provides many additional capabilities.

- **Emacs**: `http://www.tug.org/mactex/` is extensible and very customizable, though not easy-to-use for everybody. However, it's great together with AUCTeX: `http://www.gnu.org/software/auctex/`.

- **vim**: `http://www.vim.org/` is based on commands given in a text interface. It's enhanced by the vim LaTeX-suite: `http://vim-latex.sourceforge.net/`.

Windows

These editors are specifically for the Windows operating system, running on most versions:

- **TeXnicCenter**: `http://www.texniccenter.org/` is an enormously feature-rich editor, a great tool for developing complex TeX projects.

- **LEd**: `http://www.latexeditor.org/` is a free-to-use multilingual LaTeX editor with project management.

- **WinShell**: `http://www.winshell.de/` is a free and multilingual customizable editor, also with project management and wizards.

- **MeWa LaTeX editor**: `http://www.meshwalk.com/latexeditor/` is another LaTeX editor with a graphical user interface similar to TeXnicCenter.

- **WinEdt**: `http://www.winedt.com/` is powerful and very popular. This one is distributed as shareware. Also see the WinEdt community site on `http://www.winedt.org/`.

Linux

Besides the cross-platform editors, TeXworks, Texmaker, TexmakerX, Emacs, and vim there are:

- **Kile**: `http://kile.sourceforge.net/` is very powerful and designed for the KDE window system, but also runs on other window managers like GNOME, if KDE libraries are installed. Just this editor is worth using KDE also on GNOME.

- **gedit**: `http://www.gnome.org/projects/gedit/` is the light-weight GNOME standard editor and there's a LaTeX plugin: `http://live.gnome.org/Gedit/LaTeXPlugin`.

Mac OS X

Though cross-platform editors run on Macs, there's one very popular Mac LaTeX editor:

◆ **TeXshop:** `http://www.uoregon.edu/~koch/texshop/` is believed to have led many new users to LaTeX because of its outstanding usability.

LaTeX archives and catalogs

There are websites archiving and sharing LaTeX tools and packages and providing catalogs for easy look-up.

CTAN – the Comprehensive TeX Archive Network

`http://ctan.org/`

This network consists of many servers world-wide, which store the biggest collection of TeX-related material. Nearly every serious LaTeX package can be found in this archive. On the homepage, you will find search features or you may just start browsing the archive directories.

The TeX Catalogue Online

`http://texcatalogue.sarovar.org/`

This catalog offers a topical, a hierarchical, a brief, and an alphabetical index to nearly 4,000 TeX and LaTeX packages and tools. It is closely related to CTAN, which actually stores the software. This site is great for browsing especially if you work on a topic, but don't know which packages may exist for that purpose.

The LaTeX Font Catalogue

`http://www.tug.dk/FontCatalogue/`

Nearly all fonts available for use with LaTeX are listed here. About a dozen categories, such as Sans-Serif, Typewriter, and Calligraphy fonts, assist in finding the right font. The fonts are displayed both briefly in overviews but also extensively with several style and math examples. The cherries on the cake are concrete code examples.

TeX Resources on the Web

`http://www.tug.org/interest.html`

This extensive collection of TeX-related Internet resources is maintained by the TeX users group. An index and a substantial amount of links point you the way to helpful material on the Internet.

Friends of LaTeX

Some software builds on LaTeX or is closely related and offers different interesting approaches.

XeTeX

`http://scripts.sil.org/xetex`

XeTeX extends TeX by Unicode support and modern font technologies for using OpenType and TrueType fonts and Apple Advanced Typography. It natively supports Unicode.

The LaTeX version is called XeLaTeX.

Initially developed for Mac OS X, XeTeX is now available for Windows and Linux/Unix as well. For example, you can use it with TeXworks by choosing XeTeX, XeLaTeX respectively, as typesetng engine

LuaTeX

`http://www.luatex.org/`

LuaTeX is an extended version of pdfTeX. It uses Lua as its scripting language. The LuaTeX project aims to develop an enhanced TeX version while keeping downward compatibility.

Lua is a fast and powerful but light-weight and portable scripting language. You can read about it at `http://www.lua.org/`.

ConTeXt

`http://wiki.contextgarden.net/`

Like LaTeX, ConTeXt is a document markup language based on TeX. Unlike LaTeX, it offers a direct interface for handling typography giving the user more control over the formatting. It supports both pdfTeX and LuaTeX.

LyX

`http://www.lyx.org/`

LyX looks and feels like word processor software, but is built on LaTeX. It combines an easy-to-use graphical user interface with the power and structure of LaTeX. You can develop documents mainly using LyX's toolbars and menus, but you may insert LaTeX code at any point.

The LyX wiki offers an extensive documentation at `http://www.lyx.org/`.

On one of the LyX homepage's, you will find links for download, news, and support. As LyX is very popular, it's also the subject of discussions at `http://www.latex-community.org/`. Questions about LyX are also welcome at `http://tex.stackexchange.com/`.

LaTeX blogs

Are you interested in LaTeX news and expert opinions? Then LaTeX blogs may supply you with current LaTeX reading.

The TeXblog

`http://texblog.net/`

This is the blog of the author of this book. It regularly brings LaTeX-related news, offers a lot of tips and tricks, and provides a structured link collection, sorted by subject. And of course, it contains all code examples of this book, plus supplementary material.

Some TeX Developments

`http://www.texdev.net/`

Joseph Wright, a member of the LaTeX project and author of LaTeX tools, writes this blog.

LaTeX Alive

`http://latex-alive.tumblr.com/`

This is the blog of the LaTeX developer Will Robertson. It provides interesting insights.

LaTeX for Humans

`http://latexforhumans.wordpress.com/`

This blog supports LaTeX in the humanities, with a special focus on Middle Eastern Studies.

The TeX community aggregator

`http://www.texample.net/community/`

This page summarizes about 30 TeX and LaTeX-related blogs and may keep you updated.

Summary

While you have learned about the LaTeX fundamentals in this book, this chapter gave an overview about further reading online.

Now you know about:

◆ Finding and downloading LaTeX software

◆ Accessing the world wide LaTeX community knowledge

◆ Getting the latest news from blogs

◆ Asking questions online if you would encounter any problem that you cannot solve alone.

TeX friends will welcome you on any community website. As you have learned much in this book, you may soon become an experienced LaTeX user who supports LaTeX novices. At some time, you might be the advisor who answers questions on LaTeX web forums.

Pop Quiz Answers

Chapter 2: Formatting Words, Lines, and Paragraphs

Commands

Question	Answer
1	d.
2	b.

Lines and paragraphs

Question	Answer
1	c.
2	c.
3	b.

Chapter 3: Designing Pages

Question	Answer
1	c.
2	a.
3	b.
4	d.
5	d.

Chapter 4: Creating Lists

Question	Answer
1	c.
2	b.
3	c.

Chapter 5: Creating Tables and Inserting Pictures

Tables

Question	Answer
1	a.
2	d.

Pictures and floats

Question	Answer
1	b.
2	d.

Chapter 6: Cross-Referencing

Question	Answer
1	b.
2	c.

Chapter 7: Listing Content and References

Question	Answer
1	a.
2	c.
3	a.

Chapter 8: Typing Math Formulas

Question	Answer
1	b.
2	b.
3	d.

Chapter 9: Using Fonts

Question	Answer
1	b.
2	c.

Chapter 10: Developing Large Documents

Question	Answer
1	a.
2	b.

Chapter 11: Enhancing Your Documents Further

Question	Answer
1	d.
2	c.

Chapter 12: Troubleshooting

Question	Answer
1	a.
2	c.

Index

X

About Packt Publishing

Packt, pronounced 'packed', published its first book "*Mastering phpMyAdmin for Effective MySQL Management*" in April 2004 and subsequently continued to specialize in publishing highly focused books on specific technologies and solutions.

Our books and publications share the experiences of your fellow IT professionals in adapting and customizing today's systems, applications, and frameworks. Our solution based books give you the knowledge and power to customize the software and technologies you're using to get the job done. Packt books are more specific and less general than the IT books you have seen in the past. Our unique business model allows us to bring you more focused information, giving you more of what you need to know, and less of what you don't.

Packt is a modern, yet unique publishing company, which focuses on producing quality, cutting-edge books for communities of developers, administrators, and newbies alike. For more information, please visit our website: www.packtpub.com.

About Packt Open Source

In 2010, Packt launched two new brands, Packt Open Source and Packt Enterprise, in order to continue its focus on specialization. This book is part of the Packt Open Source brand, home to books published on software built around Open Source licences, and offering information to anybody from advanced developers to budding web designers. The Open Source brand also runs Packt's Open Source Royalty Scheme, by which Packt gives a royalty to each Open Source project about whose software a book is sold.

Writing for Packt

We welcome all inquiries from people who are interested in authoring. Book proposals should be sent to author@packtpub.com. If your book idea is still at an early stage and you would like to discuss it first before writing a formal book proposal, contact us; one of our commissioning editors will get in touch with you.

We're not just looking for published authors; if you have strong technical skills but no writing experience, our experienced editors can help you develop a writing career, or simply get some additional reward for your expertise.

Linux Shell Scripting Cookbook

ISBN: 978-1-849513-76-0   Paperback: 360 pages

Solve real-world shell scripting problems with over 110 simple but incredibly effective recipes

1. Master the art of crafting one-liner command sequence to perform tasks such as text processing, digging data from files, and lot more

2. Practical problem solving techniques adherent to the latest Linux platform

3. Packed with easy-to-follow examples to exercise all the features of the Linux shell scripting language

OpenVPN 2 Cookbook

ISBN: 978-1-849510-10-3   Paperback: 356 pages

100 simple and incredibly effective recipes for harnessing the power of the OpenVPN 2 network

1. Set of recipes covering the whole range of tasks for working with OpenVPN

2. The quickest way to solve your OpenVPN problems!

3. Set up, configure, troubleshoot and tune OpenVPN

4. Uncover advanced features of OpenVPN and even some undocumented options

Please check **www.PacktPub.com** for information on our titles

OGRE 3D 1.7 Beginner's Guide

ISBN: 978-1-849512-48-0   Paperback: 300 pages

Create real time 3D applications using OGRE 3D from scratch

1. Easy-to-follow introduction to OGRE 3D

2. Create exciting 3D applications using OGRE 3D

3. Create your own scenes and monsters, play with the lights and shadows, and learn to use plugins

4. Get challenged to be creative and make fun and addictive games on your own

Agile Web Application Development with Yii1.1 and PHP5

ISBN: 978-1-847199-58-4   Paperback: 368 pages

Fast-track your Web application development by harnessing the power of the Yii PHP framework

1. A step-by-step guide to creating a modern, sophisticated web application using an incremental and iterative approach to software development

2. Build a real-world, user-based, database-driven project task management application using the Yii development framework

3. Take a test-driven design (TDD) approach to software development utilizing the Yii testing framework

Please check **www.PacktPub.com** for information on our titles

Made in the USA
Lexington, KY
20 August 2014